I0152196

A FIELD OF MY OWN

a memoir of place

WRITTEN & PHOTOGRAPHED

BY

CYNTHIA MCVAY

To the land and all its original inhabitants — those leaping, burrowing and soaring — and the Esopus tribe who made their lives here long before the rest of us

CONTENTS

PART TWO

LIVING IN A PLACE

IN THE LAND

EPILOGUE

ACKNOWLEDGMENTS

PREFACE

Field Farm has been my muse for close to a quarter century. When we first met, I had no idea how our relationship would unfold, how this land would teach and heal and humble me, how I would miss it when I wasn't in it. As I willingly surrendered to its predictable yet fickle nature, as I worshipped and adored it, Field Farm has offered unfathomable adventures and rapture in return. Friends and Airbnb guests seem to agree there is magic here and suggested I share my story.

I did not set out to write a book. It started with a couple essays a decade ago. I wrote in fits and starts when I found myself moved, ruminating, narrating a walk, or wanted to capture an observation. I woke one day with a book's worth of words and thousands of photos. It felt indulgent not to get them out there in a more coherent way.

When Covid hit, and New York City dwellers fled to the Hudson Valley seeking space and green, it seemed the right moment. The pandemic challenged assumptions about how and where people reside and work, socialize, and spend their time. Trends that were already in the works accelerated —the gig economy, social media use, concern for and impacts of climate change, freelance and remote work, home projects, tiny houses, living off the grid, migrations from urban settings to more affordable and healthful communities. Folks started cooking from scratch and baking sourdough bread again, or for the first time, planting tomatoes, running chickens, setting up videocams of birds building nests and the emergent hatchlings. Instagram helped. In the Hudson Valley, trail-use (and home sales) increased exponentially. Many dug in their boots and have no desire to go back to the office or metropolis. They look out at their backyards and wonder how and where to begin.

My life changed little during the pandemic. I was fortunate to not be an essential worker. But more: I was already here. This is my life and how I live. I genuinely want to share what I've learned in the hopes more people can find joy in their lives and in the natural world while treading lightly on this earth. I believe people feel less stress and more alive when they live in nature, authentically and for themselves, rather than for others. It is possible to live frugally and luxuriously, without sacrifice or compromise. The 28 percent of Americans who live alone—and those lonely even while partnered—might find solace and community in a garden or on a trail.

A Field of My Own is a loosely chronological collection of stories and essays, part memoir of both this particular place and of the Hudson Valley, and part "Do-It-Myselfer." I couldn't write a DIY manual. I'm not an expert, just someone who has learned a lot from doing, considering options, taking risks, failing, flubbing, and, possibly, flourishing. I wanted to show it's doable, even for a single working mother on a modest budget. My hope is to inspire and offer practical guidance to others seeking fresh, thoughtful ways to live.

For work, for years, I was a strategy and management consultant. I have in many ways behaved exactly how I advised clients not to be—responsive, rather than strategic and deliberate. Although a cohesive vision and framework were my guiderails, I let Field Farm and curiosity lead the way. I learned to trust. And so, I encountered and took on things that were not part of any plan. At the start, I knew little about the Hudson Valley and homesteading. We picked berries in late summer, but foraging was not a word in my vocabulary or the cultural conversation. I likely tread on a skunk's conical explorations for years until a friend pointed them out and identified them. After spotting a bright orange bird flitting by, I now look for the woven, hanging sac of an oriole nest. I stepped by thousands of glistening, slimy, proud, pock-marked, bald mushrooms springing from the forest floor without noticing the first hundred times. Early on, I didn't recognize and was not disturbed by the invasive bittersweet strangling the dogwoods on the forest's edge. I had no interest or notion of wielding a tractor through the high grass. Or that I would summon and erect an old barn and now be gazing through enormous windows at an exuberant garden chock full of hibiscus, black-eyed Susan's, hydrangea, and Echinacea. But here I am.

Often, while sitting overlooking the field or by the pool, an appreciating friend tells me how lucky I am. Yes, I am, but I also believe Field Farm is lucky to have me. I can't imagine anyone else loving it as much as I do, obsessing about it, treating it with such tenderness and respect. And to be fair, oodles of sweat, splinters, and broken fingernails went into creating this place, my home.

PART ONE

HOW TO LAND
IN A FIELD

"Love sharpens the eye, the ear, the touch;
it quickens the feet, it steadies the hand, it
arms against the wet and the cold. What we
love to do, that we do well. To know is not
all; it is only half. To love is the other half."

— John Burroughs, *Leaf and Tendril*

SMITTEN

The first time I saw Field Farm, in February 2000, it was the dead of winter, snow-less and charmless, but even so, something about the soft curves of the land and open space captivated me. As the realtor fumbled for the key to the modest house, with thick plastic tacked to its windows, I turned my gaze to the short-cropped, amber field, unfazed by the fierce wind that came from all directions at once. I wrapped my scarf around my neck and head and stuffed my bare hands into my coat pockets. My shoulders lifted to my ears to close out the cold. I could barely hear the realtor's answer when I pointed and announced I was going *there*. And then the wind swept me into the land.

A slight difference in the quality of the grass might have indicated the path off to the right, but I didn't see it that day. I cut a diagonal across the expanse, under the large white-gray sky, to the field-room behind, around the corner, past the trees. I charged across that frozen smaller field too, by the dozen old apple trees I probably didn't notice that day (how much can an overwhelmed person take in?) but came to know individually and for which I have provided hospice since. I found the opening at the other end of that field that took me, through the brush, to what looked like an unending grass driveway, which I later learned was the gas line and property border. I crossed it, continuing into an orderly stand of silver-trunked maples, to an old stone wall with an ancient sugar maple at each corner demarcating a two-hundred-year-old cemetery.

How did I know? How did I know—when there was no path, no markers, no trail—where to go? I am not suggesting it was destiny or intuition or a higher power that drew me, unless destiny is defined as the pull of curiosity, the need to claim, to grasp. But I found it just the same. Further, how did I know this patch of earth was it? What joy this mildly domesticated piece of the universe would give me over the years, how the land would draw me back, demand my attention, make me long for it when I was away? I was introduced on the least hospitable day of the year that first time, with no inkling of the terrain's full-blown magic, its relentless lures and seductions, and yet I knew I had found what I was looking for. I did not, could not, project onto that barren brown field, with all my imagination, what happens here every spring and summer and fall. And every year, even though I know it's coming, I am awestruck, somehow forgetting, despite experiencing it fully every year and trying to sear it into my memory and hundreds of photos.

As a single working mother of five-year-old Tess, I had been looking for a weekend escape from our small apartment in New York City, a piece of green, sky. After staying with friends of friends near Hudson, New York, I was leaning toward the Hudson Valley. One thing I knew was important to me: If I was going to be in the car Friday and Sunday nights, I wanted the drive to be scenic. And the drive north of New York City was, unlike the drive to Princeton, New Jersey, where my parents lived, and which would have been a more logical choice.

Before *The New York Times* featured Rosendale and Hudson and Rhinebeck every year, I had seen cabins on top of mountains; old summer camps for which the Catskills were famous (*Dirty Dancing* helped), one with a tree growing in the empty, cracked pool and a suitcase full of vintage bottle-bottom eyeglasses; small, stone schoolhouses; dressed-up doublewides with magnificent mountain views; clapboard ramshackle Victorians overlooking the Hudson River. I had thought I was looking for a modest house. There were some contenders among them, some I lay awake thinking about at night, but many had unseemly or scary neighbors, roads whipping by too close, or intimidating projects for houses (a retired public school?). My budget was tight so I knew I would have to compromise on one dimension or another, but none of the dozens of properties I had seen took my breath away like this one. When I say I don't make decisions, this is what I mean. There was—I had—no choice.

 That day I knew I would become the steward of this land—
82 acres!—taking on a huge responsibility, one I would take as seriously as everything else I have done in my life.

 Even at its barren low, I fell hard. It was true love.

* * *

That first year I was excited to see how the seasons would roll
across the field. A few years earlier, when I lived in Bedford, New
York, with my then husband, our antique home came with well-es-
tablished, formal gardens and century-old specimen trees. In the
perennial borders, gracious peonies, elegant roses, sturdy hosta,
hundreds of tulips, and sweet lilac gave me such pleasure as they
revealed themselves that first spring. It was there that I first began
to garden, taught by the flowers themselves.

 I missed the country. I had moved back to New York City
when my marriage ended. It had been several wrenching years
starting out all over again, financially and emotionally from scratch,
on my own with a toddler. Eager to not lose career momentum, I
had been working long hours as the head of strategic planning for
a large corporation in downtown Manhattan, traveling monthly,
spending time in airports and abroad, leaving little Tess with a
wonderful, loving, live-in sitter, the only way I could make things
work in my new life. I received a small bundle of stock options I
wanted to turn into a weekend home, enough to buy a two-bedroom house on an acre, so I was astounded where we landed—in a
field.

 I had no idea what would come from the property I just
bought. On our final walkthrough, the previous owner Jim pointed
to a couple of aromatic heirloom rose bushes, one faded pink, the
other electric, which had been his grandmother's. Two crimson king
maples and a blue spruce, now immense, had been planted near the
house and, although beautiful, seemed suburban in the rural setting.

Jim noted that taking down the stand of trees at the base of the field would reveal a sliver of Hudson River view, which was only a couple thousand feet away. It never seemed necessary nor worth the sacrifice.

Spring came with an innocent confidence. Dogwoods embraced the field. The eager, bright green and red buds of the maples and poplars brimmed with excitement in April. The apple, pear and peach trees flowered, fleetingly.

As the first summer pulled in, I found that the fields were one part grass and one part poison ivy. Jim had not mentioned that the fields were impenetrable, untouchable, that we would have to stick to the trail on our daily walks. I was so disappointed—angry—and thought Jim should have told me. These were not fields to run through or for hosting picnics! I came to realize that this information would not have discouraged me from purchasing the property, nor was Jim dishonest, only how naïve I had been, how poison ivy and bramble were the norm for an under-kept meadow. My city friends would be aghast if they could identify the poison ivy and were aware of just how much there is. Enthusiastic and shiny red in the spring, with a matte finish in the fall, poison ivy helps paint the Hudson Valley foliage visitors adore. I lend my guests boots, long socks, and work pants to avoid the topic altogether. I rarely hear of any of them falling victim to the three-leafed predator, and I really am only infected by the venom when I yank it from the garden or trees. Despite what the literature says about the longevity and trans-ference of the oil, I never caught a rash from our dog or my clothes.

Once though, early on, I was clearing an apple tree of a poison ivy vine that was as thick as the tree itself, some six inches in diameter of furry centipede. I cut through the vine with a handsaw, separating its infinite grabbing feet from the bark, yanked, and the entire poison ivy canopy fell on top of me. The following week, the skin all over my body was raised an inch with red bumps rendering my face and hands unrecognizable. The faint brush of my clothes on my back was unbearable. I took hot showers to scorch it, to bring momentary relief, then suffered as the heat made the rash itch even more. In the end, I was given steroids. I had been hazed by Field Farm.

*   *   *

Weekends and those early summers we came up when we could. We walked, every day, the path that cut through the field and around the property. With Tess's little legs, and, soon after, puppy Charlotte's, that seemed enough for us to take on. We walked slowly and breathed in every leaf of grass along the way.

We cut bundles of flowers, which I carried back with Charlotte's warm, small, exhausted body cradled in my arms. It seemed each day brought new blooms, or we saw them for the first time. Many will never have names, only descriptions—"the small bluish ones with heart-shaped leaves near the sun-liking ferns." I am not good with names and don't feel the need to know what we humans call things that exist for themselves, not us, although naturalist Robert Pyle makes an excellent case for why I should, as stories are embedded in the Latin as well as indigenous names. But I knew when and where to find the flora and kept an eye out for the sturdy orange milkweed, the no-nonsense clusters of gray-white flowers with lace leaves in July in the same places. I also learned which flowers don't like to be picked; they would be spared next time, next walk, next summer. Many wildflowers stink up and sully the water more than conventional cut flowers, so I vase them in ceramic rather than glass. I transplanted some flowering plants to my garden, since they seemed to do well in this difficult clay soil, and I wanted to see more of them.

Every January I get used to the meadow in winter-mode, which has its own austere beauty, sculpted by history and topography, and shadows thrown by the empty trees which surround it. But it's hard to believe—impossible—what will happen in a few months' time. But it does. Each year, spring unfolds with predictability and regularity. Without fail, nature delivers boldly and with nuance. The field wakes and stretches, and from a dry, brown, sleeping mass, emerges a five-foot-high maze by July. Every day, every hour of the day, holds light and beauty uniquely. I never tire of watching the grass grow and the morning light hitting the back field sometimes through fog, the stand of trees beyond, the shadows, the spring foliage, the horizontal flowers of the dogwood, the turning leaf of the poplar in the wind, the white bending lines of the birch. In mid-spring, I will jog my memory:

Do the apple trees bloom before or after the dogwood?

BLUE BRIDAL FARM

In the early part of the 20th century, six black Angus grazed the meadow and sheltered in a barn at the base of the field. When lightning struck the electric box, the barn and cattle all went up in flames. A few charred boards and barbed wire and barrels still snarl in the corner of the field as evidence of that wretched event. The image flashes through my mind pretty much every time I watch the sun set. I imagine how the fire smelled.

Jim, the previous owner, had horses, and called this magical place Blue Bridal Farm. His wife rode with Barbara Lockhart, a neighbor, over the fields and through the woods, although I sometimes wonder how much riding there could have been. My 82 acres, plus her 150, is a lot of land, but could be covered in minutes on horseback at a gallop. I think about the trails they might have ridden; maybe they just walked the horses and chatted in a leisurely sort of way.

I never met Jim's ex-wife, but I sought out Barbara when I first bought the property. She had been one of the first landowners in the area to put her property under conservation easement, for which I was grateful since her woods bordered mine on two sides. That protected land was one of the reasons I decided this place was worth the gamble over the long haul. With the young artists and handy types that lived in a tenement-like structure on her farm, she organized Earth Day clean ups on our River Road, handing out plastic bags and serving apple cider and donuts as incentives.

To visit Barbara, I had to exit my driveway and enter hers three quarters of a mile from the other side, although going through the woods is the deer's shorter path. While a half-dozen defunct cars, rusting refrigerators, and unstable barns could be found in the woods between us, there was no car in the driveway, so I wasn't sure if Barbara was home. I knocked tentatively on the door of her white 1930s farmhouse.

"Who's there?" an alto shouted from inside.

"Hello, Mrs. Lockhart. My name is Cynthia McVay. I'm your new neighbor." I projected through the door tentatively.

"Come on in, then!"

Barbara was seated in the kitchen next to her potbellied stove on a late winter day. She looked as though she never moved from that chair, that was where she held court. Among the many knickknacks and wall hangings, a sign read: *MY BITE IS MUCH WORSE THAN MY BARK.* She had a reputation for being tough but good-hearted. A character. That she had preserved in perpetuity her forest and farm, in the middle of nowhere, long before conservation easements were fashionable, and many other African Americans were still fighting for their restitution and civil rights, marked her an iron-willed visionary.

I mumbled answers and admiration. I trembled in awe. Eventually I got around to asking her about the use of pesticides, which I had wanted to do before I bought my property. I had been reading about old orchards that had been turned into developments only to discover their lawns were laden with so much poison, four feet of soil was dug up and carted away.

"Never had any goddamn mosquitoes when we used DDT! 'Course the pond is totally dead now." The small, green pond was not entirely dead, but I wondered what the frogs looked like and how they might jump. Near the pond, behind her farmhouse, a thick, rusting chain draped casually around a crumbling square asphalt scab that had served as a boxing ring. Her late husband had been part of Joey Lewis's brigade.

Her answer wasn't the one I had wanted to hear, but it didn't sway me from loving my field, and her. And what I heard wasn't surprising. Everyone was using DDT at the time. That's what I had been afraid of, but it no longer seemed to matter.

I got to know some of Barbara's tenants and dropped in occasionally over the years. When her legs could no longer carry her, Barbara moved to a retirement community a few miles down

9W. She turned the property over to a couple of folks who had helped her with her chickens and tomatoes. River Road Earth Day cleanups have been replaced by Riverkeeper's organized sweeps of the Hudson River's banks. Barbara passed in 2012. I still refer to that property as Barbara Lockhart's although it's been years since her name was on the NO TRESPASSING signs on our shared border. I later learned from neighbors that Barbara was a graduate of Hunter College, a registered nurse, and an activist since she was a seventh grader, working on community and civic causes. I was honored to know her.

*   *   *

As much as he seemed to love his meadow, Jim sold the property to developers in the mid-1990s. Those buyers returned it to him when they were unable to get approval to drop in 42 trailers as the zoning went from two to three acres per lot. Simultaneously, in 1994, IBM closed their offices in Kingston, New York, reducing the need for housing. I was lucky to stumble across the property when I did—snapping it up for one-third the price it had been sold to the developers a few years earlier. The developers had done extensive survey work on the property, assessed the water and soil, and dug four wells. Jim gave me a box full of topographical maps and plans. One of the wells is now the source of water for the house. Two are in the woods. One is buried in the field and every year creates havoc for this tractor rider when it comes time to take down the field.

We decided to rename the property since horses were no longer part of its profile. Tess came up with something that seemed to capture its essence: Field Farm. That's what we have called it since.

EYES WIDE OPEN

The day I closed on the property in the local law offices of a nearby town, May 5, 2000 (*Cinco de Mayo* and unknowingly our future puppy's birthday), I drove to my purchase. I sat on the rotting stoop of the "front" door—as much a back or side—and looked over the field. I could not feel the warmth and welcoming, only the jitters that consumed me.

What had I just done? What made me think I could do this—take on 82 acres as a single mom, already stretched by a challenging and demanding job and a young child, and from a distance? The house was putrid, could not be lived in as it was. How would I manage its renovation, the enormity of it all? The fields? The decrepit apple trees?

I closed my eyes and lifted my face to the sun. *Mmmm.* I breathed in my country air. Then I heard the crackle of gravel and an engine. A broad man jumped out of a large pickup.

"I'm Ralph. I own the orchard next door."

"Nice to meet you."

"You the new owner?"

"As of an hour ago."

"Here." He threw a couple thick, bound documents at me. "That there is the agricultural code. It says I can do whatever I want, and you can't complain. Furthermore, your trees over there have branches hanging over the fence onto my property, and I'm going to cut them down."

That was how Ralph introduced himself to me.

Ralph's rumored $1 million investment into ten-foot deer fencing around the perimeter of his property and planting dozens of dwarf apple trees had factored into my purchase. Although I didn't love his fence—I was outside it like the deer—I was happy to know that the land uphill from me wouldn't be turned into a development any time soon.

Despite that introduction and even though Ralph sprays his orchards at sunset (I later surmised to avoid killing the pollinating bees who are in bed for the night)—especially when I have friends over, it seems—I appreciate how hard he works to make an honest living. As with many orchards in the region, he hosts family-picking events on fall weekends, and recently opened a farm stand down the road. He has since diversified his crops with heirloom tomatoes, plums, peaches, garlic, and a hillside of blueberry bushes and may be moving to organic. Chinese apples became impossible to compete with commercially, and apple cider can no longer be wrung from fallen apples.

I became friendly with the Jamaicans who work in Ralph's fields—wave when I see them, go up and talk to them through that deer fence—and often wondered whether Ralph is as stern with them as he was with me. But when I hear them in the orchards, seems all's well. Their conversation and laughter tumble down hill with the breeze. Eddie appears to be the patriarch, and his sons come from the islands during high season to help.

When Ralph "welcomed" me to the neighborhood, I didn't know what to say. I don't know what I said. I just know the tremble in me has persisted a couple decades, and I've never challenged Ralph on anything, and not because of the agriculture code. What Ralph didn't know, but perhaps he has come to learn, is I want him to succeed and wouldn't give him trouble. I am on his side.

Four days later, a severe storm hit with alleged 150-mile-an-hour winds (is that even possible?). The old walnut tree and the two crimson king maples by the house were left standing, but the storm whipped the 18-acre wood patch on the hill, toppling dozens of large trees, easy victims given their shallow root systems in shale beds. Tess and I weren't here for the storm but noticed the damage as soon as we came up the following weekend.

I sought lumberjacks in the yellow pages, someone with a portable sawmill who could make boards of the "blowdowns" in situ, to use in the reconstruction of the little house. A hefty logger came with The Wife (his name for her) and eight children for a visit, a Sunday outing. He rode his ATV across the field towards the hill, his family running behind. They passed the afternoon on the property, thanked me, but I never heard from him again.

My dream of rebuilding with wood from the property remained just that—an unrealized dream. The blowdowns were a mixed bag, a few each of tulip, oak, maple, beech; the local experts saw no value, no attraction in the assignment. And I learned that portable mills need accessibility and a flat area to work, neither of which were possible.

I monitored the blowdowns informally for a few years as they rotted in place, the huge vertical root systems—gripping rocks and dirt and shale—stood six feet above ground and left craters where water puddled, and other plants and mosses found refuge. I remembered what I'd learned in biology class decades earlier: When a tree comes down in the forest, it creates its own micro-ecosystem, letting in light for vegetative pioneers to move in.

Walking in the woods, beyond and around the freshly toppled trees, I noticed dozens of rock mounds roughly the length and shape of interred bodies, conjuring up a graveyard, death. Who was buried, here, in the woods? Then I put it together: Those shallow root systems of the downed trees, which lifted with them shale and rocks, over time, rotted away. The rocks sunk in place, creating lazy piles beside the holes they'd created. The mounds, in fact, were tree tombs.

*   *   *

Field Farm was a piece of land, with a humble house overlooking an intoxicating meadow. No barns, silos, or outbuildings gave visual homage to a productive past, other than a couple of leaning lean-tos, the softened walls of fist-sized stones in the woods and the pile of boards and oil barrels at the base of the field from the cattle barn that burned down a half century earlier.

The raging storm responsible for the dozens of blowdowns had also lifted a three-bay lean-to—which before me had housed a motorboat for nearby Hudson River jaunts—and wafted it into the field. Large, flat pieces of corrugated metal and fiberglass were strewn across the meadow hundreds of feet from their origin. I was happy the demolition of the unseemly lean-to was the only "real" harm that occurred, although, to be fair, there wasn't much to damage.

I had contemplated whether I would keep that nothing-special lean-to in the middle of the lawn. So, in a way, I was thankful the decision had been made for me. I received and pocketed $4,000 in insurance for the loss, with no intention to rebuild. The posts remained standing, fortified with concrete, stubborn and unmovable.

We hung an eight-foot deer fence on the posts to create an enclosed vegetable garden. Many topsoil dumps and mulch bags later, we squeezed out a tomato or two, but mostly battled the encroaching meadow and lawn outside the fence. Even topped with better soil, the clay beneath and myriad of springs rotted the roots of anything we planted.

Nearer to the house, in all its ramshackle splendor, gaped another five-bay lean-to, of similar architectural provenance, which inexplicably has remained standing. Every couple of years, the handyman in my life—a boyfriend, a caretaker, a hired hand—buttresses the leaning structure with weather-treated four-by-fours, re-secures the corrugated fiberglass roof or siding, which allow in light, or sprays poison into the holes drilled by the hundreds of super-sized, voracious carpenter bees. We nod at that year's Band-Aid, and say, *guess we can get another year out of it.*

The five-bay "garage" is a study of what accumulates when given the room to do so over a couple decades, a little like a huge kitchen junk drawer. It houses a tractor and accoutrement; piles of leftover wood from deck, fencing and siding projects; a regulation-size soccer goal my sister gave Tess when she graduated from high school, not used once; a rolled up badminton or volleyball net; gardening gloves mud-crust-dried into acrobatic poses; an injured and dormant basketball stand; several extendable apple-pruning saws and clippers; shovels and spades, plastic and metal rakes missing tongs; oodles of hoses; spray dispensers; a couple of stiff, dull hand-push lawnmowers; piles of rusty nuts and bolts most of which predate me; organic fertilizers in compromised boxes; a bag of leaking grass seed and very fine grass growing beside; orange life vests and wooden paddles, two kayaks, and a porous canoe.

Every caretaker has asked if he can clean out the lean-to—*yes!* —but has never gotten to it—and not because they were too busy, that's for sure. I have come to believe they ask me that during the interview, and express excitement about the use of the vegetable garden, to impress me. Or perhaps they do have intentions and dreams. But generally, they don't get around to either. Rather, when they eventually move out, they leave behind another pile of stuff with no immediate utility that is not quite garbage.

THE HOUSE

The 1930s house was a wreck. Shag wall-to-wall carpeting from the 1970s shouldered up against the woodstove with aluminum foil as a protective shield. The low ceilings had been dropped further with Styrofoam tiles. The basement was under a half foot of water most of spring. On closer inspection, the quaint, dusty blue shutters with stenciled moon slivers were plastic, and dumpster bound. The view of the field was squandered through a single aluminum door and a "picture" window that could not be opened. The tiny bathroom was filthy and awkward, like a badly designed ship WC. Under the blue plastic wood paneling and the extra walls that chopped up the living room, and after excavating decades of mouse nests with varying degrees of activity, I discovered the original one-room cabin built by a squatter, a hundred years earlier, initials scratched on the weathered siding. Removing the woodstove revealed a decent fireplace that drew well.

While I did not buy the property for the house, I spent close to a year renovating it to make a weekend home for Tess and me. Tess was a trooper, taking hose-cold baths in an antique tub in the lawn, too young to expect anything else. She thought that was normal. We slept on futons on a platform, without walls, open to the elements, not knowing yet about the coyotes, but certainly aware of the mosquitoes, and later, the unpredictable workmen that slept nearby.

I didn't realize that the house was a candidate for razing until we were halfway through its reconstruction. I hadn't set out to buy a vacant piece of property and start from scratch, but that's essentially what happened. The contractor, Patrick, who came recommended by a friend in Hudson, was a tall, even-featured blond, with translucent skin, with whom I shared palpable but need-to-squelch chemistry. Patrick assigned a couple guys to live and work at the house during the week since Hudson was too far to

31

commute from every day. Patrick showed up on Friday afternoons, just as we did from the city, in time for dinner. So, Patrick often shared a candlelit dinner, on a little makeshift table in our wall-less home.

The main carpenter, grungy, beefy, heavily-tattooed (before it was fashionable), and red-faced, who lived on site with Tess and me, turned out to be an ex-convict and drunk most of the time. He worked with a cigarette hanging limply out of his swollen, sunburnt face, and rubbed the butts out into the gravel, twisting his metal-toed boot with a certain intensity. Although he never physically harmed us, he had a threatening edge. Once, he screamed bloody hell and fell off the ladder. I ran to see what had happened. A black rat snake had dropped through the ceiling from the attic onto his head. I found it amusing that such a tough guy could be unnerved by a harmless reptile but came to learn that most locals fear snakes just like the rest of us, even we nature-kind environmentalists who pretend nothing scares us.

The carpenters sanded down seven wood doors to remove unseemly crackling, peeling brown shellac. When they came to ask me what color to paint them, I was bowled over. The sanding had revealed three to four layers of paint, spanning decades, blues and whites and natural wood, specks of red and yellow and green, akin to fired pottery. We left them in that state, each an original piece of Raku-like art, born of an honest process, without self-consciousness, but out of function and deliberateness. If I had asked the carpenters to sand down the doors to achieve that effect, I doubt such beauty would have been cajoled from them.

The open living room with the old squatter's cabin inside shares a view of the meadow with the airy, raised-ceiling kitchen. We stained the hardwood floors—which had been protected for decades by carpeting—and the window moldings dark brown. We built a deck with prime meadow views beyond a wall of windows.

As with any old house, there were discoveries and unforeseen complications. When I asked how much an alteration would cost, the answer was *about $150*. I have no idea how those small adjustments summed to $100,000 more than what our contract stipulated. All told, the renovation cost four times the estimate. When I asked Patrick about it, he said, "All my projects end up being four times what people budgeted," not realizing he had incriminated himself.

Although it made me seethe, I was beholden to him. I fired Patrick and his crew in September, finally, given the many delays and mishaps and extra costs, but he begged to return to finish the job, for his own conscience, he said, for free.

After much pleading on his part, I acquiesced, wary. I had no alternative, no contractors in my hip pocket. All I had was an unfinished house on a big piece of land, and I lived two hours away.

His small team worked for another six weeks, without billing me, and then, just as frost bit in November, he held me by my female balls. With no doors and the radiators spread across the lawn, he demanded I write another $20,000 check or he would leave me to deal with winter—a house open to weather and freezing pipes. I cried my way through writing that final check, with little Tess, thigh-high, oblivious to the charades around her.

A couple years later I heard that Patrick had been thrown in jail—and I thought, *Yes! Someone finally got him*—for having two silos full of marijuana. Ah, so.

*   *   *

The two-bedroom house, once renovated, had some recommending features. The brick fireplace, asymmetrical but functioning, throws heat back into the room much like an efficient Rumson. Years later, we covered the tacky brick with vintage forest green shutters to create a mantel. The master bedroom has three sides of windows which furnish generous light and a gentle cross breeze.

I did not replace the unseemly asphalt roof until it leaked, six years later, and did so with metal standing seam, which promises to have an infinite life and can be recycled when the house is gone. The standing seam roof redeemed the house aesthetically in an instant.

For years, I didn't paint the exterior, given its modest profile and dimensions, fearing that if it were too cleaned up it would look like a trailer. After replacing the asphalt roof, painting the house became a possibility. Initially, we went with a pale lichen-mossy color that blended in with the landscape and more recently repainted with a dark greenish brown, like the forest floor. Although not an historic or architectural gem, the house, which we now call "the cottage," both roomy and cozy, possesses its own unpretentious charms.

Tess found a baby bird that had fallen out of its nest under the black walnut tree by the house. It was just old enough to identify as a cedar waxwing. We put it in a box with leaves, water, berries and small insects. A couple days later, when it seemed ready to be reintroduced to the wild, we returned it to where we'd found it. An identical cedar waxwing stood on the tree's root and didn't budge as we placed our rescue down beside. They stood with the same posture, neat and erect for a moment, swung their heads one way, then the other, in unison, in an instinctive choreographed moment. We thought we were seeing double.

One brutally cold winter, we arrived on a Friday night to water gushing through the walls. After a week of negative twenty-degree nights, every radiator had frozen and cracked—apparently along with a quarter of houses in the region. In all the confusion, I didn't question the oil company delivering oil the next morning. Had they missed a delivery? Was the gauge on the tank unresponsive? Had it been empty? I didn't try to recreate why the house had frozen or pursue the oil company for damages; there was too much mayhem to ascertain what had happened. The insurance company sprayed preventatively for mold and wrote me a $40,000 check for the water damage and cracked radiators. As allowed, I did not install a new heating system at the time, not keen to invest further in the house, nor feel beholden to Field Farm in the winter the way I did the other three seasons.

We drained the water in the late fall and, in spring, once frost had passed, turned it back on. Tess and I occasionally came up from the city during the winter, sometimes bringing adventurous friends, and camped in the living room with a fire, closing off the hall to the bedrooms. Newly insulated, the room reached eighty degrees even with frigid temperatures outside. We played Apples to Apples or Scrabble, melted snow for cooking water (ratio of 20:1 snow: water, a little better than maple syrup). We showered in the city before we left and flushed the toilet with buckets of water dragged from the stream. Those were cherished times.

THE POOL

Once the house was done, almost immediately, Tess and I decided we needed a pool.

The red-faced, pointy-nosed pool man tried to convince me to plunk the pool right off the living room's deck so I could go in and get a beer whenever I was overcome by thirst. Not interested in beer accessibility nor looking at the pool cover off season, I wanted to create a separate experience, an outdoor room. So, a 20' X 40' pool went in two hundred feet away at the far end of the lawn, beyond where the three-bay lean-to had been, a little down slope from two productive Bartlett pear trees, into the same gently curving rock bed on which the house sits. This turned out to be the perfect site. Later, I would build my barn-home beyond, but I didn't know that yet.

I had assumed I'd be putting in a Gunite pool, but they were hard to come by in the region, very expensive, liable to crack in winter given the topography, so not a viable option. The pool company offered an array of white and turquoise liners, with fake tile decorating the waterline, which seemed incongruous in the organic landscape. When I grimaced, they showed me a black liner—soft and velvety like an inner tube. The decision was easy. Over the years, the black faded to dark, mottled slate, which renders the pool, even as a rectangle, pondish. That felt right for Field Farm.

Saline systems were not yet available, but when the pool pump failed a decade later, we replaced it with saltwater filtration. No smell of chlorine hovers in the air or on the skin. The salt concentration is the same as that of gentle, joyous tears.

The standard issue aluminum deep-end ladder that came with the pool found its home in the basement—where it still is twenty-plus years later seeking something to scale. A typical diving board didn't seem quite right either. The pool remained a simple, unadulterated rectangle for years. Eventually, a Maya Lin-designed outdoor coffee table, oblong, of gray concrete, became a diving platform. Other Maya-Lin pieces from the same store-closing-sale purchase, smaller and taller, are strategically placed to rest a morning coffee.

The building department mandates a four-foot fence around pools to keep small, unattended children from falling in, even though this pool is thousands of feet from any neighbor and the road. A fence discourages deer from falling in too (a small anxiety I harbor), and there are plenty of those. White plastic nor a solid picket fence would work in the open landscape. I settled on split rail, which seemed appropriate to the farm's visual vocabulary, with a barely-visible 4" x 2" metal garden fence tacked on to comply with regulations.

Digging holes was onerous. Two crews worked sequentially on the 360-linear-foot fence and quit. One broke a tractor-powered hydraulic auger drilling. The third and final crew cut off the bases of some posts and secured them in the ground with concrete because they couldn't dig deeper. Without the integrity of depth, the fence leans this way and that, not quite comfortable with itself.

The fence project confirmed what I had already learned in the garden: Not only is Field Farm sitting on a rock shelf, but the soil is either rock-hard dry or slippery-when-wet clay packed with fist-sized rocks. With the stone walls surrounding the fields and squaring off property boundaries within the woods, you'd think all the stones were removed a century ago. But there are more—layers and layers. You can skim off the surface and there's another layer. With the exception of the alluvial plains around meandering waterways—orchards and animal husbandry are abundant in the Hudson Valley, I believe, because it is so hard to till.

Around the pool, I envisioned a clean modern concrete patio of large smooth squares. Purveyors suggested pressing "decorative" fake rocks into the concrete (*otherwise very slippery!*), which I could not warm up to. They described a scratching process, and I wondered whether I would end up with a sidewalk or what might feel like a public pool. My inclination to install a bluestone patio seemed foolhardy given the disturbed earth would be settling for a year or two. But the raw dirt needed something.

We laid a six-foot wide path of pea gravel around the pool, and then built a three-foot-wide path-deck of pressure-treated 1 X 1's atop running 2 X 6's and a larger platform for lounge chairs in the shallow end, where Tess and I played Scrabble— and lost half a dozen Scrabble pieces over the years through the slats. The deck worked off multiples of three, including 9' X 9' gardens and a gravel bed for relief. It had a sophisticated, Japanese vibe.

Over time, the wood slats warped and separated from the anchoring 2 X 6's. The oversized truck inner tubes we'd brought home for pool play (the same velvety black as the liner) wilted, pierced by the screws. The man at the industrial tire center apologized and patched the inner tubes for free, multiple times, even though I insisted it was not his fault nor responsibility. Every spring, we assessed the pool deck, re-secured any outliers, and eliminated pointy culprits, concerned the screws might puncture more than just inner tubes.

A decade later, we replaced the warping deck with two-foot-square local, organic bluestone. We visited the quarry in the foot-hills of the Catskills to pick the stone. Along the dirt road, as we approached, mammoth pieces of stone scattered, leaned, piled on a spectacular hilltop with 360-degree views. The owner's home, walkways, *everything* was made of stone. Atop the hill, oblivious to the prime views, the owner had burrowed an underground passage between the house and the rock shop hundreds of feet long, lined with—yes—stone. He was ready for the apocalypse. One couldn't help positing that he possessed far too much stone, possibly too much time, and likely a dose of paranoia. He was, after all, in the middle of nowhere. Who was coming after him?

When I saw dozens of cylindrical cores of different heights and widths that had been punched from tabletops for umbrellas, I asked whether he had plans for them. They came home with me, as my own miniature Maya Lin sculpture, along with a large stone tabletop that sits atop a wrought iron base poolside.

The mason did an excellent job laying the stone and creating a bulbous nose rim around the pool edge. He had never laid stone square on square—he usually staggered them—but I liked the straightforward linearity of it, and he seemed convinced in the end too.

At the start, I had asked the mason whether we should keep on the pool cover, and he declined. I understood he needed access to the pool edge and could not work around the cords. During construction, concrete and stone bits ended up in the pool rendering the bottom of the pool moon-like. The filter was caked with concrete. The pool guy attempted multiple times to get the pool functioning again with little success. The mason, defensive and irate, revealed his racist streak, blaming my (Black) pool cleaner of many years. I was livid. I insisted the mason remediate the situation, which he eventually did with his pool-keeping brother-in-law, netting out buckets of rocks and debris, and bypassing the pump. Half our pool time was lost that summer in the process, but it was resolved.

I always learn something, but wonder, how can I anticipate all the issues that can go wrong? Yes, the mason fulfilled his promise of installing a patio, but as an experienced mason, someone who had laid dozens of pool patios, I assumed he knew what the project entailed. This couldn't be the first time he dropped concrete in a pool.

This is part of a pattern. Over the years, tradesmen deliver the contracted work but are blind to the impact their work has on other things. Lawn mowers snare a hydrangea or throw grass seed into the garden. Painters drip paint on a new floor. Floor guys splatter wood stain on freshly painted walls.

A year later, we discovered that the mason had left chunks of stone and wire and boards in the field at his staging area, buried in the tall grass, damaging a tractor that ran through it.

In the end, it didn't matter. This too passed, tucked away in four weeks of mayhem a decade ago, a distant memory. The blue-stone patio, which I live with every day, has created an extra dose of tranquility and elegance, and lends legitimacy to an otherwise out-of-control display of floral abandon and a modest liner pool. I wish I had done it earlier.

The pool became the draw for urban dwelling friends and later Airbnb guests. Gratuitous physical contact during water polo matches July 4th and Labor Day parties was a highlight until I felt all the bodice ripping was inappropriate in my mid-fifties. The games were rough and rowdy, with more dunking and holding people under water than passing or scoring. But the pool, and comparatively lazy volleyball games, was sheer jubilance.

POOL GARDEN

A Sanctuary of Orphans and Strays

The bare earth around the pool, inside the fence, was an invitation to create a garden from scratch without the interference of deer, who could jump the four-foot fence but wouldn't, I was told, deterred by the size of the enclosure. This was generally true, except in winter, when anything green was irresistible.

It didn't occur to me to hire a professional landscaper. This was the kind of thing I undertook on my own, with whomever's help was on hand. I scoured books with garden photos, maps, ideas. I talked to the folks at the local nursery and came home with a variety of junipers to anchor the empty beds. A friend gave me a "blue" Rose of Sharon as a pool-warming gift. (Am I colorblind or is blue really purple in gardening parlance?) It has spawned dozens if not hundreds of bushes of varying colors, creating a dense privacy screen; many found their way to other gardens.

While visiting a friend, I saw her gardener digging around her ice pond. Irritated by their abundance, she was giving dozens of irises the heave-ho—yes, throwing away a huge stash of Siberian and bearded iris. I'm not sure what would be more lovely and suitable around that body of water, but I wasn't going to convince her to keep them. I backed up my old Volvo and brought bags full of tubers to Field Farm.

Irises are easy and not fussy. They like to be at the surface without mulch, and don't mind wet feet, which the clay soil provides in spring, particularly in low spots. I dedicated a nine-by-nine-foot bed in the pool enclosure to Siberian irises. The tidy leaf blades push up in April in organized clumps, develop purple cocoons which open into a sea of purple, precious in their ephemera. These graceful stalks control my movement. I don't travel, barely go grocery shopping, because I don't want to miss the irises

41

for a day, an hour, a moment. At times, a lone red poppy stands among them punctuating and competing, in color-wheel contrast.

The large, floppy bearded irises spread across the garden at the deep end of the pool among spirea and false indigo. Voluptuous and fleshy in soft champagne, amber and salmon, their scent allures and invites closer inspection. They bloom at the same time as the false indigo and are lovely together in the garden or in a bouquet.

Being something of a novice gardener at the time, I had not fully appreciated how early in the spring irises emerge. To accommodate and enjoy their enticing display, I open the pool for the irises—and to get out ahead of the weeding—in early April, well before Memorial Day, the traditional pool-opening time. Climate change has been shifting spring earlier too. I don't swim in the spring chill but prefer sitting and gardening by the water to a pool cover and not having to worry about tripping on the cords and stakes that secure the cover.

Bright, greasy buttercups float above the mulch in spring, too. Why not let them? They are full of cheer, when so little else is happening. I transplanted a sturdy clump of purple coneflowers— Echinacea—from the house's existing garden, and watered it diligently through that first dry, hot summer. That Echinacea plant, joined by additional seeds and plantings over the years, proliferated and now marches over a good part of the shallow-end garden and beyond, three feet tall for much of midsummer.

The native Echinacea, in the composite daisy family, is considered a holistic miracle plant. It is believed to stave off a cold, be an anti-inflammatory and relieve the side effects of cancer treatments. On occasion, when my current dog Dexter has an upset stomach, he chomps at Echinacea leaves instinctively. It would be convenient to use the Echinacea in its raw state—that is, grab a leaf as you go by, like he does—but experts recommend drying leaves or flowers or tubers to make tea. I sometimes wonder who drinks all that tea people recommend. I have so much Echinacea that I play with the idea of making a medicinal tincture. In the end, I am loath to sacrifice the plants at peak, which is what is called for. I wouldn't mind so much if I could use the flowers once they've faded from deep purple to burnt bluish pink like a bright sock that's been thrown in the wash with new jeans, or when I behead them anyway at the end of the season. But I do like saying, *Echinacea tincture*, so I talk about doing it from time to time.

I dug up feral daylilies from along the driveway and surrounded the Echinacea with a border, offsetting the purple with orange. I unearthed sun-loving, wetland ferns from the field and brought them in. I transplanted red and pink tallish bee balm in from the field and planted it towards the back of a couple beds. Round, large-leafed Italian oregano plants have immigrated from the meadow on their own and emerge in generous clumps, with small lavender-hued flowers. Self-planted native concord grapes grow yards a day in summer, grabbing the fence and bushes along the way. Asters, golden rod, and milkweed have joined the others to make their home in this and other gardens.

After cutting through the cottage garden while mowing the lawn (another example of a man's singular focus), a boyfriend compensated me with eight perennial stout black-eyed Susan's, whose leaves and countenance are like Echinacea, along with a perennial late-blooming seven-foot yellow-eyed varietal, which I planted toward the back of a couple gardens. The annual black-eyed Susan, a byproduct of my attempts to sow a wildflower meadow, self seed and squeeze through wherever they can—including patio cracks.

*   *   *

"I hate Lily of the Valley," a friend said a few years ago, with a grimace.

She couldn't mean it. "How can you hate Lily of the Valley?" I asked.

"I just pulled hundreds from my garden and threw them

43

away," she said without audible remorse.

"You threw them away?"

"They're so invasive!"

"I would've taken them! I love Lily of the Valley!" and it's invasive, aromatic beauty. After the bloom fades, the foliage creates a pleasing groundcover.

"Well, they're gone. Gone," she said with finality.

My heart sank.

I had few places to plant them as most of my gardens are full-on sun. But I would have taken them in a heartbeat, walked them into the woods and let them have a run of it there. Or maybe planted them beside a puddle-pond on the edge of the field, which I posit was dug to water cattle a century ago. I have a fantasy of turning that spot into a shady, moss garden for mid-August escape.

I eventually received a stash of Lily of the Valley from another friend who, too, was exasperated by them. Undeterred, I planted them in the shade of the large sugar maple by the house where, because of the maple's roots, the soil is shallow and generally unwelcoming. I am pleased to report that they have taken over and a couple times each spring I cut a dozen stems and stick them in a small vase in the bathroom.

I gave wildflowers a go of it around the pool initially. Handfuls, pounds, balls, tubes, packets of seeds thrown on bare earth. Over the years, some California orange poppies survived and indeed thrived, moving from the garden to the pea gravel beside the garden where they seem to prefer the radiant heat and open space. A few tall, broken-necked, red poppies pop up in different beds, beside dusty blue cornflowers with their silver sheen—perfection! When the poppies start going to seed and the cornflowers dry up, I face a recurring dilemma: If I want seeds for the following year, I must allow them to go through their sad, unattractive demise.

A friend held an unopened, drooping poppy bud in her hand, and said, "I must come get seeds from you," not understanding that I rely on them to seed themselves and I sacrifice my aesthetic to do so.

"Eden is offering 100,000 seeds right now," I say, to protect my diminishing supply. I couldn't imagine asking someone for their precious poppy seeds, although I am happy to part with many of the other abundant and escaping flowers—iris, spirea, obedience, rose of Sharon. But not poppies.

From the cottage I transplanted a local sedum which was being regularly clipped by passing deer. Inside the pool fence, the sedum filled out and multiplied. The sturdy plant provides contrast in deliberate, stoic clumps and bloom in the fall when the Echinacea and most everything else begins to flag. That is, except the native sunchoke—also known as Jerusalem artichoke—whose stalks tower more than ten feet, a golden sunflower angling against the clear blue late September sky. I relish eating the divine tuber packed with nutrients in November. The more I excavate, and eat, the healthier the stand. I am happy to accommodate.

Animal sanctuaries in the Hudson Valley welcome injured and abused animals. I have a plant sanctuary. Most of the flowers in my garden are habitat-proven, transplants, orphans, free. They are modest, plentiful, informal farm flowers. They tolerate clay soil and droughts. They are aggressive survivors. My garden—and I—cannot be fussy. I have been disappointed by blights, rot, drought, fungus, mites, Japanese beetles, rabbits, deer. Whatever comes up, and makes it or flourishes, wins my admiration and a place. And many of them remind me of my generous friends.

The native American high-bush cranberry, or Viburnum, has become a personal favorite. I planted several foot-tall saplings in the pool area, which are now fifteen feet tall with abundant, white clusters of flowers in May, succulent dark red cranberries in late summer, and beet-red maple-like leaves in fall. They please year-round. When a branch laden with berries becomes too heavy, I prune it back, bring it inside, stick the cutting in a vase and locate it centrally to catch the light. After a few weeks of bliss, I pitch it along the edge of my lawn or garden, where some berries self-plant to produce more bushes. One year, the berries were so heavy and plentiful, I made cranberry sauce for Thanksgiving. Unlike the bog berries we purchase in the grocery store, the fruit has pits, so must be sieved. A deep beet crimson, and more sauce than jelly, it is slightly pungent and something of an acquired taste.

Our neighbors in Princeton, where I grew up, had a traditional, large yard with box hedge and hosta and a formal rose garden outside the living room, below the master bedroom. When I think of roses, I think of that well-mulched elegant garden, and Mrs. Wilson out there sculpting and spraying and watering the bushes. I have planted a few rose bushes here and there, more informal varietals. A tiny rose bush I bought for a spring Easter table has become one of my favorites, standing four feet tall with a lovely deep red flower and polished dark green leaf. A generous, loose rose bush has an abundance of open pink blooms and a delicious aroma in the early summer outside the living room window.

Until Michael. We met on Match in 2006—when online dating was still new and carried an air of desperation. I had consulted for Match for several years so knew the algorithms and had a comfort level, but Michael never wanted to admit that we'd met that way, so he'd say we met at a gallery— which was true, on our first date. To be fair, he felt like someone I should have met in the regular course of events but hadn't. Divorced for ten years, Michael was an environmentalist and in the soil business; his ex-wife was a landscape designer and gardener. He had a lot of credibility when he suggested rose bushes to climb the pool's split-rail fence. It went against my grain to make such a deliberate, risky investment. Nonetheless, at his insistence, I bought thirty-five deep crimson climbing rosebushes from his business partner, who swore by their no-nonsense hardiness. Even with a generous discount, I forked over hundreds of dollars. We spent a day planting them at the base of each fencepost around the pool and at the end of the driveway. We spoiled them with topsoil and fertilizer—something I rarely do for other plants. Even so, only a half dozen survived.

They put on a fabulous show in early summer before they succumb to losing every leaf to black spot fungus or Japanese beetles, ending the season gangly and naked. A precious few produce flowers throughout summer.

One morning, lying in bed, I asked Michael, "What about that arbor we were going to build?" Michael, who had mentioned the arbor idea months earlier, barely groaned.

After we sipped our coffee and watched the sun rise over the meadow, we measured, bought materials for, and built an arbor skeleton of cedar posts and beams and wire to frame a 9-foot by 18-foot area along the pool. We planted one orange trumpet vine, and two wisterias at either end. The wisteria wasn't expected to bloom for years, but to our delight, drooping, aromatic flowers emerged the following spring.

Today, a ridiculous tangle of vines shades the arbor space. Both vines throw off hundreds of pods every year; young plants push up through the pebbles beneath, in the garden and the field behind the pool area. The trumpet vine crawls along the ground, while tender wisteria shoots grow straight out from the vine trunk, reaching, looking for something to grab, perhaps an unsuspecting reader lounging by the pool. I don't cut them back because I hope these shoots will yield more blooms, which are increasingly scant. In the battle of trumpet vine vs. wisteria, the trumpet vine is winning. It's hard to get a handle on the proliferation; I will have to deal with this soon.

But not quite yet. When I sit in the arbor's shade, ruby-throated hummingbirds dart about, ricochet into one another, in invisible territory disputes. I am in their peripheral vision. They pay me no mind until I pull out my camera-phone; then, of course—*zoom!*—they're gone. Males catch the sun, with their splendiferous translucent sapphire breast; females are shades of gray. Some mornings, sitting in silence with my laptop and coffee, these 0.1 to 0.2-ounce helicopters buzz so fast I fear one may spear me. They are the only birds able to not only hover in place but fly backwards, accounting for their helicopter deportment. On occasion, one hangs above me, looks me in the eye, cocks its head to study my ear to see if it, too, has nectar. *No!* They fly back and forth, back and forth, at up to 60 miles per hour, persistent, relentless, almost bouncing off one another, like magnets of the same persuasion. I am not concerned about their ability to keep up with their fructose demand—given their high velocity and metabolism—as they have plenty to pillage. But it is hard to imagine that after they've spent the summer on Field Farm, these fragile, high-tech birds make their way thousands of miles to Mexico and Texas to overwinter like Monarch butterflies.

And so, the pool became a rambunctious, overwhelming garden attracting not only bathers and meditators, but all manner of pollinators and other wildlife: green and gold finches, sweeping purple swallows, courting mallard ducks in spring, vocal, brazen mockingbirds, paired cardinals, tumbling butterflies, hovering dragonflies, garter and black rat snakes, twitching bunnies, and chirping chipmunks, all of whom are as surprised and delighted as I when we bump into each other.

THE BARN PROJECT

*"To be a philosopher is not merely
to have subtle thoughts . . . but so
to love wisdom as to live according
to its dictates, a life of simplicity,
independence, magnanimity, and trust.
It is to solve some of the problems of life,
not only theoretically, but practically."*

—Henry David Thoreau, *Walden*

EXPLORING

Weekends Tess spent with her dad, I dropped her off at school on Friday morning and headed north from New York City to the Hudson Valley, to Field Farm. Michael met me later in the day.

Those weekends, Michael and I made headway on our *List of a Million Things to Do*. We were both early risers. He was handy, and I was a motivated, eager sous carpenter and gardener. We fixed and made things, battled the poison ivy and grapevines under the rubric The Invasive Species Management Program.

Being with Michael was like belonging to the country club I had always longed for. He smelled like antiques. The Chippendale grandfather clock in Michael's 18th-century house had been passed down from his grandparents and the oversized oil painting crowding his living room wall depicted a colonial-era aristocrat with Michael's features. Or vice versa. Michael grew up playing with the Forbes sons, and summered on Martha's Vineyard, in the same rental house, for close to six decades. He wore handsome, padded Barbour jackets in autumnal colors outdoors and a German boiled wool jacket to formal events. An avid environmentalist, he hung kestrel boxes on Field Farm, where we spent most of our time, and was studying falconry. It stood to reason that Michael hunted and fished. He brought his reel and spent a weekend fishing Esopus Creek near me with his ex-parents-in-law, on a weekend that I couldn't join them, which I never understood or got over. This is what he did: Michael eagerly shared and contributed to my world but continued to live in his own, previous life, without me. His ex-wife, divorced ten years prior, was everywhere I wasn't, and often where I was.

Michael came with Rocks, his chocolate Labrador, who behaved like an exposed nerve, with a big knuckle head and, even as a six-year-old, a surplus of puppy enthusiasm. I always said, *if you like dogs, you'll love Rocks. If you don't like dogs, you won't.* We loved Rocks and he was part of the package, and de facto our lab Charlotte's boyfriend, so we double-dated quite a bit, especially on walks through the field. Charlotte was full-blooded, she had papers, was beautiful and refined, but was not pedigreed like Rocks. Rocks came from exceptional lineage and was trained to hunt. Charlotte cowered at the sound of a shot and found solace in a closet, something I totally understood.

I am indebted to Michael for his unbridled enthusiasm, encouragement, and the sweat equity he put into Field Farm over many years. We collaborated well on projects and genuinely enjoyed working outdoors in the land together. I was happy to do grunt work—hand him tools or hold logs while he wrangled the power tools to cut or screw them together. Unlike many men, he understood that I wanted to help design, discuss, and weigh options. Importantly, he didn't mansplain.

A resourceful partner, Michael found new trails to hike nearby. He won a kayak at a benefit and restored a handsome 30-foot vintage "war" canoe we lowered into the Hudson River with a dozen friends. We headed to small hamlets all over the Hudson Valley to listen to music or taste-test a new eatery. We made a habit of pioneering new territory, drove down dirt roads pretending they weren't driveways, particularly intrigued by those with NO TRES-PASSING signs.

In my search for Field Farm, I came across a simple wooden church for sale in the tiny town of Krumville. The church, no longer in use, filled most of the footprint of the land that came with it, making installation of a well and septic field near impossible, and city water nor sewage were available in that rural setting. Converting the church into a home in situ would be difficult. Plus, the neighbors, who didn't seem particularly friendly, were *right there*.

I continued to think about that church for a couple years and imagined moving it to Field Farm in the meadow around the corner, not far from the two-hundred-year-old cemetery. I liked the idea of recreating history, in a way, confusing future historians by giving the cemetery a church. I toyed with the idea enough to write the minister of the shuttered church, to see if he would accept $10,000 for its removal and conservation, but never heard back. A part of me knew the church would likely not make the trip nor renovation unscathed. The siding was worn and would need replacing, the windows and roof required serious repair. Having just lived through the renovation of my simple house, and seeing how much was rebuilt from scratch, I wondered what would be left of the charming church after its travels and conversion.

I mention the church because it was a spiritual predecessor to what would become The Barn. So was the silo, for which I researched many standing silos and silo plans, both wood and concrete. IKEA was selling a round bed one year which made a silo even more intriguing. Someone told me that people who live in round rooms go insane. I didn't believe him, but stopped obsessing about silos. I also loved the notion of disappearing into the hill with an energy efficient berm dwelling, and considered container homes, sleek glass boxes, modern prefabs, years before they became widely popular and available. But they were pricey.

One day early on, I called up Smith & Hawken—the now defunct garden catalog company—about their greenhouses, after dog-earing that page for years. The conversation went something like this.

"Hello, this is Molly. How may I help you?"

"Hello, Molly. I wanted to know more about the 8′ X 10′ greenhouses?" I asked.

"I'll see if I can answer your questions."

"So, how hot do they get in the summer, say, in the northeast, and what kind of ventilation is there?"

"The windows can be opened, and there is a fan as an add-on option."

"And in the winter, how cold do they get? How well do they retain heat in twenty-degree weather?"

"There is a heating unit available, as another add-on option."

"Is the glass insulated?"

"People don't start using them for seedlings until February or March. So that isn't usually a problem. And they keep plenty warm then."

". . . If I wanted to live in one."

Silence. "Ma'am, they are greenhouses. They are for plants, not for people."

"I realize that. Please bear with me. Can you imagine three or four scattered in a field, like glass tents or houses?" I'm not sure she could, but I still do.

I looked at yurts, too, although not seriously; their overwhelming seventies vibe was a put-off. I joked about using them for strategic planning retreats, which I was still doing as my day job. Imagine retreat attendees—the top eight to ten company managers—getting together to build a yurt the first day of a strategy session, and then holding the meeting in it the second day. They would learn about each other on a personal level, how to communicate, trust, and collaborate, while working with their hands. After a few strategic planning sessions, Field Farm would have a yurt colony. This amused me for a nanosecond but was not something I coveted or really wanted to live with.

We began exploring barns just for fun, abandoned ones in fields (also often bearing NO TRESPASSING signs). Michael shared my love of barns and had always harbored a desire to live in one. Barns—and embarking on a big project every three years—are in my blood. I approached the project in a *Fountain Head* kind of way. I wanted the barn unadorned, authentic, minimalist.

As we explored, we found that each barn we visited had its own story and soul. Many were loaded with couches, antique fridges and cars, fluorescent lights hammered into beams; sloping additions and rooms were carved into smaller spaces. I wanted to be true to whatever barn I ended up with. Like old trees, they were sculpted by time and weather and utility.

Many barn conversions done in the 1970s felt tired and uninspired. When I looked at books on converted and renovated barns, or visited those of people in the business, I was disappointed to see that most were covered with new clapboard which, to my eyes, detracted from the barn-ness, making them big drab boxes. I loved the old barns the way they were, in their original setting, generally atop a stone foundation, naturally nestled into a field or hill, laden with a rusty roof and faded red siding, possibly askew with a lazy slope. I wasn't crazy about the *conversion* part, although in recent years, with architects involved, some very interesting homes have been built from barns, which celebrate the barns' integrity while introducing contemporary elements.

Michael and I canoed the Hudson River one day, as we did on occasion. We stopped at the breezy, abandoned Esopus Lighthouse halfway across the river for a picnic of smoked salmon on little toasts, an apple, a square of chocolate. We continued.

On the other bank, when we got close, barely visible in the shadows, we saw a dark barn in the woods a hundred feet in.

"Let's go look at it," I said.

I had never seen Michael hesitate when confronted with an adventure like this one, but he did, briefly. We parked the canoe on the sliver of bank and clambered up the retaining stone wall. A sign posted on the tree said, "Scenic Hudson," our local non-profit designating preserves and conservation easements, which gave me courage or chutzpah; we could explain our being there if we bumped into someone. We approached the shy barn, small and compact and elegant. Likely built in the 1880s, based on the hand-hewn posts and beams, it had a clover-shaped window like others I'd spotted on the east side of the river in Rhinebeck and Rhinecliff.

Michael said. "Look!" Wooden beams piled inside were curved. "It's a boat barn." This is one of the reasons I adored Michael. Maybe I would have put it together eventually, but he knew these things. He knew stuff I wanted to know.

Although neglected, the barn seemed happy where it was, and being dark, the barn was suitably buried in the woods, and would not seem quite right in a field. Nonetheless, I wanted it.

"We should float it across the river and roll it up the hill to my property!" I joked.

"In the middle of the night." Michael quipped.

We were captivated. Michael and I continued up the hill, trespassing further. We crossed abandoned railroad tracks and what looked like an old train station. More barns and other structures were buried in the woods. We came across a giant's compost hill, with enormous trunks of trees, some five feet in diameter, many with root systems, that seemed to have just been tipped over the edge onto the slope we were ascending. Poison ivy crawled everywhere we did.

At the top, in a clearing, we found ourselves among a small village of barns around a plaza, with a tower off to the side, which seemed maintained, in use. Peering into the largest barn through a small-windowed grill, we saw a collection of dozens of antique carriages and cars. Now we really were trespassing, but we didn't see any movement, any actual live people, and our curiosity pulled us further. We walked beyond onto the sloping back lawn of a major estate. A gardening house or toolshed was built into the slope, cave-like, strewn with broken clay pots and tools. Further up the lawn, enormous weeping beech trees had limbs that drooped and dropped back to the ground to create Dali-esque outdoor rooms. Huge, injured trees hundreds of years old around us explained the giant's compost heap at the start. We came upon a neoclassic spanking pristine white house with scaffolding. It was hard to determine whether it was new or under renovation.

I felt my pulse quicken. Something about its newness, its presence, signaled someone was nearby—had just left or was returning, or possibly was inside right then. And we were exposed on the lawn. Without saying a word, we turned around, retracing our steps, at double speed, our hearts pounding in our chests.

A few months later, while driving on the other, east side of the Hudson River at about the right latitude, Michael and I passed what we took to be the entrance to that estate. We looked at each other. Our eyes nodded. We pulled into the driveway, slightly more legitimately, but timidly, to inquire about the boat barn, which I had been contemplating since we'd laid eyes on it.

Through an open door to the white house on that gorgeous day, we could hear the distinct, syncopated *plop, plop, plop* of a ping pong ball. A gorgeous man with fabulous brown curls in a blousy linen shirt and rolled up pants held a paddle and was playing in the foyer of the house with a young girl, the height of the table, presumably his daughter. An elderly, elegant woman—mama? —sat on the chair beside.

"Hello! Sorry to interrupt! Looks like fun! . . ."

"Alo?"

I smiled. "You have a barn down by the river. A boat barn?" I paused. I couldn't tell if he understood me. I assumed he was Italian.

"You fix barn?" he said, his eyebrows raised, smiling.

"No, no. I was wondering whether you'd like to sell it?"

"Fix!"

I really, really wanted to stay and play ping pong with him, and maybe eventually fix his barn. After fumbling for another minute or two, Michael and I left. We retreated the way we'd come. All my dreams about curved boat barns and curls flattened.

Years later, I found out that we had been on the estate of Bob Guccione, founder and owner of *Penthouse* magazine. At some point, Andre Balasz, a New York real estate tycoon and celebrity, who dated Uma Thurman, purchased the property. I never figured out who the cute Italian was and how he fit into the puzzle of ownership and what he was doing there.

With most real estate purchases—and mate seeking, sofas, shoes, and hiring decisions—I generally consider 30 to 40 options before I decide. Much of the initial exploration is background research, warming up to the idea, getting to know the market, fact-finding, so that when I come across the right one, the decision

is visceral, obvious. I know it. And when I can't decide between two
contenders, I know I haven't found The One yet. I maintain that
the best decisions are not made under duress or need but born of
informed passion.

I get to know the roads traveled, lay of the land, the neigh-
borhoods, particularly if new to an area. I saw dozens of properties
in the Hudson Valley before I homed in on Field Farm, before I
knew what I was looking for. And I would see dozens of barns
before I found one that was perfect. In the process, I educated
myself on barns in general, what makes them special, or not. I
started to think about size and dimension differently after standing
inside a dozen.

Years earlier, before finding Field Farm, I had considered a
property in Pawling, New York, consisting only of the outbuildings
of an old farmstead. The farmhouse had been siphoned off as a
separate property. An awkward plateau without a driveway hosted
three silos, two enormous barns and a dozen ravaged cars parked
among and inside them. I was drawn by the way the buildings
nestled with one another, and, if I'm honest, the mess of it all. I am
drawn to complexity, things that have potential or need to be saved.
The same with people, too, I suppose.

I often wonder why I can't keep things simple, buy something already done. A friend bought a place in Maine and was so
pleased—smug—that it was completely renovated, turnkey, even
furnished! When he told me he wouldn't need to buy a sofa, I realized that "solution" holds no attraction for me. Where's the challenge, the creativity in that? No. I like to burrow for the soul, reveal
its beauty, save it, and that was part of that barn clutch's appeal.

I loved the faded green barnwood siding, and the huge cavities of space they offered, their elegant relationship to one another,
the way the adjacent silos lent verticality and unique, spiritual, interior space with only a small circle of light forty feet above, which I
not only still remember, but feel. It was religious.

I invited barn expert and childhood mentor, Elric Endersby,

from New Jersey to look at that Pawling property. In an instant, he told me the barns were nothing special. I was crestfallen. Elric showed me that the posts and beams were not hand-hewn, and they were sitting, in part, on concrete blocks, not stones. These barns were not worth all the work—to build a driveway up that hill, remove the junkyard, stabilize and render inhabitable—that would be required. I learned that day that it is the frame, not the siding, that makes a barn valuable. Elric is a bit of a barn snob in the best kind of way, a purist, having moved and rebuilt dozens of spectacular barns for the likes of James Taylor in Martha's Vineyard. I was embarrassed to have wasted his time.

Ten years later I contacted Elric again, thinking he might know of a barn that needed to be saved. He graciously invited me to tour a few barns in New Jersey, near where I grew up, that he had restored and created, all lovely in their way. When we stepped into a barn that was still raw, employed, with an enormous, heavy central beam, he said, "This barn is about the right size. Most people want really big barns, like McMansions."

The barn we were standing in was about 30′ X 40′. I realized at that moment, and I was ashamed to confess to him, that I, too, wanted a bigger barn. Not a McMansion. A cathedral.

So, I learned a little something from every barn and carried it to the next one. Many barns we looked at were never candidates, but Michael and I collected them as reference points. A square one in the middle of a field outside Rhinebeck had a wonderful feeling, boasting sofas and cars, and an old-fashioned ice chest. It was in bad shape; it wouldn't last long without roof repair. I couldn't get in touch with the owner, nor that of the one on the way to the Rhinecliff train station. I left a note on the front door, but never heard back. From an ethical point of view, I feel strongly that I move a barn that was going to be razed or fall anyway—since thousands meet their demise every year—rather than remove them from their natural setting or gainful employment. I expressed interest just in case but didn't follow up.

I heard that a religious retreat a couple miles down 9W from Field Farm wanted their barn removed. I wasn't sure why, but possibly because of the risk it posed to visitors and because it was no longer used for farming activities. Built in the late 19th century, it was, again, a little too new but I liked the idea of procuring a local (and organic? grass-fed?) barn, in the neighborhood. It was more complex, built in the shape of a blunted cross (intentionally?) with singular potential. I ultimately passed.

"Barn porn," in the form of barn websites, became an obsession as I spent nights, weeks, months culling through hundreds of options online, including small log cabins, round barns, and chicken coops. Most were out west and had already been disassembled, piled in a barn warehouse or graveyard, so there was no way to visit, step inside and feel the space. I wondered, too, whether a barn from the west or mid-west would be out of place in the northeast, perhaps architecturally or from a materials standpoint, and so inappropriate to the Hudson Valley.

I came across a barn for sale in Lancaster, Pennsylvania, and left a message at the number provided. An Amish man called me back while I was cooking dinner. *I thought they didn't have phones.* He told me that I needed to come the next day. The posts and beams would be converted into planks and boards unless I bought it.

The next morning, after dropping Tess off at school and arranging for her to be picked up in the afternoon, I drove eight hours to Amish country through torrential rains. I had to pull over a couple times because I couldn't see out the windshield. I arrived as the sun broke through the clouds just as it set, wondering if this was a sign. Located right off the highway, neighboring a landfill, a barn frame stripped of its siding, a skeleton, stood against the orange sky. I parked the car and approached.

I walked inside its footprint, around it, trying to feel the space. The frame was old and noble, in excellent shape, with an honest rectangular simplicity. It was a good size, long and slender, but there was nothing remarkable about it, nothing to work with.

It was getting dark. I needed to decide. I poked around the edges, the stone foundation, for clues. I didn't regret having driven through all that rain all that way—I chalked it up to more education—but I could not envision going through all the trouble of making this frame my home. It didn't beckon. I wondered if it was already too cleaned up for my taste; all the siding was gone, as were the sofas and cars and hay and stories. I wanted to save this barn from the saws, the blades, but I just could not fall in love with it.

I got in my car and drove back to New York City.

I was scared. This vulnerable, nude structure was a warning. I wasn't ready to take on a project of this magnitude. If I bought it and hauled it to my field, I feared it would rot in a pile without the wherewithal nor a handyman in sight. It was just too much of a risk, too early, and yet its fate still summons remorse and guilt within me. I let an old barn and all those beams get chopped up.

Michael knew a barn expert, we'll call James, who had restored a barn near him in Westchester. James had fled because of something akin to not paying workman's comp or taxes. James was no longer in the barn business, but introduced us to Chris, a younger barn guy based in a village twenty minutes from Field Farm.

With big, brown, soulful eyes and a subtle drawl, Chris put on a song and dance of his portfolio of houses and invited me to see a couple barns he had erected and "designed." One had become a French chateau, with plaster walls, a Tudor outside and highly lacquered beams inside. I was aghast. Chris also showed us his own barn-home, dark and cluttered, which he had chopped into a million pieces and which no longer read "barn." It could have been anything, but mostly it was one of those tired, butchered seventies barns I feared.

As I was exploring possibilities with Chris and continued to look at Mount Alphonsus and barns online, James contacted Chris. He sent us photos of an Amish barn near him that was coming down. James was fifty miles south of the Canadian border, near Fort

Drum in Gouverneur, New York.

Intrigued, Michael and I drove up the following weekend, a bleak and inhospitable wintery weekend, not dissimilar from the day I had met Field Farm, only with snow. After five hours of driving, signs on the side of the road profiled not just tractors, but buggies, signaling we were in Amish country, mixed in with some God-fearing folks, as the billboards on trailers attested. I tried not to take their accusations personally ("SIN HAS SEPARATED YOU FROM GOD") and kept my eyes on the map and road. Would the barn be lovable, despite its neighbors, its provenance? Perhaps my destiny was to save it from going to hell.

From the road, the dark structure looked low and long, sunk behind a small hill-mound and a bank of snow. The barn appeared unfriendly, austere, solemn, maybe, I thought, unhappy in its current site. As with many barns, over the years, leaning additions had been built on two sides adding a modicum of complexity.

We ducked through the service entrance and stood up inside, and as soon as I did, I knew I was home. The space was generous and cathedral-esque, but not cavernous. Small square windows at either end of the barn, near the peak, gave light to hay piled in the lofts. And the mechanics worked: With a solid roof, and two layers of siding, the posts and beams were rot-free; the structure was in excellent shape.

Functional elements created visual rhythm. On either end, the vertical posts of the loft railing were echoed by the horizontal rungs of built-in ladders hugging the post climbing towards— although not quite reaching—the roof, heaven, in a perpetual state of hope and tension. The barn housed distractions too—an internal room and a catwalk that ran halfway across and fed down a stair-well.

What I wouldn't know until later is that in part the barn felt good, felt *right*, because a sixteen-foot square could be drawn on the floor between the four center posts, twice, which repeated verti-cally, defined by the central bays, confirming that balance and good design work in subliminal ways. Even if the barn were constructed of steel, and not hand-hewn beams, it would have had integrity. And while the barn was symmetrical and exacting, who would have assumed all seven bays measured to the inch down its 90-foot length?

My barn was strong, quiet, and handsome, with broad shoulders.

This was it. This was the barn I had been looking for. I knew immediately, and Michael agreed, allowing me to talk *ad nauseum*, fortifying my conviction. Over the next couple weeks, the decision focused on how much it would cost to convert, since it was so enormous, and therefore—regressively—whether. I hadn't really set a budget; I needed to decide what I was willing to spend. But I was obsessed. I couldn't stop drawing the layout on paper napkins in spare moments or thinking about how I would orient it on the land. After James and Chris sent annotated drawings of the frame, I had more to work with.

A few weeks later, I wrote a huge check, a deposit on The Barn Project, handed it to Chris, with a contract that I dissected every which way before signing, and just after he left the room, bawled. I leaned up against the cold refrigerator in the small, manageable house that I was completely comfortable in, and sobbed. I knew that this check was a commitment, and as large as it was, merely the beginning of a stream of checks and obligations and responsibilities over years, maybe decades. I was moving a huge barn onto the property. There would be unknowns and things that would go wrong, decisions and choices, that I didn't even know yet, to be made. If Patrick, my former contractor, were involved, I could expect to pay four times whatever I thought I was going to, no matter how conservative (that is, generous) the projected budget.

But that's not why I was crying. My fear, which I could not voice, was amplified because I knew Michael and I were unraveling—fighting about his escalating drinking and everything that went with it: the pretense, the arrogance, the lies. My inability to reach him at night when we weren't together. The vodka bottle, three quarters empty, rolling under the seat of his car and the red, denying cheeks and nose he arrived with on Friday evenings. I kept letting him back into my life, again and again, because we were so good together, and he was fundamentally a kind and generous man, but I knew that at some point—not then, but eventually— I would cut him loose. Although Michael had no financial stake in The Barn Project, he had an emotional one. I knew I would never have had the fortitude to move forward on it without him in my life. Maybe he knew that, and thought The Barn Project was his relationship security, would keep us together. And yet I knew that we would not survive in the long term. And then what? What would I, a single woman, do hanging around in an enormous barn with Tess for a couple years, and then by myself? What was wrong with this little house? Nothing! This was enough for me—plenty—more than I needed and more than I could handle as a single working mother.

Where had this idea come from to build a barn? It had crept up, in incremental steps. Was it really Michael's idea? He had always wanted to convert a barn and, so, had resurrected the barn urge in me. From thinking about moving a church, to casually exploring barns in other people's fields, to bringing a colossal barn from five hours away to Field Farm and building an humongous home from scratch. If we had not gone down some of those driveways or pulled the canoe out of the water to check out the boat barn across the Hudson River, maybe none of this would have happened.

But it did.

ORIGINS

Growing up, we weren't poor but we were frugal, pinching pennies and clipping coupons. I wore hand-me-downs not just from my older sister but family friends. My childhood was steeped in education and devoid of American pop culture. We listened to Pete Seeger and classical music. We read. My German mother was head of the math department at our school. My environmentalist father worked for Princeton University and co-discovered that humpback whales sing. My mother was a founder of an organic, bulk grocery store, one of the first of its kind, which still thrives. We ate organic peanut butter on whole wheat bread while bologna on white bread was the norm. We cooked from scratch.

Even from a young age I could tell my parents were cool. They read *The Village Voice* in our house of Scandinavian mid-century modern furniture, which they collected as newlyweds on their honeymoon through Europe, including a Hans Wegner dining room table, double-decker sideboard, and Papa Bear chairs. We didn't summer in Martha's Vineyard or Cape Cod, belong to a club or own a summer house. We traveled, on the cheap, as a family—I think of my father testing the mattresses before we committed to a motel—and brought back art, pottery, and textiles from distant places. We wrote reports about the countries we were going to visit. We kept journals documenting our travels.

The house where I grew up and spent my formative years—and I adored— burned down while I was in college. Hand built in the woods by a squatter Scotsman, it was a charming compendium of repurposed materials. Railroad ties and bulky river stone formed its core and character. The front door—salvaged from an old Trenton Church—had to be bolted from the inside before we raced through the side door to catch the bus. The oscillating orange and blue roof which looked like Spanish *tejas* came from an old Howard Johnson. My sister and I played Monopoly and endless War in a small, elevated loft in the den. Alongside the fireplace, sparkling Moroccan mosaic doors covered deep ovens, to roast a potato, say. I always thought it odd that a stone house could burn down almost entirely—it was less stone than it looked, I guess—but it did. Other than the front façade, the two-story house and wing out back and everything we created and coveted (original art, childhood photographs, journals, poetry) turned to ashes. The little that survived was warped and smelled of smoke. An hour after the oil repairman "fixed" the furnace, a dripping valve ignited a raging fire. We never got over it.

We knew personally and visited every year woodworker and furniture designer George Nakashima in New Hope, Pennsylvania, at his showroom-compound nestling and cascading down a small hill of serene beauty and flowering cherry trees. We ate dinner on Nakashima chairs, and had original art framed by him.

Frank Lloyd Wright-influenced and subterranean house architect Malcolm Wells (and his artistic family) was also in the swirl. His holiday cards were works of art incorporating his bold block print, line drawings, and wry sense of humor. Ceramicist Toshiko Takaezu was a dear friend. In 2024, an extensive retrospective of her work was on view at the Noguchi Museum in Queens. The Museum of Modern Art in New York City exhibits furniture and kitchenware I grew up with.

All these inputs influenced me, my style and approach, along with considerable time spent studying and working all over Latin America, and in particular Mexico, in open air courtyards and sculptural Corbusier-like adobe structures. I developed a taste for antiques and urban living in prewar apartments and raw lofts in Soho and Tribeca in New York City, Cambridge, and Philadelphia. I was never happier than when I spent two college summers deep in the Peruvian Amazon jungle studying monkeys, living in a small tent, only a screen between me and the nocturnal jaguars. Those summers reinforced my love of the outdoors and desire to live with and in and for the natural world. We lived simply and close to nature. *Very* close, intimately so. I didn't intentionally try to recreate my jungle life, but in retrospect, it seems to have played into many decisions.

In high school, my art teacher allowed me to use the art room beyond the curriculum, and I did. I had always dreamed of becoming an architect. When I was in my late teens, in the seventies, my well-intentioned parents introduced me to a local architect with a large New Jersey firm. The architect told me it was a difficult profession, very competitive, and she spent her days placing bathrooms in large corporate buildings using a software program. It was the beginning of the digital age; we were still typing on electric typewriters. The notion of working on a computer in an office was vague and uninteresting, compared to the hand-drawn architectural renderings I had envisioned and romanticized. I left feeling discouraged. It didn't square with the vision of architecture I'd formed over the years from people I had known.

Nonetheless, in college, I had taken so many courses in architecture, sculpture, graphic design, and painting that I ended up minoring in Harvard's equivalent of studio arts. I have been an artist all my life and, indeed, put myself though business school selling my large collages. My relationship to design and space and beauty is not casual. I renovated a half dozen homes of architectural interest over the past three decades. At the time of The Barn Project, in 2009-10, I had under my belt, an 18th-century Hiram Halle house in Bedford, NY, where I had lived with my then-husband, and the cottage on Field Farm. I would go on to revamp an enormous 1840s stone house near Stone Ridge, NY, once the site of the New York State Assembly, with five outbuildings including a smoke house, chicken coop, and a complex barn, which was part of the annual Vernacular Barn Tour. In 2018, I coaxed back to life a windowless, door-less, roofless mid-century modern home in St. Croix, in the US Virgin Islands, owned originally by Fritz Henle (a German photographer) and Atti van Berg (a Dutch modern dancer and artist). This last house was a completely different experience not only because it was a pile of rubble, but because of the hurricane issues inherent in Caribbean living, security, water catchment and cistern systems, and a mix of tropical and desert ecosystems.

As I undertook The Barn Project in 2009, Tess and I were living on the top floor of two adjoined townhouses on the Upper Eastside of Manhattan. The two sides had been pulled together and renovated in the 1970s by a forward-thinking, design-oriented, art-collecting 86-year-old couple with visionary industrial designer Ward Bennett. The wife wore designer sneakers and oversized glasses and was a docent at the Natural History Museum. He was a tax accountant. I purchased the apartment in 2004 at a significant discount because it wasn't marketed properly.

When the sellers moved out, they asked if I'd like to sell their art collection, including over eighty paintings, sculptures, and tapestries, by the likes of Picasso, Miró, Grey, Chagall, Modigliani, Zúñiga, Calder, and Van Gogh. They handed me an annotated price list, assuming I knew nothing about selling art, which I didn't. But I called friends who did. I did research. Most of their prices were higher than comparable pieces I found in retail stores on Madison Avenue or in recent online auctions. The unsigned Van Gogh propped on a stand in the living room with ambiguous provenance was suspicious. I almost sold the entire collection, twice, and eventually unloaded a couple of pieces—a Picasso plate and a Miró tapestry which once hung at the Museum of Modern Art. Living with and among museum-grade art with young Tess and her friends who came over for play dates created considerable angst. It also seemed odd that the owners would leave the art with me. They explained that they were consolidating three homes that year and had nowhere to store it. His being an accountant and the possibly illegitimate Van Gogh made me a tad wary of the whole arrangement.

One afternoon I came home, and several small Zúñiga sculptures were missing. I panicked. What had I been thinking? Who is responsible for the art? Was it insured? Later, I learned that the owners had dropped by and taken them. *(They still had a key!?)* It was too much for me. I asked them to come take it all away.

They arrived with a young insurer armed with a clipboard, wrapping and numbering every piece going into storage. I saw the couple duck out with a couple of Modigliani sculptures and squirrel them away in their car trunk. Would those pieces be "lost"? Would they be reimbursed for them? I don't know. But I'm glad I didn't live in a museum anymore and it was no longer my problem.

Over time, I saw other New York-based couples of a certain age, like them, featured in *The New York Times*, who had accrued tremendous collections of a particular era just after WWII.

While I never would have ripped out the original wood floors and molding of the historic townhouses, the resulting apartment was important in its own right. Gray industrial tile and wall-to-wall carpeting were underfoot. Ward Bennett was the designer known for creating conversation pits. In his final years, in the 2000s, he designed the restaurant in the basement of Lever House. The apartment had built-in lounging sofas the size of daybeds; carpet climbed the walls. The sellers had asked if I would like to purchase two velvet sofas designed by Bennett for $8,000. I declined. But after I moved in, I found, on an online mid-century modern site, a couple of secondhand Ward Bennett sofas in Texas for a tenth the price, with beige and ribbed fabric like what he had designed for the conversation pits in the living room and platform mattress in the bedroom. When the sofas arrived, an attached tag said "Enron." It was not long after Enron's collapse. The sofas must have been in their lobby. Maybe those crooks sat on them, or the FBI waiting who busted them did. High design and history collided in my living room in a couple mud brown sofas.

The kitchen's entire countertop was molded of stainless-steel and had a swinging restaurant kitchen door with a window, to see approaching bussers and waiters. The stainless-steel counter backsplash also had built-in, labeled compartments for aluminum foil, plastic wrap and wax paper. The front of the brown 1970s refrigerator did not supply water and ice but had a frozen orange juice dispenser! When I finally replaced the quirky fridge for a new one, the electric bill dropped by two-thirds. The cabinets needed an update, too, but I was loath to change anything in my landmark.

Heavy, solid, tall doors enclosed huge closets, an anomaly for New York City, and everything was tucked away, including a mirrored bar. It had many cutting edge features of a bygone era: track lighting, central air, and piped sound. Inside the radiator boxes, we found a tangle of dozens of telephone wires, a futuristic notion of where cable was headed.

The dimensions and flow worked with wide hallways and open expanses, but the colors were stark and dreary. Ward Bennett designed to showcase art and people. To liven things up, inspired by a friend's home from the Bauhaus era, I painted a wall in each of the main rooms an off-basic color: one tomato bisque, one marigold and one deep sky blue. Eventually, I replaced the worn, faded blue-green rug with a dark gray tightly woven one. I otherwise altered little.

I had to redo the bathroom when the shower tiles were dropping from the walls and a hole was developing around the drain. When I could see my downstairs neighbors through the floor, I could no longer delay. As much as I respected his vision, Ward Bennett's "meditative" gray tile in the shower stall and throughout the apartment were depressing and tired. I was relieved, in the bathroom, to replace it with white industrial tile, something I figured Bennett would have approved of if he were alive. I channeled him when I chose the Kohler hatbox toilet and deep, jet-laden bathtub, too.

Tess's room was small and awkward. There didn't seem an easy, conceivable way to increase its size, given the overall dimensions, without making major structural adjustments to the entire apartment. Tess's bed rolled under an ample, walk-in closet the footprint of a full bed. She had her own bathroom and a lovely sitting nook with a Bennett-designed cushion overlooking gardens in the city block's center. Her Eames desk was in my enormous bedroom, parallel to my own, and we worked together every afternoon after school. As fabulous as the apartment was, when Tess was angry at me, she reminded me that she slept in a drawer. I couldn't argue with her.

When it came to building my barn-home, I drew on all these experiences and previous renovation projects. I understood a little something about signaling entrances, room and window placement, traffic flow, lighting, plumbing, materials. I appreciated spare, modernist lines with the warmth of natural materials. I would stay away from industrial, matte gray. It was the first time I was starting with an almost clean slate rather than a renovation, although the barn was an existing structure of an imposing sort.

I acted as designer and general contractor. It never occurred to me to hire an architect, to hand over all that fun. I credit the Amish as the true architects, who had given the barn its structural integrity. I didn't want to mess with it. I used the existing floor plan, expanses, and openings—where a tractor rolled up to the hayloft—to map my windows and doors and created a bedroom and bathroom where the barn's office had been.

From the get-go, the intention, the vision, the conceptual glue for The Barn Project was to keep things as simple and authentic as possible. And so, it would be green, low maintenance, outside-oriented, flexible. To my mind, these tenets merge and support one another, but even with clarity of vision, there would be nuances and judgment calls. I would be hands-on in every facet of its design and process. I couldn't imagine it any other way.

THE CONCEPT

SUSTAINABILITY

By employing a barn and using reclaimed wood, many of the materials are by definition reused, re-purposed, and from natural sources. I explored in detail what it would mean to be off the grid and the options available to harness sustainable, renewable energy, with some surprising results. The walls and roof are super-insulated, and given the barn's orientation and large windows, is passive solar. On a sunny twenty-degree winter day, the space warms to sixty degrees without the heat kicking on, which is what geothermal will get you, consuming a lot of energy, generally provided by solar panels. Open windows in the summer cool the barn, without air conditioning, creating a welcome cross breeze, for all but a few stultifying high humidity days.

A large part of sustainability, in my view, is to minimize consumption. In any given situation, I consider what I already own to solve a problem. When I deign to purchase, I naturally lean toward vintage, garage sales, or items found in open air markets all over the world. Early on, I went to a local flea market down the road and bought lamps (functioning!) for 10 and 25 cents. A large, rusting iron agricultural vessel was anointed The Cauldron, long before fire pits were ubiquitous and manufactured. A half dozen vintage green and red maple sugaring buckets serve as trash baskets. The end stumps of beams elevate indoor plants and retain the large swinging windows when they are open. The kitchen cabinetry is an assemblage of antiques, many of which occupied previous homes, including a workbench I bought at the Rhinebeck Antique Fair in 2000 and was the kitchen island in the original house.

My contractor Chris claimed to be a "green builder," and drove a hybrid as if to prove it, but Michael— who was still on the scene, in and out of my life for a couple more years— wondered about his sincerity and convictions. On the construction site, Chris's outdoorsy crew threw barnwood scraps into the dumpster along with cans, bottles, and paper—if they didn't leave them to blow across the field. Weekends, Michael and I excavated the dumpster, separating the recyclables, and piled the old barnwood off to the side to later use to build internal walls or fuel cauldron fires. Process efficiencies were lacking, which led to wasted time, resources, and money. With my McKinsey consultant background, and German upbringing, and being born under the Virgo perfectionist stars, I was all about efficiencies. I had to keep on Chris.

MINIMALIST—OR NOT

> "When you think about design as the bringing together of a number of materials and parts, letting them interact—and not as the expression of your own personality — the demand must be made that it answers the purpose, no matter how complex."
>
> —Charles Eames

I wanted the barn up in its most basic form, to be livable, but not much more. Delayed decisions, incremental change, and evolution were tantamount, although some decisions left doors open to future possibilities. For example, extra footings were built into the slab for a potential fireplace in the dining room. My plumber and I decided to put an extra drain in the kitchen floor in case I wanted to add a half-bathroom at some point. This drain would also save us from having to excavate roughly 70 feet of concrete floor if the current kitchen drain failed, as it runs under two-thirds of the barn.

In the construction process, I aimed for efficiencies to minimize waste, adornment, and energy use. I tried to use readily available, industrial solutions when possible. I asked the tradesman why they did things a certain way and whether a better, more streamlined approach existed. I learned that some processes or features in construction seem extraneous and discretionary have functions. That's true of aspects of window installation and flashing. Along with wall sheathing which wicks water, trim keeps seams air- and water-free. I realized that a green architect, with connections to suppliers I did not have, may have come up with better solutions.

I am minimalist from a process, consumption, and maintenance perspective, as well as aesthetic, and I agree that "conventional" minimalism has a lot of appeal. When the barn was first erected and empty, the barn possessed a spare quality, but no longer. I found that, for me at least, minimalism in look is hard to achieve and live in comfortably, and it often requires *more* work and resources to hide things. I know "minimalists" who tuck away life's mess in closets and cabinets, although I'm sure that out there somewhere there are purists who learn to live with little. I swear I am not a hoarder, but it is hard for me to let go of scraps of wood, fabrics, and tools because there might be a use for them in a future project. If I finally break down and buy a new pair of sneakers, I keep the old ones for a muddy or beach walk.

I tend to forget about clothes, food, and other objects when they are out of view. Shoes are on display near the door on an old pasta drying rack I bought from a four-star restaurateur when he closed his kitchen. I find myself wearing whatever is on top in the drawer, or fresh out of the dryer. Spices are lined up above the stove on a barn-wood shelf. Having worked in retail at the time that big box retailers were the craze, I learned to keep all inventory on the floor, in sight, and eliminating backrooms. That's how I live. The result appears maximalist.

Be True

I stood inside the newly erected barn looking up at the catwalk with a sense of doubt. I voiced my concern. "That's the only beam that didn't exist where it was."

Michael stood beside me. He said, after consideration, "No one will ever know."

"That's not the point. *I* will know. I will know every time I look at it."

The only wood that did not belong to the original barn (aside from the tenons, which one of Chris's guys carved by hand) was that one beam that was used to create the catwalk from one loft to the other. All the external siding, boards on the ceiling, and the internal walls that Michael and I built came from the original barn.

Authenticity comes from natural materials and embracing but advancing the familiar design adage, *form follows function*. I cringe when I see an old beam in a new house, as a decorative element, divorced from structural import or intent. I would not replace moldings in an old townhouse with new moldings that "look the same," especially if they are plastic. If old moldings are salvageable, I cultivate their imperfections. I try to be true to the object and honor the material. And I have a hard time when realtors voice triumphantly an apartment has been "gut renovated," which means, generally, it's been taken down to the studs and stripped of anything with charm and soul. Old glass windows and creaky floor-boards are gone. I assume the quirks that gave the place character have been eliminated. I steer clear.

There are many interesting new materials in the market-place, such as concrete panels. I would use them in large swaths, and let them be what they are—concrete— not pretend they are wood, like grain-printed vinyl siding does.

And in keeping with the Japanese wabi-sabi aesthetic, *true* may not be perfect. We often fall in love with another person for their imperfections and vulnerabilities: the gap between their front teeth, a mole, a peculiar gesture, an awkward laugh. We like lumpy hand-knit sweaters and holey sourdough bread. And so, hand-hewn beams carry a certain charm, remind us of the humanity, of the person who worked that chestnut trunk a couple hundred years ago—by hand. The beams were cut to meet a need, that didn't require "perfection." On one beam in the barn, someone penciled in lavish cursive. When, who, I don't know, but I won't erase it. The script seems from another world, another time. The natural blotches in a polished natural-toned concrete floor give it more depth and contour; the sculpted banister in an old home reminds us of those who gripped it before.

Not everything should be broken and scratched and worn; nor should imperfection be an excuse for inferior craftsmanship. Imperfection works when it has room to breathe, when it contrasts with clean lines and there is a sense of deliberateness, and when it's authentic, not the result of a manufactured process, as in pre-ripped jeans. There's nothing genuine about those.

I also believe in being true to oneself. To live your life in your space, not for resale value or convention. I design for how I will live every day, not for the occasional guest. I don't separate the living from the entertaining spaces. I populate spaces with personal collections and objects imbued with stories and meaning, not someone else's idea of decorating or a trend.

I vowed to honor the old barn the way it was when I found it, keep it intact and as close to how it was in its original form, to the extent possible. I even considered, for a millisecond, making sofas and beds out of hay bales, like those we saw in the loft before it moved.

In my estimation, many renovated and converted barns are overbuilt, losing their "barnness." Like many farmers' utilitarian relationship to the land, many "barn people" enthusiastically exploit barns and wood. Without hesitation, they chop them up into rooms or replace or add posts and beams from other structures. They clad interiors with additional wood, often to excess. Although they appreciate barns, they favor their own craft and ingenuity.

My barn was sacred.

In Favor of Flexibility

Most memorable travel moments occur when I stray from the itinerary and guidebook. I do my homework: figure out what I need to see, plot where I am headed, but then. . . .Pick up hitchhikers in southern Brazil and get invited into a dirt-floored family dinner; join a wedding parade in Oaxaca; dance until 4:00 AM in Firenze with four men who turn out to be security detail for a Russian oligarch.

Flexibility is also a key ingredient in cooking. I rarely shop with a recipe in hand. I might make a mental note that I need milk or olives, but when preparing for a dinner party, I see what's fresh, ripe, and abundant at the farmer's market and take it from there. If I am in the islands, I focus on fresh wahoo, tamarind, local avocados, plantains, and mangoes rather than force-fit my northeasterly habits on the Caribbean bounty.

Life seems richer responding to cues and clues outside the lines, whether it's the fresh catch of the day or discovering a new way to get somewhere when confronted with traffic, along the lines of *necessity is the mother of invention*. Stepping outside one's comfort zone because of circumstance or competing desires forces new experiences, innovative solutions, and personal learning. The pandemic, too, altered our approach to both planning and space. Like many, I was forced to be more flexible given frequent cancellations and adjustments.

A few years ago, a relationship with a man that seemed like it had potential stumbled shortly after I heard about his plans for built-ins. He had so much to recommend him: he was intellectual, athletic, financially secure, his time was his own, he lived nearby. He had recently bought a house that was oversized for a single (or even coupled) person (although who am I to judge?), with multiple bedrooms, office and workout and media rooms, full and half bathrooms, associated closets and foyers and two-car garage. The land was lovely; I figured we could work around the house over time.

The pile of Restoration Hardware boxes for all the furniture he had just bought to fill the house gave me pause. As he described the shelves and cabinets he was going to have built here and there and everywhere—he was very particular about how he would set up his stereo system and everything else—I felt my body tense. I couldn't put my finger on it immediately, but it dawned on me our approaches to life were miles apart. I could not imagine filling my home with furnishings and decor overnight. I understand the need for a sofa and a bed—which he already had. This went far beyond that. His desire for order and control, I suspected, would (and did) permeate other parts of his life. The boxes and built-ins were a red flag.

For me, joy comes from acquiring unique pieces over time, discovering a wicker set at an antique fair or an Eames desk on the side of the road. Do cushions have to be on a sofa the minute you buy a sofa? The kitchen in the barn is an ever-evolving collection including an antique French sideboard, an old workbench, a blue metal industrial cabinet, a turmeric-colored Chinese cabinet housing special-occasion plates and stemware.

There's a strong dose of opportunism baked into flexibility and how I set up my life, but I *plan* to be flexible. To be clear, flexibility requires thought, something of a vision, and an elaborate just-in-case strategy. I have a lot of stuff in the trunk of my car (and pantry), just in case. Just in case I stop at the beach and I need a change of dry clothes, or if I drive by the recycle bin, the wind calms down and I can row, or if my dog's leash breaks.

When I renovate or design a home, flexibility is a core philosophy, both in the process and result. If I can, I live in the structure for a while to see how the wind blows and how the sun moves through the day and seasons. I take advantage of different views during the day. Rooms have multiple rather than single or dedicated use. Living in an expensive urban setting like New York City forces people to rethink the need for an extra, idle room that can cost upwards of $300,000 in the purchase price of an apartment, and in ongoing monthly fees to the cooperative or condominium.

So why have a vacant bedroom or dedicated guest bathroom in the suburbs? Is it just part of sprawl? Or are there really plans and hopes for visitors or an Airbnb business? Many guest rooms lay fallow a good deal of the year, although during the pandemic many became offices. I have day- and sofa beds in common areas which accommodate visiting friends and family over the holidays. And I have one bathroom. My mother often comments I should install a second one—for the three days she visits each year. I remain unconvinced. But I do have that extra drain in the kitchen if I change my mind.

I incorporated temporal flexibility into bathroom design as well. Why dedicate ninety cubic feet to an enclosed shower stall used once a day? In my barn-home, I waterproofed much of the bathroom and placed the shower head and a drain in the middle of the room with a view of the field. When the shower is not in use, people walk through the shower space to get to the toilet or sink without noticing because they are looking out that window too.

Flexible solutions are also more environmental, reducing need for space and consumption, through thoughtful re-purposing and reusing, rather than buying and building with urgency.

Flexibility can apply to many but not all things. Theater, dental work, and getting a babysitter require planning. I am dutiful about being on time and respecting deadlines—not flexible there. I heard a speaker once try to make a case that procrastination increases flexibility. I disagree. Flexibility is lost in procrastinating. If you get your work done early, then your time is your own, to pursue other things that come up, such as windsurfing when the wind picks up or meeting friends for a spontaneous dinner.

And there's little flexibility when it comes to ethics and integrity. And I guess, for me, with men.

THE RESURRECTION

The barn was sited beyond the pool, on the same rock ledge that gently curved around the magical field and would also open views to an unsung meadow to the north. Beyond the pool, and a rash of purple thistle, this meadow—longer, less appreciated, ran along the orchard next door and backed into a stone wall and a dark forest, the property line. The meadow had always been there, sitting quietly, but it didn't demand attention like the grass bowl that one naturally sinks into, given the topography and orientation of the existing house and pool. The raw terrain naturally sloped off and away beyond the pool, so the building site would be positioned more *in* the land. The 35-foot barn peak would serve as a backdrop but would not dominate views from the pool.

The excavator prepared the site, leveling and pushing the dirt, leaving bare earth (and thousands of fist-sized stones) a hundred feet wide and two hundred feet long. I contemplated a full or partial basement for the mechanical room, but decided against it, given the extra cost, impenetrable rock bed, and likelihood of basement water.

The crew dug and poured footings for each of the 36 posts, a potential future fireplace, and foundation wall. They dumped and raked gravel within the building's outline, my future home. Plumbing, electric, gas lines, insulation and a radiant heating system would live below or within the concrete floor to be poured on this gravel footprint. As with any house, everything had to be thought through upfront—where the industrial, satin-finish, round floor outlets would be located to host light fixtures, where the kitchen sink and the toilet would drain—but the overall structure would not be altered.

With something akin to addiction and obsession, whenever I sat for a moment, I drew small sketches which became architectural renderings and plans for the crew. The barn's dimensions and posts, as well as the views and general orientation, dictated many of the spaces and places and natural flow.

Since I'd been coming to Field Farm for a decade, I knew how the sun and seasons moved through the day and the year across the meadow. I knew how the swing of the sun's arc changed, how the beginning and ending points of the sun drifted across the tree line and orchard behind. I knew the wind and rain usually came from over the hill, the orchard, from the south and west. The roof line would converse with the rock ledge, the existing contours of the land. Each window would frame a view, an ever-changing image.

Once a few critical decisions were made (i.e., placement of the mechanical room, bathroom and kitchen), most of the other decisions fell into place. I knew I wanted my bedroom to have a view of the sunrise, and the dining room to have a sunset. The posts and beams dictated where doors and windows could go, the range of possibilities. I voraciously flipped through *Dwell* and other design magazines for kitchen and bathroom ideas.

An Amish crew, overseen by upstate, almost-in-Canada James, dismantled the barn and assigned each post and beam a letter and a number, scrawled on a small piece of white metal and nailed to each. The barn arrived over a couple days on three forty-foot tractor trailer flatbeds. Posts and beams and boards were packed and stacked high and bound tight. After the final delivery, the truck driver asked, through Chris, if he could park on the property and stay the night before he headed home. When I went to speak to him, I found his teenage daughter in the front seat, where she'd ostensibly been for hours during the unloading, and of course the long drive. I encouraged her to come down and stretch her legs, but she just said *thanks,* and stayed put. She and her father shared a mattress on the floor of the cab before pulling out in the morning. Awkward. I now view trailers differently when I pass them at highway rest stops.

The posts, beams and boards were piled a hundred feet

from the barn site in the field near a big apple tree where most my apples come from. With the foundation and footings poured, the barn frame went up quickly. I would have preferred to have had the Amish re-raise the barn, but Amish travel only if they can sleep in the homes of other Amish, which I could not offer.

During our visit to Gouverneur, James recounted one significant difference between the Amish and the Mennonites. When Mennonites started using buttons, Amish continued to fasten only with hook and eye. Amish, too, sport untrimmed beards and drive horse and buggies. Although I've heard of Amish who run to a neighbor's house to use electricity or a phone (such as the one early in my barn search), they do not typically own modern day "conveniences" themselves.

I don't know many Amish personally but got to know an ex-Amish in the summer of sophomore year of high school when I attended a National Science Foundation marine biology program in Chincoteague, Virginia, famed for the pony water migration that occurs every July.

Titus, a tall, broad camp mate, had run away from home, from being Amish, as an 18-year-old. He was by far the oldest in our group and was physically a man, all grown up, farmer or military strong, but gentle. He even had a thin Chaplin mustache, among all us kids. He didn't have *Playboy* posters on his wall, like the fisherman from Maine, or sneak off for a smoke like some of the others. Titus had a playful, endearing side, perhaps owing to his stuck-in-time innocence. If I'd understood where he'd come from with more clarity, I would have asked more questions. All I knew is he'd struck out on his own, and I liked having him on my volleyball team.

After weekdays of living at the army barracks and studying brackish water, we were awarded an afternoon at the beach with our very thin and very tan, smoking, bikini-clad counselor, who was off-brand for the geeky adolescents in her care. At the beach, Titus dug a hole. He dug deeper and deeper, until the cavity was three feet deep. He brought over a snorkel and mask to the edge, then dropped into the hole, pulling his entire large body and head below beach grade. He piled sand on top of himself. Mostly self-interred, he grabbed the mask and suctioned it to his face and asked us to cover the rest of him. I hesitated, not sure if it was a good idea. But others threw on sand, as requested, and packed it loosely around the snorkel, which was Titus' only connection to the world—and oxygen—above. The sand pinned down his arms so he couldn't dig himself out.

We backed off, sat on our towels, and watched beachcombers walk by. Titus screamed through his snorkel, which came out as a strange, muffled noise. This became our regular go-to activity on our weekend visits to the beach and never ceased to amuse, although poor Titus never saw the reactions of the startled passers-by. I worried that one day he might get crushed, or sand would go down his snorkel and suffocate him. Or we would walk away, as we sometimes started to, forgetting he was there.

Titus has nothing to do with my barn. But my Amish barn and its broad shoulders makes me think of him occasionally. So does the beach. I wonder where Titus is now, and whether he ever got all the sand out of his ears.

*   *   *

The barn was reassembled exactly as it originally stood by a team of handy-types and rock climbers from the Mohonk area. Its simple, stark, regular lines against the blue sky inspired awe. It was magnificent. I wanted to stop everything right then, leave it as an enormous, elegant sculpture, an ode to negative space, framing the sky above and field beyond, but I knew it would not last that way. The two-hundred-year-old wood needed to be re-enclosed to protect its ancient fiber. I dreamed of cladding the frame with glass to keep the look and feel of the naked frame, but it was unrealistic from a structural and financial standpoint.

Through the summer, the grass and poison ivy grew around

the idle boards and beams that lay prone in the field, which the crew didn't get to for months. I had purchased all the barnwood I could from the original barn. I coveted and many times requested the rolling barn doors, but they were not available, with no explanation. I suspected they were sold separately for a good sum. Nonetheless, my newly erected barn would be reconstructed with wood only from the source barn, which was important to me, and gave it integrity.

ON THE GRID

At the end of a washed-out road in Maui, Hawaii, where I traveled in 2007, I noticed a little cafe-hut buried in the tropical forest. I pulled in.

"Could I get a smoothie?" I asked the woman behind the counter when I was able to get her attention.

"What do you want in it?"

"Papaya and pineapple?" I wasn't crazy about papaya or pineapple but saw no other options.

The woman scooped pre-cut fruit and some ice into a blender, then pointed at a bicycle next to me, I had stepped around without thinking, and said, "Get on."

I looked at her, not understanding.

"Get on," she said, "for the blender," in a *duh* voice.

I mounted the bicycle. I pedaled and so powered the blender to make my smoothie. A crosswire in my brain wanted to believe the pedals were spinning the blades, but of course, they weren't—they were just powering the electricity to do so. But that little smoothie place suggested that my old bike whose tires were shot might be in the kitchen in the barn to make espresso in the morning, while getting exercise and watching the sun roll across the field.

I had envisioned that the barn would be off the grid. But as I explored alternative energy options, being off the grid seemed onerous. Pre-Musk, batteries were not where they are now. The whole building process, codes and permits, are set up to do everything according to common standards, and it would take a lot more work to build off the grid than to stay on it. I just didn't have the energy to pursue being unconventional on one more dimension, given all I was juggling (demanding work, a child, a complicated relationship, and this project, from two hours away). And although I had hoped that connectivity for phones and internet would have been more evolved by then—that is, no need for cable or satellite dishes—it wasn't. So, if I had to run a cable underground for the internet, I might as well run electrical wire while I was at it.

I researched geothermal energy for heating and air conditioning, although AC was not something I deemed necessary. Geothermal was in the news, in a few early LEED-certified buildings in New York City. It made sense: Use the natural, stable temperature of the earth, of about 54 degrees, in a thermal exchange system, to get air or water close to usability, and then raise the temperature the last few degrees.

I interviewed four or five geothermal installers, all relatively new to the business, who were promoting the latest fad and exploiting tax incentives for renewable energy. Options and choices abounded: open vs. closed loop, vertical (deep into the earth) vs. horizontal (a system that would run under a large field, for example). One provider described a system like a huge spider that fanned out into the earth.

The geothermal experts provided references of presumably their best, enthusiastic customers. One woman I spoke to removed her geothermal system because it never really worked. Another told me his electric bill increased by $700 a month to power the pump, and that was after several adjustments to the system. I surmised that installing geothermal makes sense only if you use another renewable energy source like solar to power the pump. Since I use so little energy otherwise, my break-even for solar panels was forty years out. If I had gushing water from my new well, I would consider an open geothermal system which I posited would use less energy to pump.

When it came time to drill a well, I hoped to find water near the pool, so water would be on hand for the pool and surrounding garden. I had mistakenly assumed that the pressure tank would be at the well head, and the water would go straight from the well to a spigot. But the well water went to the pressure tank inside the barn, of course, and would go through all the filtration systems like the house water and go back out to the spigot near the pool.

The well driller used a divining rod—I am not kidding—to locate the specific place to drill, oddly where I had hoped to find it: near the pool. That rod didn't divine so well. They drilled over 400 feet before they found water. Another 50 feet and we would have had to apply for a mining license! The water contained a very fine white clay and sulfur, so a filtration system was immediately installed to make it potable and to avoid gunking up the new pipes at the outset. The water ran far too slowly for an open geothermal system.

Over the years, dozens of solar companies have sent me proposals to rent 20 acres for 20 years to install panels for $1,000 an acre per year to feed the grid. While I am a huge supporter of solar and other forms of renewable energy, it pains me to see bucolic meadows covered with them. There are enough rooftops and parking lots that could be used for solar panels, which could also shade cars from the sun in summer and snow in winter. They can go on top of malls and big box retailers, closer to where the energy is used, or on every house and apartment building, like we saw in Turkey. Distributed rather than centralized, on-site energy would also reduce transmission loss, which last time I checked ran at 40%. Why not put a panel on every electric car? Vermont's farmland has been sadly altered by solar (and veal) farming. Even understanding that it is hard to make ends meet as a farmer, I grieve the loss of meadows and deserts—and stands of trees, when cleared to make way. I can only imagine what solar farms do to wildlife and habitat. I am convinced industrial solar farms will come back to bite us environmentalists.

I also considered wind energy, both a small residential mill to power my own activities, and briefly explored the idea of installing three industrial turbines on the hill to feed the grid. I found a directory of windmill installers and began calling.

"Hello?"

"You install wind turbines?"

"Yes."

"Could you tell me a little bit about your process?"

"I charge $200 to come do an assessment," he said.

"Oh, okay. . . Could you give me an example of a wind project that's worked?"

"I don't know. . . . I don't know," he stumbled. "You know the one up off route 28 near the Sky Top Motel?"

"Near 87?"

"Yeah."

"The one that's been there since the seventies?"

"Yeah. That one."

"That's the most efficient one up?"

"Yeah. That's a good one."

"How many wind turbines have you put in?"

"None."

One eager salesman came to the property and doubled his price of installation once he stood next to me. It would be close to $22,000.

"So how many windmills have you installed?" I asked.

"I have five projects underway."

"Do you have any up and running?"

"I have the pole installed in one, and the concrete poured in another."

"You don't have a single wind turbine up?"

". . . No." I had heard that the main manufacturer at the time, that everyone was getting behind, was delayed months in meeting demand. It turned out that there was not a single (new) residential wind turbine in Ulster County at that time. I would not be the first.

Chris didn't like the contractors I had found for electricity and heating and recommended his own. I acquiesced assuming he would get along and work with them well if they were his own pick. Electric Man, a good-looking, affable pothead like Chris, rarely showed up as scheduled. Since many other systems relied on power, his casualness had real costs. Even though he and Chris claimed to have done many, *many* concrete floors before, Electric Man installed the electrical wires in the wrong layer, so the insulation and plumbing had to be pulled up and redone. The building inspector discovered the error before the concrete was poured. Phew.

When Electric Man eventually installed the electric meter, he put it exactly where I said I didn't want it—on the path to the pool, visible and blocking the entrance. And he either did not know, nor informed me, that the meter required driveway access. So, before the utility company approved and turned on the electrical system, I had to get a dump of gravel and extend the driveway thirty feet across the lawn to the pool.

The hot water heater didn't work for the first few months. I had moved into the barn as my home, and had someone living in the cottage. Heating Guy blamed Electric Man and Electric Man blamed Heating Guy. Heating Guy clenched his teeth so the muscles in his jaw and cheeks flexed, while he "listened" to me. He had an attitude and an air of danger, which made me enormously uncomfortable, since in those early months, he spent a lot of time at the barn with me, alone, trying to fix all the problems he'd created. If this guy were found to have limbs in his freezer, people would say, "I knew there was something off about him." At one point, when he couldn't figure out why one heating zone didn't work, he told me it was my fault for messing with the thermostat wiring. I assured him I don't touch anything electrical.

He installed three complicated (and expensive) programmable thermostats to control the three heating zones, and when I asked him how they worked he threw a brochure at me and said, "I don't know. Here's the manual." When I finally figured it out, I discovered he'd left the heat on all spring.

I informed the company owner that I could not have Heating Guy come to my house anymore, but it still wasn't working, so the owner came himself. He was baffled by the mess his guy had created. He didn't know how the thermostats worked either and couldn't figure out why one of the zones didn't work. Heating Guy was fired. I am sure there was more (like limbs in his freezer) to that story.

This went on for months until Michael figured it out: One of the valves had been installed upside down.

So, at the end of the day, the barn is not off-grid, and I didn't install renewable energy at that time. A friend of mine is contemplating geothermal now and believes that some of the issues that I encountered have been resolved, but she decided not to go forward with it either. Over the past decade, solar has become more efficient and affordable. In 2018, I installed a small solar array on a two-bay garage-barn built from vintage wood and old metal roofing a friend was discarding. This array powers the cottage and pool, the greatest energy demand, especially since AC was installed. Solar for the barn still doesn't seem necessary as the electric bill has run at about $50 a month for the past fifteen years; the vast majority of the bill is "fixed costs" or the cost of delivery.

The oversized windows provide natural light. Fluorescent lights were the no-frills vernacular of old barns, including my own, and also were at that time an energy efficient alternative to incandescent bulbs before other options emerged. I installed simple, long fluorescent lights above all exit doors, and in the bathroom and kitchen. I have since replaced some with LED and found a new owner for the retired fluorescent fixtures.

The small furnace was the most efficient available at the time and uses propane to heat coils of water which feed through the concrete floor. One benefit of the radiant floor is that the heat hovers low above the floor, rather than lifting to the 35-foot peak.

And in summer the heat rises to the cathedral ceilings. Opening just a couple large windows at either end of the barn creates a breeze and aeration, and a feeling of being outside surrounded by birds and other critters. For a decade, there were only a few unbearable summer days and for those, I jumped in the pool every hour or two. With the increasing frequency of thunderstorms and wildfires—with heat, high humidity, and major winds—

and need to close the large windows, I eventually installed an energy-efficient split system, which I rarely use.

When people step into the barn, one of the first questions they ask is the cost to heat it. (Actually, men ask me whether I own a gun, wondering about how safe I feel at the end of the long driveway. No, but I have an ax by the door!) Large windows face southeast and west, triple-paned and Argon-filled, and the walls and ceiling are super-insulated. When it's sunny, passive solar keeps it fairly warm in the winter—as much as geothermal would. The low sun hits my bedroom, living room and kitchen first thing in the morning, warming the barn, and then again, just as it goes down at the end of the day from the west. The heat clicks on at 2 AM if it's less than 30 degrees outside or if the day is cloud-covered. Even as a Goliath structure, the barn is an energy-efficient envelope.

THE ROOF

The roof is enormous. So is the uninterrupted ceiling.

The carpenters clambered thirty-five feet into the sky and nailed old boards into the thirty-two trusses to create the ceiling. The boards varied in color, sometimes weathered to differing degrees, or stained red or painted with white lye. I asked them to put them up randomly. I anticipated that they might have trouble with this notion of *random*, so I watched. Sure enough: they were spacing out the whitish boards every five. I explained that whatever board they grabbed goes up. Sometimes two white boards will be beside one another, and sometimes only one red one will be in a whole section. You can't plan or pretend randomness. It just happens.

Six-inch-thick Structured Insulated Panels (SIP), R-Value-45 (an insulation metric), laid atop those boards. The SIPs are covered with Tyvek and the most simple, humble metal roof available, one notch above, or possibly below, corrugated metal. Standing seam, like what I eventually put on the original house, was expensive and too dressy.

I did not install gutters initially. I wanted to see if they were necessary. Maybe the rain coming down would be good for the surrounding gardens. Little could I imagine. When it rains, the drip line is forceful. Worse, I had not envisioned the huge snow avalanches that slide off the roof in winter, which would have decimated any gutter. When we have six or ten inches of snow at a time (rarely now), and that slides off the warming roof—a combination of internal heat and baking sun—a thunderous rumble gives a second of warning. The avalanches start on the east side in the morning and move to the west in the afternoon. The quantity of snow that comes down is stupendous. Often wet, the heavy snow angles slightly in as it drops and on occasion hits the large vulnerable windows precariously. The avalanches have moved half-ton logs—several times—

which I'd placed as benches at the garden's edge, twelve feet out. At first, I thought my caretaker had moved them, until I saw it happen. What if my dog, or I, were nailed by one of those avalanches? I park my car away from the barn on snowy days and venture out carefully.

I have thought about capturing what runs off the barn in a big wooden water tank like those atop New York City buildings—and using that for the pool and garden, employing a gravity feed, without pressure tanks and pumps and filtration systems.

Many suggest snow guards, those little stops that keep snow in place. I started looking into them again a few years ago, hesitant about additional screw holes in the roof, each a threat to the roof's integrity and a potential leak. One contractor tried to convince skeptical me that the holes are super-sealed and would not present an issue. Just as I was deciding to go ahead with (very expensive) snow guards along with simple industrial gutters for water catchment, a friend who has snow guards mentioned that the snow on her roof melted then refroze, resulting in enormous chunks of ice careening from the roof. Not just snow, ice! No snow guards for me.

WALLS

The brittle antique siding on old barns generally splits during dismantling and is discarded, but I asked for all they could salvage, not wanting new siding to make my barn look like an oversized box. I was in luck. The original barn was clad with two layers of siding and most of the boards were in excellent condition and reusable. There were enough eight-foot, one-inch thick, one-foot-wide boards not only to re-side the barn, but also for the entire interior ceiling, with extra to spare for a few interior walls.

The old barn frame provided the structure for the building, which remained visible on the inside of the barn, with SIPs up against the frame, surrounding it. Anyone who has built a house in the past decade will be familiar with SIPs, which are insulation sandwiches: two sides of strand board and hard insulation foam between. SIPs are replacing traditional two-by-four construction, as more time- and cost-efficient.

And SIPs provide excellent insulation: The wall SIPs are four inches thick and have R-values of 36 vs. the ceiling SIPs six-inches and R-values of 45. I would have preferred more earth-friendly insulation than styrofoam, but at the time it was difficult to procure and prohibitively expensive to consider obscure alternatives, given the surface area of the barn, although new materials— such as cellulose— are on the market now. If I had known then about cork's insulating, fire-retardant properties, and sustainability, maybe I would have pursued cork bricks instead of SIPs.

Chris had a sane and competent woman in the office, who held his entire operation together. I got to know her well telephonically over the year we worked together. Chris left her to calculate and place the order for the SIPs. When the order arrived, weeks later, it turned out she had grossly underestimated the square footage required, so the barn stood with a big chunk missing for months, awaiting the next delivery.

As we moved into winter, this misstep increased the cost of construction by tens of thousands of dollars. The SIPs that were up and in place were exposed to the elements. The Tyvek—the protective sheath that wicks rain off the strand board—flapped in the breeze and ripped, and would have to be repurchased or re-secured, and with diminished efficacy. For years I found black Tyvek scraps in the field. Port-a-potties and dumpster rental expenses were extended for those additional months, for which Chris tried to charge me. Meanwhile, to accommodate the concrete truck in the early spring so it could traverse the slippery clay mud, I invested $25,000 in a 500-foot gravel driveway, which I had been trying to avoid, desirous of a grass driveway like the trails in the meadow. If we had been able to pour the floor in the fall as originally planned, that driveway would not have been necessary.

Chris always had a bit of a chip on his shoulder working for me, despite his soft, flirtatious, big-brown-eyed side, which irked Michael. Like many of these guys, he was conflicted by our relationship. Some minor attraction was challenged by his having to report to me, and my being a woman—and one who saw errors. Chris literally yelled at me in the heat of one heated confrontation, "We always make mistakes, but we fix them before the client discovers!" Even though he was a decade younger and was in a completely different line of work, the financial and reporting relationship between us pained him and was awkward for me.

Chris blamed his assistant for the bad purchase order. She had, in fact, miscalculated, but in my view, it wasn't her fault. I went out on a limb and offered Chris some unsolicited advice, invoking management consultant. I explained that as the boss, he should never have left such a large purchase to someone on his staff. He was responsible. He should have triple checked the math himself—and that goes for anything larger than, say, $5,000. Unforeseen issues emerge and change orders come up in any project, but in this case, it was just lack of oversight. But more: take ownership. Don't blame your assistant and don't expect your clients pay for your mistakes.

Using the leftover barnwood siding, Michael and I built internal walls and doors around the mechanical room where the furnace and water system were housed, as well as to create a bedroom, walk-in closet, and bathroom. On the surface, it would seem easy to bang out some rustic wood walls, but it requires problem solving. We needed to secure 4 by 4's (also leftover barn posts) into the concrete, to which the boards would be nailed. Lining up the boards meant matching not only width, but board thickness. The boards had to reach those posts, so we wanted to maximize the use of each board and make as few cuts as possible. And we had to do this on either side of the post, leaving a cavity for plumbing and electric, and eventually sound insulation.

It could have been a puzzle for the Sunday *Times*.

If a board ended up on a corner, we left the weathered edge facing out, so the fresh-cut raw edge wasn't visible. We saved pieces that had shape or color interest for future projects, or used them on the backs of doors, where linearity was unnecessary. I learned a lot from Michael, who was skilled and meticulous, down to the kind of rough-hewn nails to use.

The unattractive strand board of the SIP panels needed to be covered. I got an idea from a design magazine which had a photo of burlap that had been painted over with layers of glossy black paint. Burlap! But plain. I purchased rolls and rolls of it, in different widths, through Michael, who had ready access to burlap through his work. The natural burlap blends with the color of the barn frame. Both minimal and of farm vernacular, burlap is also inexpensive. All the burlap cost a few hundred dollars. Other than keeping the strand boards bare, or maybe painting them, it seemed the simplest, minimalist solution.

I installed much of the burlap myself: measuring, cutting, climbing on a ladder, and teetering with a staple gun, folding over the edges for a clean finish, balancing and holding the rest of the fabric while getting it *just so*, and stapling some more, tucking it behind the beams and posts. The larger pieces were difficult because the weight of the unstapled burlap pulled down.

I assumed burlap was a temporary solution that would evolve with time. I thought I might change the burlap out, make an upgrade of some kind, down the line. I played with the idea of padding the walls in my bedroom like those I saw in an elegant country home in Normandy, France, using the textiles I collected from all over the world, notably Indian saris and dhotis, wax cloth from Mali, mud cloth from Senegal. Doing so, however would conflict with the art and make the barn visually busier.

While I burlapped most of the first- and second-floor walls, there came a time that I could not balance and reach and feel safe. I needed to enlist the help of someone handy who had a longer ladder and was not afraid of heights.

At the same time, as I moved from the house into the barn, I sought a caretaker to live in the original house, or "cottage." I put an ad on Craigslist for a caretaker and began fielding dozens of calls. A sampling of respondents, verbatim:

"I hear you have a free place."

"I used to mow lawns as a summer job. I been working for Burger King for the past four days. I think I'm qualified as a caretaker."

"I have friends with money. Like I know the guy who just bought that motel on 9W. Real nice place."

"I've been working on my sobriety, and your place seems like a good place to do that."

"We have four kids and three dogs and have been living out of our car for the last three months. Please, please, please."

When Peter called, he seemed perfect. For years, he had been the caretaker for a local art colony with almost 300 acres and a couple dozen buildings. He gave me the director's number as a reference. I called.

"I have had problems with Peter," the director said.

"But he's good, right?" I asked.

"He really doesn't do much. It's his friend who does all the work. So, work gets done. He's a nice guy, but I did let him go."

"Three hundred acres is a lot to manage."

"Yes and no. He doesn't do anything. He doesn't plan or think ahead or actually do the work."

I didn't think a caretaker needed to be a strategic planner. I decided to ignore her, principally because I needed someone immediately and he seemed heads and shoulders better than the ninety other people who had called and written.

Michael and I went to meet Peter at the art colony where he lived while they sought his replacement. Peter was literate—even quoted poetry—and used to work for the local radio station. He was tall and good looking, mature, personable, and had a slight southern drawl. He sweat as the warm day demanded.

I looked around. Buildings were rundown and the landscape was unkempt, as forewarned.

I had my trepidations, but Michael and I were desperate. Aside from ongoing caretaking duties, we needed someone immediately to watch our Labradors while we were away in Martha's Vineyard for two weeks.

Within moments, on our site tour of the art colony, Peter introduced us to his friend, Steve, half his age, even featured and able bodied with curly black hair. Greek God-like. My memory of Steve is without a shirt, although he must have had a shirt on that day. There seemed an understanding, but it never occurred to me that they were lovers. The understanding, it turned out, was at least in part that Steve would do all the work, just as the art colony director had said.

Peter moved to Field Farm the day we were leaving for the unforgiving Martha's Vineyard ferry, later than I had hoped and we had agreed to, so I only had time for a cursory introduction. I gave him a quick tour and instructions for the property, the house, dogs, barn, tasks. He seemed a little foggy, but he agreed to everything and nodded slowly, as if he understood.

While we were away, I checked in periodically. Reception was spotty.

"How are things going?"

"All good," Peter texted.

"How's the burlap project?"

"Almost done."

"Wow, that's great. How are the dogs?"

"They're both doing well. Stay as long as you want," he wrote.

When we returned, we found that while the dogs were fine, Peter had barely begun the burlap project.

"I didn't really understand what you wanted me to do," Peter said.

"You said you were almost done."

"We did all this here." One small piece, literally, a single piece of burlap, probably stapled as we drove up the driveway, something that would have taken ten minutes.

We discussed the project again. He nodded some more. He seemed slow, confused, not all there. Was this when I started to note the empty beer cans?

He said Steve was coming over the next day, and they would get on it.

"But I'm home now. The idea was to do it when I wasn't here. This is where I live." There were no walls, no privacy. I didn't want Peter and Steve in the barn with me for the rest of the month.

"Steve couldn't come over while you were gone. It'll go fast when he comes to do it with me."

The next day Steve arrived and got on the ladder. Peter handed him tools and cut the burlap to spec on the concrete floor.

Steve wasn't afraid to climb high.

We went through a month like that: grudging agreement to tasks that would go undone, and then a flurry of activity when Steve came over. But mostly Peter disappeared every morning. He didn't seem to understand that he had to put in hours in exchange for living gratis at Field Farm, although I thought I had made it clear.

One day, Peter was scheduled to come over to work but didn't show. Since this was part of a pattern, I didn't think much of it. A few hours later he called.

"Steve died."

"What?" My eyes stared into the back of my head, into that white space where you aren't in your own surroundings anymore and you're trying to picture something—Peter, Steve, anything—staring into voices and confusion.

"He keeled over while we were working on some things a half hour ago."

I checked in again later, "They think it was cardiac arrest," Peter said, matter-of-factly. "I should have known. I just didn't—"

"He's too young. There was no way to have known."

Steve looked about thirty-five to Peter's sixty-five and the embodiment of health. It was inconceivable that he had died, was gone. All I could think of was opioids, although they were not as prevalent or visible as they are today. There was no further explanation, ever. Peter was in shock and dealing with Steve's parents and arrangements. It was an intimate burial.

I felt terrible but wasn't sure what to do, what my responsibilities were. I gave Peter space. He kept nodding vaguely, as he always had, going about his business. I saw him drive off in his van most mornings. I felt bad for him, and I too was in shock, but I can't say I knew Steve well enough to grieve as perhaps I should have. I'd met him a few days over a month or two. He'd been a hard guy to get to know. He barely spoke, hadn't engaged, gave no openings.

Peter wrote me, "Steve thought you were the nicest person he had ever known." I reread those words a few times. I didn't know what to do with that information. Could I take it at face value? I was touched, it was so sweet, but already I was becoming suspicious of Peter's drinking and manipulation, patterns I was familiar with but kept slipping into.

One sentiment gnawed at me, which I must confess, although it pains and embarrasses me to do so: I was incredibly thankful and relieved that Steve hadn't had his cardiac arrest while atop the 25-foot ladder in my barn. For so many reasons I am glad he was on *terra firma* elsewhere.

Another thought I had was that Steve didn't die, but the relationship ended.

The summer was almost over, and Peter hadn't done much caretaking since. In fact, he hadn't done much at all, and he wasn't paying rent. I gave him room to mourn, the least I could do. But I found out he had been working at the art colony all along.

I got up my courage to confront him. "Hey, Peter, if you're working, it seems to me you should be working here too. Could you help with this gate, please?"

He nodded. His skin looked gray.

In the early fall, Peter moved out quietly, leaving a mountain of beer cans in the lean-to. He had spent three months on Field Farm as caretaker and never walked the property, never walked into the meadow out his back door. I found out subsequently that he'd been taking care of someone else's dog and readying the second room to sublet.

That was my first caretaker, and possibly my best. It was downhill from there. But that's a different book.

The burlap project continued. I finished most of what was left, but there was the very tall end of the barn where there was no loft, no second floor, to lower the 35-foot peak. Someone needed to climb way up there, and the ladder had to be more than 45 feet to reach at an angle. That person would not be me. The little triangle of bare strand board stared down, relentless. Until it was covered, the barn would not be finished.

I was still living part time in New York City, near The Metropolitan Museum of Art. One day, as I was walking Charlotte into Central Park's Great Lawn, as I did pretty much every morning, I bumped into Ric, one of the team of guys who had worked with

Chris on my barn 85 miles north.

"Ric!"

"Cynthia?" Ric tight-walked the top ridge of the barn frame when it was first erected, without being tied in, as if he were walking down the street. He had spent a couple years in Peru, so we talked Peru a bunch, and he had his furry mutt in tow, whom he'd brought back with him from the Andes. Ric and I had always gotten along. He was an adventurous spirit and, like a lot of the younger folks in the New Paltz area, was a rock climber and took full advantage of The Gunks.

"What are you doing down here?" I asked.

"I'm working on the bamboo sculpture," Ric said, pointing towards The Metropolitan Museum behind me.

Doug and Mike Starn, identical twins, and artists, had conceived of Big Bambú: "You Can't, You Don't, and You Won't Stop." They had hired a dozen rock climbers to tie together with colored nylon thread some 5,000 bamboo poles that came from Georgia and South Carolina. The sculpture was a dynamic flurry of bamboo a little larger than my barn—100 feet long and 50 feet high. I had already seen the bamboo sculpture, and it had given me some ideas.

"Wow, really? Awesome!"

"What are you doing down here?" Ric asked.

"I live here, when I'm not upstate," I said. Ric had only known me as the barn client.

Ironically, coincidentally, I had started to contemplate building a bamboo scaffold for the inside of my barn, after being in Beijing earlier that year and seeing it used to construct enormous skyscrapers. I thought it would be cool to have a three-story scaffolding structure on wheels, that moved around inside the barn to reach high places, and maybe even house a futon as an open-air sleeping arrangement. I told all that to Ric. He was intrigued.

"But mostly, I need help finishing up the burlap. Would you be able to help me get to the final peak? With a bamboo scaffolding or otherwise?"

Ric had to finish the sculpture first. A few weeks later he dropped by to discuss the burlap project. When he returned to begin work, he scaled, barehanded, up the south end of the barn on the inside, threw rope over the rafters and created a swinging platform from which he worked. It was a lot simpler and more practical than building a big bamboo rolling platform, and he got the job done in a couple afternoons. That peak had been bugging me.

The barn was finally finished. Although, I suppose, it is never finished.

WINDOWS AND DOORS

When we were first looking at barns, Tess articulated something I had absorbed only subconsciously: how, with barns, the light seeps through the linear cracks between the boards and pin holes and ragged edges. It is in part this permeability that makes a barn feel different from other enclosures. How could we keep that feeling, the rhythm, that rawness, and still insulate, keep out critters and protect it from the elements? It was such an interesting idea, but I couldn't fathom how to make it work, other than with huge panes of glass to cover the entire wall, which made no sense at all.

In fact, one of the trickiest design decisions overall was the windows. Barns often share certain proportions, a distinct slope to their roof, and a comfortable way they sit in the land, but they look like barns because they have few if any windows, and generally not for the views. Sometimes windows let in light, sometimes they buy access. Most have large, rolling barn doors, where large machinery enters.

I knew I wanted to frame certain images with windows: the field, poplars, and north meadow. Traditional, small-paned windows would fit architecturally in some ways, possibly because they hail from the same epoch, but would create visual grids, be difficult to clean and not as well insulated, unless I used the kind where the wooden grille lays atop the glass, a pretense I found unacceptable. I wanted to bring the outdoors in, both visually, and physically. I wanted the interaction with nature to be seamless.

I spent a lot of time thinking about windows: placement, style, material. I gathered information everywhere—my go-to design and architectural magazines, observation, internet searches. Michael and I went to Turkey the summer the barn was going up, a trip that almost didn't happen because of our on-and-off again relationship. But on that fabulous, adventurous trip (we traveled together well), we saw huge, elegant wooden windows on ancient buildings. I wished I could find or replicate them, with their over-sized rusty hooks and hinges that held open layers of shutters and windows.

When I spoke to window manufacturers back home, they agreed that wooden windows were indeed better for insulation than metal, and then asked what color aluminum I wanted to clad them. That isn't what I meant! But wood, without paint or aluminum, they explained, requires constant upkeep, annual oiling to withstand the elements. Wooden window frames, like those I saw in *Dwell* maga-zine, were appealing, but I noted most were in California, the Medi-terranean or under overhangs, so were not a viable option.

At the time, Tess and I were still living primarily in New York City, in the Ward Bennett apartment. The windows in that apartment were huge and simple, and they could tilt or swing open, European style. When swept open, they let in the out-of-doors. We lived on the fifth floor on a tree-lined side street, and my bedroom windows were open in fair weather. The starlings made a racket as they settled into the trees at dusk and in the morning when they woke. Even though starlings are an invasive species that notori-ously, unforgivably elbow into the niches of songbirds and wreak terrible havoc on cars parked below, their social frenzy connected me to another world, maybe the jungle, and I welcomed it over the rattling trucks hurtling their way up Madison Avenue.

In the file folder the apartment's previous owners left behind, I found the name of the window manufacturer in Queens. I called them to fix a couple windows in the apartment. I called a half-dozen times before they called back. They eventually came to fix the hand-manufactured windows with confidence and compe-tence. Despite the enormity of the glass—four by six feet—they lifted the windows out of the openings and fixed the handles and locks as needed.

Harry, the manager and possibly owner, was from Monte-negro. Harry was too young to have owned the company in the 1970s when the apartment's windows were installed. Nonetheless, after much research on alternatives, I asked him whether they could outfit the barn's windows and doors.

Although consistent with past service behavior, I was surprised Harry didn't get back to me after I called a dozen times with the possibility of a huge order. Of course, it was not a good sign, one I should have heeded. I reasoned that maybe he was diligent about current rather than future clients. Eventually when Harry did respond, I shared my plans.

A few weekends later, Harry, with his wife and two young children, spent an afternoon at the barn site. In the haylofts on the second floor, where carriages and tractors originally entered via barn doors, I envisioned four eight-foot square double balcony doors, resting eighteen inches off the second floor to meet building code. Four six-foot square windows on the first floor would create a breezeway through the middle of the barn-house. And there would be nine additional five-by-five-foot windows that tilted and turned and swung open in other strategic places—bedrooms, bathroom, dining room, living spaces in the loft.

The bathroom and two bedrooms would have a view of the northern meadow. The rain shower head is situated in the middle of the room, looking out a huge five-foot square floor-to-ceiling window, which would open, swinging close to the lip of the toilet, and so feel like an outdoor shower. People seem concerned about privacy, starting their question, "Aren't you worried about—?" and then realize there is no one, nothing, to worry about, just the field, the woods beyond, maybe a deer or turkey, a distant stone wall. One friend suggested I place two Adirondack chairs on the lawn facing the window as a taunting suggestion of audience.

I try to take my showers during the day, or as the sun is setting, so I can devote ample appreciation to that meadow and punctuating pear trees. I time my showers to not coincide with the weekly lawn mowing, being appropriately modest and not wanting to cause any accidents.

Once Harry and I put together the entire order—which

amounted to 25% of the barn's entire budget—Harry said it would take two weeks to manufacturer and two days to install. I was incredulous.

"Really?"

"Yes."

"Really?"

"Yes."

I wrote a check for the deposit on half the order, which was sizable, on what amounted to a very flimsy contract with crude drawings.

No surprise, manufacturing took more than two weeks. Four months went by. In December, Harry called, presumably to schedule installation.

"We are leaving tonight."

"To come here?"

"We go home to Montenegro."

"You're leaving the country?" I couldn't mask my dismay. I didn't even know where Montenegro was. I looked it up and realized I had been there when it was still part of Yugoslavia.

"For Christmas."

My heart sank. I literally did not know whether I would ever see my windows, my enormous down payment, or them again.

"Are you coming back?"

"Yes, of course."

They did come back. But not until late January in the middle of winter. The driveway was impassable. There was no way to install windows at that time. When spring broke, we started to schedule the installation team's migration north.

Because I was living in Manhattan and had limited time on site to oversee the work, I impressed upon Harry that it was important for his crew to leave early in the morning from Queens to be able to put in a full day. Half the time they canceled; other times, they arrived late in the day, citing flat tire, broken-down van, or traffic.

*   *   *

Tess and I had discussed all kinds of innovative ideas, like beds rolling across beams, which would never have passed inspection. One less costly yet innovative idea was to put a swing in the center of the barn, over the middle beam. We found a board and drilled four holes for the rope to pass through, then bought a hundred-foot rope, enough to hang down twice and to be tied to the loft railing. Not thinking it through very well, I found myself on a ladder on the catwalk trying to hoist the rope over the beam with a rake. After a few hours and a lot of trepidation, we had a swing in the middle of the barn, our first piece of furniture. Not long after, an older gentleman from the town's planning department visited to inspect the barn. He got on and swung, loving the barn so much he claimed it an asset to the property and the neighborhood, to the town.

Once, when the window crew of five guys came up, a young, tall, buxom blonde rolled out of the van, too, introduced as a friend. I thought maybe she was with one of the workers. With a huge smile, like she owned the place, she jumped onto the swing in the middle of the barn. She swung as high as I've ever seen that swing go, laughing and giggling, as if she were in a commercial. There was something jubilant about the whole thing, and hugely annoying.

I left to do some errands, and when I returned, the team of guys were still working, but the blond and Harry were not to be found. An hour later, they showed up with leaves in their hair. Reminder: Harry is the guy who had visited with his wife and kids a year earlier to make the sale.

Two days of installation? It was done over eight winter months. Other things were held up, too—pouring the concrete floor, which requires a specific band of temperature between 50 and 60 degrees. We eventually poured the floor, sealing the gaping openings with plastic and running huge space heaters, which bothered my environmental self. I continue to forget how to

112

stipulate penalties for time overruns in contracted work.

In the window contract, Harry had agreed to find a way to open the high, small, square windows at the thirty-foot peaks on either end of the barn. He talked about a long pole, or a remote, but never came through with a solution. I had hoped to have an escape outlet for hot air (which never became necessary) and realized later that it would also serve to let out birds that had entered the barn that were hard to cajole out other openings. Hummingbirds in particular were attracted to the lofty windows.

Because Harry's windows and doors were really for use in city buildings and balconies, they also did not have traditional hardware to lock from the outside. Although I stipulated a front door that would lock, he never solved that issue, so I had to go out a side door with a different (ugly, unmatching) handle and mechanical system, if I wanted to secure the barn when I left.

A few years in, the custom-made closures broke on the front and back doors. The handles disconnected from the locking mechanisms, and there was no way to fix them. I replaced the entire door units with doors custom made in Germany, with new, normal locks. I did not call Harry.

INTERIORS
Found, Discovered, Repurposed

The barn is big but not intimidating. It is warm, welcoming, and whimsical, in part because of the natural tones and materials, its organic-ness, gentle human marks, and informality. In part because of the swing.

Early on, Michael and I made a pact that all furniture would be homemade or re-purposed. Handles were crafted from branches and sanded so they didn't jab too much if you walked into them at night. We built a four-poster bed out of four dead cedar trees we lugged back from the woods. We lifted the trees through the 8' X 8' windows and built the bed in situ. Sleeping between the two open windows at night was an adventure. We were forever chasing bats and birds out of the barn—and slapping mosquitoes.

A confession. While I consider myself a frugal non-consumer in general, I become a rabid but discerning shopper when abroad. In open air markets and artisan cooperatives, I collect textiles and utilitarian objects unique to other cultures: lacey brass mouse traps from India, bow and arrows and gourds from the nomadic Amazonian Machiguengas. I also have a penchant for outsider "art," like a crèche scene with two baby Jesuses, and two-faced dolls I found in Peru. I try to support makers directly and value their traditions. I have no appetite for tourist trinkets.

The space has filled, in almost in every conceivable cranny over the years, with art and objects from global travels. An ancient Berber chest from Morocco found its place in the central sitting area, dusted with the same golden browns and oranges as the Mexican handwoven rug beneath. A stack of vintage suitcases in yellows and browns and oranges serves as a coffee table. I bought giant biomorphic gourds on the roadside in Morocco. Our guide at the time wondered how I'd get them home. He found out later— inside the oversized Berber chest. A large wooden serving platter for couscous, with metal straps band-aiding a crack, is laden with a dozen translucent camel skin spice containers and contracts—I was told for real estate, marriages—scratched and inked on cylindrical wooden rods. In the bathroom, hanging above the toilet, is the entire display of shoehorns, with hooks and prices, I purchased from one of two men who sell shoe horns in the Fez market. He did not offer me a volume discount, nor did I seek one.

A dozen six-foot dried great mullein cut in the field splay from an oversized bamboo vessel. A three-dimensional tic-tac-toe from Panama made of palm nuts sits atop a delicate, gilded 19th-century French side table. Handpicked textiles from markets in Ghana, Senegal, Thailand, Cambodia, The Gambia, Guatemala, Mexico, China, and India hang on the rungs of three apple-picking ladders leaning against the loft.

My penchant for textiles may have come from my mother, a talented seamstress, who sewed us matching Marimekko dresses and collected fabrics, but also early exposure. In 1980, after freshman year in college, I spent the summer doing anthropological work in San Cristóbal de las Casas, in Chiapas, Mexico, as Professor Evon Vogt's final student researcher in the 400-person Harvard Chiapas Project. San Cristóbal is surrounded by dozens of Mayan hamlets. The women generally wear square, elaborately embroidered tops, called *huipiles,* unique to the village. I purchased dozens that summer, many already antiques, concerned they might disappear within the decade as polyester fabrics and Day-Glo dyes were arriving. Thankfully, I was wrong. When I returned to Mexico a few years ago, I found a surfeit of pride in Mayan crafts, even among the mestizos—inconceivable a half century ago— who had previously distanced themselves from traditional indigenous culture.

I also collected masks and hats when I wrote for *Let's Go: Mexico* from Mexico's west coast and northwest; in Cuzco, nestled in the Inca highlands, on my way to the Amazon to study tamarin and capuchin monkeys; and in Brazil when I was there a few years later for studies and work. They frame windows, and peer from the upstairs loft. Decades later, I could not resist saris (pricey, but well worth it) handwoven by nonagenarians in a Rajasthan cooperative which I feared would no longer exist in a decade. And from Morocco, I sent home a luggage rack-frame used on the backs of camels, which now is an elevated side table, easily transported on my own back to create an outdoor bar-counter during fireside parties.

On shelves made of old crates: a collection of wood clamps, piano hammers, and vintage paint brushes. An old trowel stands in as a toilet paper holder. On walls: conceptual art and oil paintings, most of my own or Tess's making. I store Christmas decorations and wrapping paper in a huge Chinese chest I found in a local consignment shop for $150 similar to those that go for $2000 online. An Indian doorway was turned into a shelf unit for books and display. A dozen old foggy bottles stand at the bottom of the stairs next to the window, catching the morning light, casting blotted shadows.

The summer Michael and I went to Turkey, on the first day in Istanbul, I fell in love with felted tribal rugs used to insulate nomadic yurts. I was concerned that it was the first day, and I should see more options before I made such a large purchase, but I couldn't imagine loving anything more, or anything more suitable for the barn, especially for the price. I bought 13 of them, most of a certain ilk, but three were of a different era and style. They are soft relief on the splintery barnwood floor in the lofts and put bounce in one's step. Ten years later, I came home from Morocco with a dozen 3' X 5' tightly-woven rugs in neutral taupe and cream, each subtly different. One has a single line of red thread, another a small blue dot. It is, of course, these idiosyncrasies that make them special.

The bathroom counter is made of barnwood scraps and leftover stone tile from the house's bathroom. Vintage picnic baskets contain bathing suits, construction tools, and supplies. An Indian blue steel drum stores dog leashes, treats, and other canine paraphernalia. Reams of vegetal-dyed wool (a sustainable fiber) purchased at the annual Rhinebeck Sheep & Wool Festival became pillows on the living room sofa. A sea-foam green piano, I purchased for $50, entertained Tess for years. It has great tone—at least to my untrained ears— but has never been tuned. I promise myself I will take up piano again one day. Two oversized stainless steel dumpling steamers from a New York Chinese restaurant serve as enormous planters on either side of the front door.

Outdoor furniture cushions that lost their luster have a second life sound-insulating the walls between the bathroom and the bedrooms. Discarded linens and clothes are stuffed into what were Moroccan hanging cribs to create ottomans. "Horizontal closets" were made from leftover barnwood and double as coffee tables. I often reuse other people's abandoned canvases as a point of departure in my own paintings. The concrete kitchen sink, which looks like slate or stone, likely hails from an old art or laundry room. It's gray and mottled, and has two very deep basins, one allocated to dirty dishes, one to rest clean ones to dry. Appliances include a sage-colored professional range, mint-colored dishwasher, and a cobalt blue glass refrigerator. Water and wine glasses come in all shapes and forms, textures, and colors—red, blue, brown, pink, green, and clear—and are shelved on a high barnwood shelf to catch the light and stay out of harm's way. They come from all over—my mother's cabinet as she downsized, garage and flea market sales in Martha's Vineyard, Guadalajara.

A ping pong table, built from wood scraps and a couple pieces of white birch plywood, rolls around at the far end of the barn. Without the net, it doubles as an alternate dinner table, and otherwise provides a handy utilitarian surface to fold laundry, pack for a trip, or serve as a horizontal easel. During an energetic party, we roll the ping pong table into the central space and conjure up summer camp. Competitors grab the paddles and take wild, wide swings. Dozens of white and yellow balls are provided so momentum is not sacrificed. The unsuspecting inanimate parchment globes are whacked and slammed and bounced, given names and curses and points. They find air and then hiding places all over the barn. For weeks, I discover balls, testimony to a good game, a good party.

When a lumber company went out of business around the corner, we picked up dozens of old fence railings and cedar boards. We lay the rails on the ground to demarcate what would become an enormous garden on two sides of the barn in fifteen-foot increment squares. We used cedar boards (rather than burlap)—which can withstand water—to line the bathroom wall, covering the strand board. We designed and built chaise lounges for the pool out of additional cedar boards and a long dining room table for twelve, also able to take the elements. The table operates as the dining room table inside, but it has so much wax from breezy candlelit dinners, I will soon move it outside where it belongs.

Tess has her own space, a three-quarter room, a slight step up from her drawer-bed in New York City. One wall is missing, so it opens to the main space. A thick, dark-blue-and-white handwoven cloth we purchased in Chiang Rai, Thailand, curtains off the space when she visits. It does not afford complete privacy, even compounded by a rolling closet we built and a telephone booth cum closet. I don't want to close that wall for the week a year she visits, because from the other end of the barn, on entry, you can see all the way out to the field beyond. Enclosing her room would not permit that light, that view.

My parents love the barn, and when it was finished, I think they finally believed I could accomplish almost anything I set out to do. Applying for research grants and doing original research on monkeys in the Amazon at age twenty, getting into and graduating from Harvard and Wharton Business School, and landing a job with and surviving—indeed enjoying—McKinsey for seven years until I decided to move on as a young mother, producing art, buying the property when few other single moms did that kind of thing, all these things were just steps. Along the way, they warned me how difficult things were, how I might fail.

But after the barn was up and they sat by the pool among the abundant fauna and flora, my parents finally believed that I could do just about anything. The Barn Project was my coming of (middle) age. An artist friend of my parents who was visiting, summed it up, I think, when she said, "You are the most self-actualized person I know." At the time, I wasn't sure if that was good, or bad. I didn't know what she meant, but I think I do now.

LAWN, GARDEN AND OUTDOOR SPACES

It rained in the night. The earth is dark, moist, hangs in the air. I dip to pull crabgrass from the garden's edge. Crabgrass appears every year, in the heat of summer, where the rain licks away the mulch or there's an opening in the grass. In the lawn, crabgrass avoids being cut by laying low, expanding—walking—sideways like a . . . crab, rather than sky-ward. It and the broadleaf plantain populate the well-trodden places in the lawn: the path to the pool, around the garden and house, where the dog races. I am not a fussy lawn person, but I have little affection for crabgrass and plantain. The voice of a friend who is a fussy lawn person is always in my head; she sprays and over-seeds her lawn. I wonder what she thinks of my lawn. I stoop to yank a couple easy loose weeds, but I won't stoop to use an herbicide. An informal farm setting is a little more forgiving on that front, I hope.

I didn't want a lawn around the barn, knowing how a grass mono culture is environmentally detrimental, reducing biodiversity and requiring fuel to keep short and water to keep green. Initially, I hoped to have a wildflower meadow rolling up to the windows and just a six-foot wide grass path loping around the barn for access.

Years earlier, I had tried to sow poppy and lupine seeds into the field, to create snaking lines of color in the distance like a Degas painting. Even using a tractor with a rotary tiller, the grass clumps were too solid and deep for anything to take hold. Each clump of grass root was a cubic foot of stubborn, dense mass. There was no persuading the grass to move over, to share.

This time, I started with bare dirt around the barn. I spent a week collecting all the fist-sized stones that lay atop the earth and rolled them away in dozens of wheelbarrow loads. I threw pounds of poppy and cosmos and cornflower seeds and watched for a wildflower meadow to spring to life. This would be my chance. I was a little concerned the FBI might track me down for buying pounds of poppy seeds thinking I was up to something else—I did receive warnings—but a poppy field was worth that risk.

Creating a wildflower meadow is work, certainly more work than a lawn and a well-mulched perennial garden. Even starting from bare dirt, wildflowers, which are often seed-based annuals, find it hard to compete with the naturally encroaching weeds and grass and invasives which quickly dominate. After spending far too much time weeding and cultivating an occasional poppy, the "meadow" devolved into a lawn, with five-foot native grasses, and lichen-painted pear trees beyond.

So, I have a lawn—an imperfect lawn with seasonal visitors like dandelions, crabgrass, and clover. And I have learned to be content with naturally occurring wildflowers in the existing meadow, which hosts many desirable natives and pollinators which tend to be more subtle and play second fiddle to the dramatic and nuanced grasses. Over the years, the garden, both around the barn and the pool, has become more and more wild, somewhat meadow-like in its countenance, welcoming buttercups, violets, wild oregano, strawberry, yarrow, Queen Anne's lace, golden rod, and milkweed.

Often when I ask someone whether they have a garden, they say, "I may plant a few tomatoes this year." They assume *vegetable* garden, something I find impossibly difficult. Tomatoes struggle here—and who can contemplate a vegetable garden without tomatoes? Even if a few green balls appear late in the season, the slugs get them. Basil, despite the full-sun instructive tags, seems to prefer partial shade—and, now I'm learning, only morning sun—and don't do well in my garden no matter what I try. I inter them or keep them in a pot. I water them, I let them dry out. If they don't turn yellow and scraggly, they are eaten by Japanese beetles or rabbits. Someone nibbles. They go to seed.

So, rather than plant a deliberate garden every spring, I

support local farm stands and I rely on bushes and trees. I forage and enjoy what seems to work and the land offers: high-bush cranberry, sunchoke, apples, pear, asparagus, watercress, a variety of mushrooms, hazelnut, walnut, purslane, nettle, sorrel, and other nutritional weeds.

Every year, the Department of Environmental Conservation offers a deal on native trees and shrubs. A decade ago, I bought 400 vulnerable, bare, foot-tall saplings, mere wisps of trees, for $1 a piece. I planted hundreds of evergreens along the property border to block the neighbors' roof lines, visible in winter. Many of those small pines could not compete with the deeply rooted field grass and succumbed to invasive vines. It was hard to keep up with them from a distance. The pussy willows in the driveway turnaround have grown to over twenty feet. I delight in the little velvet pods, among the first signs of spring.

It is likely evident that my decades as a strategy and management consultant influences me little in my personal life and how I garden. There is no vision, mission, and game plan, just an unwavering set of values. I garden on the fly, in a spontaneous way when I have the urge, which is whenever I walk by or get up to stretch my legs, almost every day, five times, in the spring and summer. The garden is a work in progress, an evolution, which allows me marginal participation. Bushes and perennials get bigger over time, lose their shape. A hundred giant allium I planted ten years ago are down to a handful. Some years, everything seems enormous; others, I lose a tree or a bush to disease or drought or frost. Indeed, I try not to invest too much in any decision, emotionally or financially, because of the disappointments brought on by the uncontrollable—soil, weather, predators. Some gardeners insist that you can amend your soil. True, but not without fighting what naturally occurs. And the most successful approaches seem to involve animals.

I think more about a plant's strategy than my own. As a biologist, I learned how flowers use different tactics to survive and dominate, how they attract pollinators, reproduce, spread their seeds or roots, or crowd out others. Along with the hundreds of seeds that are blown into the wind to the frustration of fussy lawn people, dandelion, whose roots are long and stubborn, make extraction difficult; even when a small piece remains, they return. There's some urgency to extract weeds going to seed, or if they are elbowing out plants I care more about. I pull poison ivy from the same places every year, even though each time I've done my best to eliminate it. And when I do, my mother's voice is in my head telling me how to use the occasional plastic bag that has entered my home to do so: I glove my hand with the bag, grab the vine, turn it inside out and stuff it with great care into the garbage.

I observe patterns in the insects and birds on the plants, too—as pollinators, reproducers, or consumers. Some have mutual relationships, or parasitic, in which one relies on one without benefit to the other. The invasive Japanese beetles obliterate rosebuds and leave mid-summer but seem to aid in pollination of the Rose of Sharon.

Given my German background and efficiency-focus, I bring a bucket from the pool and drop it off by the wheelbarrow on my way to the driveway to save a trip. I confess to optimizing and employing the 80/20 rule without thinking about it. I will weed a visible area at the front door for maximum impact and work towards the edge in case I don't finish.

One spring I devoted a week to opening the flowerbeds around the house and the pool, in anticipation of dozens of people who would lounge poolside with rosé in hand Memorial Day weekend. (Rosé, a subliminal design feature, would match the orange California poppies and the pillows of the pool furniture.) I woke in the middle of the night with screaming pain, first in a couple fingers then both palms the following night.

"No more extreme gardening," my doctor said, the explanation for a case of painful carpal tunnel. That it was possibly triggered by Lyme disease I wouldn't know for another week. His prescriptions, his admonition, confirmed my notion that a doctor tells you what you already know, or what you just told them, like what many believe of management consultants. My ex-father-in-law quipped, *They'll take your watch and tell you what time it is.* I didn't take it personally.

My doctor delivered the admonition with a smile, not understanding, being urban, how extreme gardening in early May was necessary both for mind and spirit, a rite for most eager gardeners coming out of winter, and a requirement to achieve summer garden results, in a stitch-in-time-saves-nine kind of way. Even so, every year, as aggressive and extreme as I am, I don't get to everything—mulching, for example, before the perennials push up—and I pay dearly down the line in weeds, naked parched beds, soil quality, and dirty, broken fingernails.

We gardeners are a breed who fall on the spectrum of obsession. But many of us will insist that gardening is relaxing and meditative. Our flowers offer a therapeutic sanctuary with rewards both in the process and the results, despite the frustrations. A garden gives, emotes, emits pleasure.

With over 82 acres to tend to here at Field Farm, an acre is flower garden. I am open to ideas and help; Lord knows I need it. But in the end, I'm not sure I could hire anyone to do what I do. No one looking at the bobbing, chaotic color bands and bumps would think I was particular about anything regarding my garden or that I tend it much. Many unarticulated rules guide my yanking hand and snipping shears, many rules that bend with judgment, time, and season.

For example, I am kinder to flowering weeds than most gardeners. After the self-planted buttercups, an abundant spray of daisies—hundreds, if not thousands—joins the garden late spring, early summer. I enjoy them, until I don't. When other, more precious intentional flowers emerge and are lost to the white daisy haze, I heave the daisies into a pile, multiple wheelbarrows full. With a little rainwater on the bottom of the wheelbarrow, I may let a pile of fading daisies sit on display in the distance.

I congratulate myself when I hear the emphasis recently on planting milkweed and golden rod for Monarch butterflies. I have acres and acres of both in the field, and the sturdy, fragrant milk-weed, with their handsome leaf and compound, pinkish aromatic globes, also fill in among the Echinacea and black-eyed Susan. In September, I welcome golden rod, always abuzz, and aster in shades of purple in early October.

Around the barn I envisioned a modern garden with simple blocks of color and form. In Turkey, I'd seen acres and acres of sunflowers roadside tracking the sun with their large, open, dark faces. Inspired, I planted hundreds of sunflower seeds in the long, southern bed that first year. I waited all summer. Only a few small sunflowers came up, mostly nothing. That's when I lowered my expectations and adopted a different approach, something akin to a diversified financial portfolio, to manage risk. I rarely plant things in rows, for fear one might die and leave a gap tooth. A variety of flowers is more apt to deliver. Something comes up. *Something* won't be eaten, rot or dry out.

In that same bed, I planted twelve shrubs—butterfly bush, hibiscus, rose of Sharon, roses, blueberry, hydrangea—and dozens of other perennials. There is so much happening in that bed I forget what will push up and when. It's full of surprises.

Although most have survived and flourished, I lost the butterfly bushes a few years back to frost. I miss them, but I recently learned they are non-native, so I may let them go.

I consult gardening books and online resources. One shows how to create interest in the garden with objects—little gates, benches, water baths. Although the photos are convincing, such objects seem a little cute for this landscape, and I think may work less well in a sun-drenched garden than in shade bordering woods. But friends unloaded a concrete bird bath on me, which hasn't moved from the place I put it a decade ago. And in the 9' X 9' square of pea gravel by the pool, between two flower beds, I created a sundial, arranging twelve half-stumps with angled tops, left over from another project, into a circle in ascending size, and a broken piece of sandstone in the center pointing at the tallest stump. Initially, I adjusted the stumps, that is, set the sundial, every time I walked by, but it never really told time. I looked at my watch, then moved the sundial so it, too, read 2:30, say. It was, nonetheless, an object that drew attention, or at least queries, a focal point.

When the stumps began to rot, I redeployed them as a border on one edge of the pea gravel square, and then eventually as wood for the fire pit. In its place, I tossed twenty rusting barrel bands and one stainless steel loop of metal. They fell at a rakish angle, with little need for arrangement. Orange poppies that escaped the garden self-sow every year among and around them, which I cannot bear to extrude as I love them dearly, and they complement the "sculpture" and gravel.

A few years ago, a magnificent "object" for my garden arrived when my parents downsized. Being the daughter who lives in the country, along with my mother's gardening tools, I received a bell made by esteemed ceramicist and sculptor Toshiko Takaezu, which is now situated beyond the roof's snow avalanches, in a place visible from most vantage points on the way to the pool.

Here I am in nature, a lot. But, I wonder, is this garden, this field, "nature"? Where does "nature" begin and end? Is a cultivated garden, no matter how wild, truly nature? Is this farm, which was cleared a hundred years ago and is brush hogged every year "nature"? How about this stand of woods, which likely didn't exist? Stone walls in the forest are evidence it was once a field but returned as secondary or tertiary habitat. How have the invasive flora and fauna altered our understanding and our definition, or the grazing, over-abundant deer, as they munch on the understory? It's green. It's vibrant and pulsing. There's an ecosystem and a habitat. But is it nature? Is it natural? Further, what is my responsibility? How much should I actively or sleepily "manage" rather than leave it to its own devices?

This is what runs through my head as I stoop.

I read gardeners live longer and are less likely to get dementia than, I suppose, non-gardeners. The article drew on several studies from around the world and elucidated other benefits of gardening: physical, emotional, health. But as an antidote to dementia? Being upside down in my garden hardly feels like the brain puzzles that are being pushed on those of a certain age, but maybe the blood keeps the grey matter nourished.

Separately, but I believe related, there is significant evidence that correlates living alone with a shorter life span, largely because of the stress of loneliness. I submit that we gardeners think of plants as if they were family and friends, nurturing and caring for them with empathy and tenderness. We absorb the sweet tension of hope and optimism in a bursting bud. We take in the hues and forms in different light. We work in the still gentle morning air, the warm summer afternoon breeze. We cannot keep ourselves from honing, pulling weeds, moving plants, deadheading, and trimming, watering in a pinch. As with parenting, we might approach things differently, but we share our love of persuading life from the soil in three dimensions—four dimensions, including time. We are in awe of how a brown garden will push all that color and form and biomass into the world every year. We may not suffer from dementia, but I for one forget all I've planted and am in wonder every year at what comes up.

When I was a student and financially strapped, I promised myself that when I had money, I would buy myself flowers every week. Who knew that I would wind up with a field of my own and gardens full of nosegays?

PART TWO

LIVING IN A PLACE

"He who is not everyday conquering some fear has not learned the secret of life."

—Ralph Waldo Emerson

VISITORS OF A THIRD KIND

On a still, humid evening at dusk on Field Farm, just after the barn went up, Michael and I were stoking a fire out back, as we often did, overlooking the field. We had enjoyed a drink and some salted cashews as we put the sun to bed. To be clear, the contours of the land dictate an eastward orientation, and the sun sets into the apple orchard behind on the hill. We witnessed the elongating shadow-hand spread its fingers across the meadow grabbing mounds and trees in its clutch. Sometimes we craned our necks or twisted to see the sky painted pink above the army of apple trees at our backs, but the real show was on the field of wildflowers and grasses, the distant poplars, and in the reflecting clouds.

We fed the cauldron leftover barnwood from the construction of the barn and, being 200-years old, it burned fast and completely. Two-hundred-year-old nails accumulated in the ashes. At that point in the evening, the raging fire was calming and becoming a bed of coals. We finished the fire with apple wood we'd dragged from orchard-pruning activities. Michael poked around, breaking up any log or board remnants, threw on some soaked wood chips to give our meal a little smoky flavor and lay the grill shelf on top to burn clean. I finished chopping the zucchini, eggplant, and red peppers on my lap.

We went into the kitchen to gather the rest of the fixings for dinner. I headed back out with plates, forks and cloth napkins, and the bowl of chopped vegetables, tossed in Greek olive oil and coarse sea salt. Until that moment, it was a typical, lovely evening on Field Farm after a day of working in the land.

As I headed back out toward the cauldron, I saw, dead center over the field, something that could only be described as—and I smile as I write this—a flying saucer.

But that's what it was: a flat, round dull-silver vessel, like a yo-yo on its side hovering effortlessly, silently, still. The saucer felt substantial. Four defined beams of light emanated from its belly and seemed to prop the saucer fifty feet above the tall grass below. The craft floated for ten or fifteen seconds, the way rainbows do, there, but not *there* exactly. Meaning, that while solid, the hovering object conveyed that, in approaching, it would be continuously beyond reach. So maybe it wasn't exactly over the field, but much larger and over the Hudson River; yet it felt like it was right there, a hundred feet away, above the field where I would later plant a weeping willow. Was there a ring of windows? I don't remember, and I didn't see any signs of life or waving aliens through a windshield.

Without removing my eyes, I backed up to the barn and threw over my shoulder, "Michael, come here."

Michael joined me on the stoop. We stood for a few moments in disbelief before the yo-yo-saucer pressed down slightly and briefly, gathering momentum, and pulled away as if on an invisible string.

Was it Aerodrome weekend in Rhinebeck? Were drones or other American technological feats let out to play? Had West Point, about an hour down the Hudson River, been training or testing? Or had we truly just seen an alien spacecraft? It was, by any account, an Unidentified Flying Object. If Michael had not seen it with me, I would possibly doubt myself or my memory.

That night, we searched the internet and found dozens of sightings of this flying machine captured up and down the northeast corridor. There were pictures to prove it. On December 16, 2017, *The New York Times* reported that the U.S. Defense Department spent $22 million a year on a program between the years of 2007 and 2012 to investigate sightings of unidentified flying objects, or UFOs.

Our visitors came during this time frame.

One Thanksgiving, years later, with my gathered family, we were passing around my homemade cranberry sauce and mashed potatoes, and I told my UFO story.

"I don't believe in UFOs, but I saw one."

Tess said, "Mom! You never told me you saw a UFO!"as if I

had betrayed her. Funny it had never come up. I had almost forgotten, possibly because I didn't believe it myself.

THE SHOOTING CLUB

Michael feared his firearms might be filched by a burglar who was making the rounds in his Westchester neighborhood. So, one weekend, he brought his guns and a box of skeets to stow in my shed, since we spent most weekends on Field Farm. Michael also had wanted to teach me how to shoot. I couldn't imagine pointing a gun at a deer no matter how much of the garden it consumed, but I felt hypocritical for not killing my own meat. Maybe watching the life blown out of something would finally make me a vegetarian, something I aspired to. At a minimum, learning how to handle a gun might come in handy, living as I did alone at the end of a very long driveway. I both dreaded and looked forward to my private shooting lesson, as something of a sacred rite. Maybe next time I would be invited to quail shoot at the same 50,000-acre Armstrong ranch in Texas where Cheney shot Whittington in 2006. Michael had loved that weekend—the long tables set out among the Spanish moss serving up the morning's hunt. Before he went, Michael said the event was men-only, but it turned out to be coupled; he just didn't include me.

Good friends Anne and Jacob were visiting Field Farm on an unsympathetic, bleak winter day. The sun was bound to set soon, early. Cocktail hour had begun at four. Jacob and Michael were cradling their vodkas. In the late afternoon lull, I asked Anne if she'd like to play Scrabble, since the men seemed occupied and did not possess our enthusiasm for the game. As we set up the board, Michael turned to Jacob. "How'd you like to go out and shoot some skeets?"

"What?" my surprise blurted out. Michael had never shot on my land before and had not asked me if it was okay.

"Sure!" Jacob perked up.

"Can I come too?" Anne asked in a cute voice that belied her stature and age. She put down her tile tray, smiling. Shooting trumped Scrabble.

I looked over at Michael. "It's getting dark."

"There's still some light out there," Michael said.

"Not much. And you've been drinking," I said. There were so many reasons not to.

"We're fine!" Jacob laughed, looking at Michael.

Shooting? Now? On my property?

Jacob enjoyed pushing my limits, testing me, especially when he'd been drinking. Alcohol brought louder laughter and a certain bravado. A lack of judgment. He and Michael were a team.

"I don't think it's a good idea. Please, Michael, *don't*." This is the team that "fixed" the oversized window by forcing it closed and breaking the irreplaceable hinge. The same ones that assembled and lit a raging bonfire a year earlier, thirty feet from my newly erected barn-home, and made me feel daft when I asked them to tone it down, make it smaller. When the fire got out of control, as I knew it would, because he didn't have time to get to the end of the hose, Jacob cut open the 100-foot hose to water down the blaze as it clawed twenty feet into the air.

"Come on, Cyn, let's all go shoot some skeets!" Michael said, jumping up and heading to the door.

I didn't want to, and I didn't want them to either, but I was being put in the familiar position of saying no. I looked at Michael screaming with my eyes: *This is my house and land! Don't I get a say in it what goes on here?*

The sky was getting dark, and the cavalier attitude that came with drinking provoked. Underlying my fear, though, was also hurt, an unvoiced disappointment that Michael had broken our informal pact. I had thought he was going to teach me to shoot as a way to include me in his world. Instead, he had appropriated my friends making me the outsider on my own turf.

They gathered their jackets and hats.

"Cyn. It'll be fun!" Anne said, handing me my coat.

They were through the door. Rocks bounded out while I

discouraged Charlotte, who was innocent of their intentions. *They aren't going for a walk, Char.*

Through the window, I saw Michael head to the shed to collect the rifle and skeets. I buttoned my coat slowly and caught up with them as they headed to the far end of the field. I had seen that swagger in Michael's step before.

After discussing briefly which way to shoot so as not to hit the barn, Michael set up the skeet station. He lifted the rifle, and as a bright orange skeet popped above the tree line and reached its apex, an enormous *BANG!* blasted and echoed through the still, winter evening, shattering the heavy clouds and my spirit. Michael freed another skeet, and another shot reverberated in the gray sky, and again missed. Then he hit three skeets in a row *BANG! BANG! BANG!*

Michael put the gun down, barrel on the ground, a little too hard, and turned to Jacob.

"You ever shoot before?"

"Long time ago, once," Jacob said. Michael handed the rifle to Jacob, gave him a few pointers. Jacob assumed shooting position, and Michael sent a skeet into the air. Jacob shot, missed, shot, missed, shot, hit, laughed.

"Ha!" He passed the rifle to Anne. Being a Western-born athlete she got close a few times, then nailed it.

"Cyn. Your turn." Anne handed me the rifle gently, smiling, as if she were helping me into a yoga pose. Up until that moment, I wasn't sure whether I would succumb. A part of me, the competitive venator, wanted to. But the other part didn't want to touch the angry machine.

"No, no, I'm not shooting," I said, in futile protest. Taking the gun and shooting would condone their violation and wouldn't at this point earn me admission to their exclusive club.

I was scared and hurt and cold. The sky was getting darker.

They passed around the gun and shot the entire box of discs. I was with Charlotte in the closet. In the fading light, the bright orange skeets burst and landed in the brown grass, out of place in the organic landscape, my sacred field. Shot after shot after deafening shot rang in the dead air until dark. I shivered in the winter twilight and buried my hands in my pockets, taking each bullet.

SHARING FOOD AND SKY

"A good dinner is of great importance to good talk."

—Virginia Woolf, *A Room of One's Own*

As anticipated, after Michael, I mostly have lived on my own, in what amounts to a giant cabin, on a huge honking piece of land. I am not in town. I don't bump into people. I am not within walkable distance of anything, other than a walk. As it turns out, I can handle and even enjoy the solitude, most of the time. Except for during the pandemic, and in winter in particular, it is hard to feel lonely in this lively place. But I proactively seek out companionship to keep it that way. Being a social animal and culture hawk, most evenings I go to one of the many villages within twenty minutes with a farm-to-table restaurant to meet a friend, for a book reading, opening or performance, or to catch an independent film.

Or I invite friends over to share the meadow, sky, pool, a walk, a sunset. The outdoor spaces and the barn lend themselves to all manner of gatherings: an informal fire pit cocktail party, poolside reception, birthday celebrations, cousin and college reunions, barn concerts, salons, family holidays, long-weekend escapes, and sit-down extravaganzas. Almost always, the gathering has a theme, season, holiday, and sometimes an art project or performance. The nature of the gatherings has changed over time as Tess and I aged, our circles of friends shifted, and Field Farm evolved.

Early on, we held family events centered on Tess's and my birthdays over Labor Day weekend. We imported friends from New York City with the promise of country farm fun: bobbing for apples, meadow strolls, roaring around the yard playing tag, swinging in the hammock, bouncing on the trampoline, playing capture the flag or Pin the Tail on the Other Kid. (In the latter, soft phragmites fronds were the tails. One Velcro side was on the frond, the other on each child's posterior. Everyone ran around chasing others trying to—yes—*pin the tail on the other kid*. The game ended with the smallest child (Tess) chasing the largest.) Another time, guests decorated white, lightweight painting cover-ups with paint, pompoms, and feathers, before running through the field or finding air on the trampoline. Tess invited friends up for long weekends and they made extraordinary music videos, incorporating the barn construction site, swing, textiles, paint, bales, and field.

We served simple fare like barbecue chicken and potato salad on straw plates with red-and-white-checked cloth napkins and provided fly swatters and straw hats. We played volleyball, badminton, croquet, capture the flag, water polo, and more subdued Marco Polo.

One year, I conceived of an art project called the Human Life Yard.

A little background. The summer I spent in Chiapas, Mexico, our social anthropological research focused on the layout of the town and cemetery as analogs of the town's social class structure. Since, I seek out cemeteries, which often occupy prime real estate on the edge of town or, puzzlingly, with a view. Many serve as informal botanical gardens, as they have some of the oldest (well-fertilized) trees in the region.

I am drawn to photo-document the way different cultures treat their deceased. The attraction is not morbid, but aesthetic and social interest. I enjoy the rhythm of the stone teeth or aboveground caskets in the landscape, the distinct proportions, ambiguous bumps and lumps, plastic or wilted floral arrangements, artifacts of humanity. The faint, crude etchings on ancient stones, and the cracks and lichen creeping across their faces, are veritable works of art. The names give clues as to the identity of early settlers in the region. Newer graveyards hold little fascination, and I'm not convinced they are a good use of open space. I hope never to have a tombstone, or lie in a cemetery, but to be cremated and scattered in —of course—the meadow.

For the Life Yard project, we walked as a procession across

the field to the old graveyard buried in the woods, the one I had "discovered" the first day I saw the property. We read the stones—mostly *HERE LIETH. . .* with the deceased's relationships to other people, number of years, months, days, and hours they lived. I posed the following question: *Is this the most important thing to painstakingly scratch into a stone for posterity?*

I challenged guests to make a Life Stone for a Life Yard, giving each a 1′ X 2′ canvas (roughly the same proportions as a generic tombstone), brushes, and paints. *What would you want your "stone" to convey about you?*

Some were uncomfortable—itself interesting—or thought the assignment stupid. Even so, when they begrudgingly, eventually, put brush to canvas, participants could not help revealing themselves. In essence, they painted subconscious self-portraits—rarely visages. A family of four daughters who were inseparable, made a couple canvases between them, a direct manifestation of how they entered the world as a unit rather than as individuals. One friend who was an artist, and had worked for Damien Hirst, and not yet out as gay, cloaked his canvas in black, with nuanced strokes, true mark-making. A teenage nephew who had just won a taco-eating contest painted a bright yellow taco and labeled it, "8 tacos in 14 minutes." My sister and I, who are very different people, both painted muddy paintings, oddly similar. My mother painted: *Who the hell was she? Wife to Scott, Mother of Catherine + Cynthia, Grandmother to Philip, Tess, & Matthew.* My father, in character, wrote a poem.

We celebrated many family holidays, from Thanksgiving to Christmas to Easter. When our kids were young, and Easter mattered, it often fell on me, although if I were to reevaluate, it would have made more sense to gather in New York City, since spring is two weeks ahead of the Hudson Valley and the cherry blossoms are at peak in Central Park. But we celebrated Easter here, maybe because we were able to dye and decorate eggs on the outdoor deck. Maybe just for the urge of being outside under a big sky. Maybe because the graveyard became the perfect site for the Easter egg hunt.

It was tradition: My father hid the eggs, German chocolate and marzipan in the morning while the three grandkids slept. One year he drove off, returned an hour later and without explanation began driving across the field. By then everyone was awake. From the deck, we saw the car stop, Grampy get out and walk armed with the loot in the direction of the graveyard. The grandkids shot across the field after him. Easter Bunny was busted!

When we caught up with him, we found out the car was stuck in the slick April mud. He explained that he had first ended up in the wrong graveyard. I am still not sure how that happened and what graveyard that could have been (I suspect it was the same one from a different direction), but he said he only realized he was in the wrong place after he'd hidden all the candy. He had to re-find everything before he returned and tried again from the sure-fire trail.

I ran around in bunny ears and my body-hugging yellow sequin feather-rimmed Easter dress (a retired evening dress that approximated a large chick, which no one outside the family will ever see) trying to dig out his car. We tugged and pushed, laid straw and wedged rocks, but all we heard was spinning tires digging deep divots in the wet clay.

We called a tow truck, amazed to find someone was working on Easter Sunday. A couple arrived in a pickup and, before long, they too were stuck. Surprise to me, the tow truck was not four-wheel drive! Both vehicles remained in the field until the end of the day, when the moisture was wrung from the earth.

When the barn was up, and children older, gatherings changed. Field Farm was still a weekend and summer place for us, so most of our friends came from New York City or their own country escapes. A dozen friends spent the weekend, understanding there was LOTS OF ROOM NO PRIVACY. Snorers (my parents) made it hard for light sleepers (me). Some brought tents, others slept by the pool on the chaise lounges. I cooked three meals a day for a dozen people over the course of the weekend. Some remember these adult slumber parties most fondly.

Since Field Farm became my principal residence ten years ago, I host sit-down, six-course dinners for a couple dozen predominantly local friends several times a year. With thoughtful choices and preparation, I minimize prep time, am mostly present at my own party, and guests are at ease. During informal gatherings, I slice and dice on my lap to minimize upfront preparation and time away from the conversation. I roast vegetables or a rack of lamb or wild swordfish on the cauldron during cocktail hour, then move the gathering indoors to a seated dinner.

Like meals I cook for myself, when I entertain, spring showcases seasonal and local items. If possible, I rally behind foraged asparagus, watercress, fiddlehead ferns. Summer welcomes Mediterranean, Caribbean, or Latin themes based on what I find at farm stands: tomatoes, corn, squash, cucumbers, eggplant, peppers, greens, mushrooms. Fall features roasted root vegetables, beans, warm soups, and stews. Local, grass-fed meat or wild fish is center stage, although I rarely eat fauna at home by myself. I buy only wild-caught fish, as farmed (carnivorous) fish is not sustainable on many dimensions. Field Farm pear, apple, and peach slices spritzed with lemon accompany local cheese plates or are in the oven melting in a crumble. Herbs are abundant—mint, rosemary, sage, basil, and oregano—and find their way into every dish or as aromatic adornment.

Short of growing or foraging food, the easiest ways to "do" local is to purchase from producers directly—through a CSA, from a farm stand or at the farmer's market. I live near the source in bountiful Hudson Valley with not just produce but organic dairy and grass-fed and -finished meat. My priority is to minimize packaged goods. The plastic, energy consumption in manufacturing, carbon-fueled distribution, storage, and ambiguous provenance of industrial agricculture give me the heebie-jeebies. Buying seasonal and local food is fun, often outdoors, interactive, good for the local economy and small producers. I employ little restraint when near a fresh white peach or a bin of snap peas.

Local is not always (certified) organic and may present trade offs. Large grocery store chains have an organic section or selection now. In my go-to regional-chain grocery store, the organic produce is often packaged in more plastic and comes from farther away than the piles of local vegetables, which may or may not be organic. I apply a certain convoluted and evolving calculus to my choices, involving some judgment, as I imagine all of us do, as new data emerge. I will opt for a loose, local red bell pepper over an "organic" one that has traveled from god-knows-where and is wrapped in cellophane. Organic certification is an expensive and cumbersome process and as Big Ag has adopted and corrupted the USDA's definition of organic, it doesn't mean as much to this consumer. Many smaller farms are essentially organic, but don't have the resources to comply with inspections and certification. Big Ag has interpreted and stretched the definition to include animals that are in fact confined, along with produce grown without soil, using plastic mulch. Seventy percent of organic blueberries are Driscoll hydroponic — grown mostly in Mexico and Peru and sold in plastic clams. Three chickens per square foot, contained indoors, can be "organic." The Real Organic Project is challenging this misla-beling and seeks an additional level of distinction to protect smaller and mid-sized farmers whose focus is on improving and growing food using soil.

I buy organic, bulk, local muesli, which comes in a brown bag. I won't buy precut (and packaged in plastic), when a watermelon or a cantaloupe is perfectly sealed in its natural state. A cauliflower or a head of lettuce does not require a plastic bag. I favor shelf-stable organic coconut or almond milk in cartons rather than the refrigerated almond milk in a plastic vessel because of the additional energy used for refrigerated transportation and storage. I am aware the carton coating makes the carton difficult to recycle and compost but hope it has less impact than thick plastic that likely won't be. I have been led to believe that coconut and almond milk are less taxing on the environment from a production, transport, water-usage, and carbon-footprint perspective than even a local, grass-fed, methane-emitting dairy cow, although I could be convinced otherwise. When possible, I buy milk in the few-and-far-between returnable glass bottle. I do like cow milk in my latte in the morning and I am discouraged to find that many alternative milks have significantly less protein than dairy-sourced.

I am not part of the baking movement, so a bag of flour lasts several years. Same with sugar. I have beekeeping and maple-sugaring friends who gift me extraordinary honey and maple syrup, more than I consume. Mayonnaise lasts years as well—and, no, I've never gotten sick. I don't purchase tomato sauces or salad dressings or pestos. I do buy local cheeses, grainy crackers, breads and home-made or Italian pastas.

On the "local" front, I veer from my rule for lemons, most spices (but not herbs), olive oil which are predominantly not local, but are sometimes organic. I do not collect dozens of bottles of olive oil—just a high-quality organic, extra virgin version for salad and drizzling and one for cooking. Salad dressing is easy and best made from scratch, and I've been making it since I was ten. It was my "job" in the kitchen growing up.

Guests are greeted with a signature libation such as prosecco with pureed Bartlett pear (from Field Farm trees), iced mint tea or elderflower cordial with sparkling water. Fresh apple cider is on hand in the fall. I buy a case of dry white wine and chill a half dozen bottles. Many guests arrive with bottles of red. Large pitchers of iced well water with sliced lemons or cucumbers are on the table.

We move from one outdoor "room" (pool) to another (fire pit) until we end up inside at the dinner table, which is set long before everyone arrives, with flowers, cloth napkins, flatware, an array of candles, porcelain or stone plates. There is no overhead light, no plastic, no paper. I assign seats with place cards to ensure a mix—placing a reserved person between two talkers—and conversations flow. I separate couples and mix up people who know one another. If I'm on the fence, I make the table tighter rather than spacious, in case someone doesn't show, and because it's more intimate. I serve multi-course, seated meals to cultivate energy and laughter around the table and encourage friends to stay late into the night. I remove plates and platters each time I go to the adjacent open kitchen to retrieve or check on something. I discourage guests from helping to clear dishes (although people try—not helpful!) because I don't want to interrupt conversations nor rush those who are still eating. Holes at the table alter the dynamic. Everything in the kitchen is tidy and put away, the dishwasher and sink is empty, before people arrive. Cleared plates and platters have room to roost.

Just before one late summer fete, my parents moved from their home of many years to a retirement community. My parents' taste is similar to my own (or vice versa), so I was happy to absorb half their downsizing assuming that at some point it will be passed along to Tess when she settles down. Among those items were auction finds like goblets from New Jersey Governor Hughes, mid-century plates, Persian rugs, and a whole cabinet shelf of antique floral tea and espresso cups.

These delicate vessels inspired me to make four cold soups to serve as hors d'oeuvres, with a sprig of appropriate herb: vichyssoise with chive, borscht with dill, watercress with sliced cucumber, and gazpacho. Chilled soups are easy to make and store and benefit from being made in advance as their flavors come together. On another occasion, I prepared hot borscht in two colors, yellow and traditional magenta, and served them in concentric circles in a bowl, with the requisite pinch of dill and spoonful of local yogurt. Over the years, I have learned, that one in six people despise beets, and I will return their untouched bowl to the counter. Last fall, I bought a bundle of fresh garlic scapes (the latest rage) at the farmers market. I didn't know what I was going to do with them; I just loved their comical whimsy. That evening, I served vichyssoise, and at the last second

145

put a whole garlic scape curling out from the soup giving each bowl a third dimension. Within moments of serving the soup, guests were wearing the 18" scapes around their ears and atop their heads like bonnets and antennae. It still makes me laugh when I think about it.

I am happy to bring a dish to a friend's party, but I don't do potluck and rarely encourage people to bring anything other than a bottle of wine, certainly nothing core in the event someone doesn't show or forgets. I keep being reminded of this "policy."

Last year, I was out with a couple who are caterers, and he offered to make my birthday cake for an upcoming dinner. I was excited but triple checked. "Really? You'll make my birthday cake?" We discussed it at length and agreed to an Italian-style ricotta cheesecake with hints of lemon rind.

Three days before the dinner, she texted, "What can we bring?"

When I asked delicately about the offered cake, she replied, "He was drunk."

I let them off the hook and found a recipe for a plum galette, my first-ever attempt. I didn't even know what a galette was. A friend-baker talked my ear off about ice water for the crust. To be clear, I am not a dessert person and don't bake much. But I love cooked plums, so I knew it couldn't go too wrong. I liked the fact the recipe said that galettes were supposed to be imperfect and rustic, which is on-brand for Field Farm. When it came out of the oven, it was amber and sizzling, stuck to the bottom a tad, but delicious and beautiful. It was gobbled up. I wish I'd baked two.

Another time, a professional baker friend offered to bring six baguettes to a dinner party. He called *after* the arrival hour saying he had shingles, and he wouldn't be coming. I panicked. I couldn't muster any sympathy. (Let's acknowledge that he did not get shingles that minute; he'd known for days.) As I heard the news, my eyes were scanning the pantry (that is, the old French sideboard) for crackers to substitute. I always have locally-made gelatos and sorbets in the freezer and cookies on hand if someone has offered to bring dessert. I stock things that keep for months, as back up, in case of a mishap or an unexpected visitor.

After my daughter was diagnosed with celiac, I began to take dietary restrictions more seriously and ensure the dinner party menu has gluten-, meat-, dairy-, nut- and crustacean-free options, enough to make a meal should anyone have an issue or preference.

A few years back, I returned from Sicily with a suitcase full of rare red and teal-colored platters. These are my go-to serving dishes. I also purchased thirteen stone plates from India at a vintage flea market. They are heavy and impractical but extraordinary, each a unique sculpture. (I try to buy thirteen plates, flatware, wine glasses in case one breaks or goes missing.)

While living in the Amazon, I became the cook for a dozen biologists over an open fire, without electricity or gas. When we cooked dinner, we also made lunch for the following day—that is, double—roughly 24 servings. We were deep in the jungle for three months, so our supplies were basic, requiring creativity. Produce lasted a month without refrigeration; carrots, onions, bananas, yucca, and potatoes made their way into meals early on. Month two focused on bags of dry beans, rice, flour. Canned items—tuna, peaches, peas, sardines—got us through month three. I learned to bake soda bread without yeast in an overturned pot above the flames.

I carry this experience with me. This and the times I ate at some of the best restaurants in New York City in the early nineties. Bouley made masterpieces from the lowly carrot and pea. I maintain that the mark of an excellent chef is someone who can make a fabulous meal when there is "nothing" in the fridge, on a modest budget and in little time. I accept the challenge! I do not have the patience to spend days in the kitchen in advance. But I always have onions, carrots, celery, potatoes, yogurt, milk, garlic, nuts, cheese, and beans on hand. A go-to lunch is a can of garbanzo beans and fresh herbs tossed in olive oil and balsamic vinegar. I am ever ready for spontaneous entertaining—which I did quite a bit during Covid. With a good local cheese and excellent crackers, chilled organic orange or green wine (Vinho Verde) in the fridge, maybe some pears, I amuse myself asking people if they'd prefer orange or green wine rather than white or red. I'm not sure anyone notices.

THE YARD SALE

A beat-up, rusty, white van drove by, turned around, drove by again slowly and pulled over. A man with bad teeth, creative bearding, and aggressive tattoos—including on his receding hairline—emerged with his taciturn sidekick who never took his hands out of his pockets. They left the engine on.

"How much for the sign?"

I wasn't sure what a *SPEED LIMIT 40* sign was worth. When I first bought the property, the sign lidded the gray-water tank under the blue spruce. Since I redid the septic and filled that hole, the sign collected grass-cuttings in the lean-to. It must have been filched years ago, but I wondered if it was illegal to own. What if a cop saw it?

He didn't wait for an answer; he moved on to the dusty LP's.

"Thirty," I tried to say without a question mark.

He didn't respond, just continued rifling through the vintage items I'd put out which had been left by a former tenant: a basket of gold bowling men trophy tops, old doctor's bags, a dozen vintage wooden piano hammers, yellowed shooting-target posters. These weren't fine antiques, but with an eye, a well-curated bundle could add flair to a home or fuel a gag gift or a somber art project. This was what he seemed to be after.

Maybe I should have said twenty-five. Maybe he never wanted the sign but was testing me, assessing my pricing system. If that was the case, he wouldn't have found his answer. How should things be priced for a yard sale? I priced things higher when they had some value to me and would let go of other things for much less when they didn't, regardless of market value. Was that what everyone did?

He moved quickly, a pro, threw numbers at me, and walked away with some marquee letters, three cloudy antique bottles, five wooden crates and a dusty Lion's Club crest.

"Do you want the sign?"

"Next time."

There would not be a next time. Although I believe in reuse and would rather have someone take something home than heave it into a landfill, I am not a yard sale person. My gardening friend Nancy is. She made thousands of dollars and unloaded lots of stuff at her yard sale.

"My parents and I spend weeks preparing for a yard sale," she said. "We fix things—put a new handle on a broken shovel. Put price tags on everything," Nancy told me as she cut back a persistent sumac. "I won't even stop at a yard sale unless they have prices. I'll help you with yours when you decide to have one," she offered. I wondered why she wanted to unload a fixed shovel.

I tried to price many things with little post-it's that didn't stick, but I did not let Nancy know I was having a yard sale. A part of me didn't want anyone I know to come by, and yet it seemed inevitable: I was holding it in my yard, in my neighborhood. When we had a yard sale a decade earlier, no one we knew came, but we didn't know anyone at the time. Tess and I sat an entire hot day in the driveway. Only three people scowled at and scoured over our wares even though we advertised with Day-Glo signs at both ends of our road. We wore yard sale shackles on a beautiful summer day that would have been better spent poolside. Tess was too young to be on her own at the pool, and we didn't have the gates on the driveway then to officially close the yard sale down, not that it mattered. Why would people start to come suddenly when they hadn't come all day?

I reasoned that the driveway was discouragingly long. This time, I was at the driveway entrance near the road for timid or lazy scouts. I also learned that yard sales occur on certain days, which was why I was holding mine that day; it was Yard Sale Day in our town. Still, there had been zero activity for the first two hours. The guys in the white van were my first customers.

I did not hang signs this past week. I assumed people would

be out and about and somehow down this road and so find me.
I closed the gates the night before on the driveway just in case. I
saw someone write NO EARLY BIRDS on their listing, as if flocks
arrived, although no one would have known about my yard sale
unless they consulted the town's building department's website,
and who does that?

At 8:00 AM, I raced around trying to find a piece of card-
board and paint, imagining how and where I would secure the sign
at the main intersection. I hoped that my across-the-street neighbors
would have a yard sale and that they would advertise. They seemed
to have them all the time. But not that day.

So here I was at the end of the driveway contemplating the
situation.

A sort of shame and humiliation bears down on a yard
sale. A yard sale is a day of reckoning, of judgment, after all. We
present the attending public bad decisions, mistakes, things we've
outgrown; we expose ourselves. We judge these physical mani-
festations of weakness or time's passing as no longer worthy of
possession. My wise friend Russell said judgment distances you
from the judged. The yard sale provides impetus to judge and so the
distance. Once the decision has been made, and the item is deemed
yard-sale bound, carted to the end of the driveway, it is hard to
reabsorb that item back into the closet or cabinet should it not find
a new owner. The emotional separation has occurred, the commitment to liberation marks the item an outcast. The item withstands
further judgment by potential purchasers and neighbors who assess,
poke, look down at it, both literally and figuratively.

I find myself internally and sometimes outwardly defending,
buttressing, describing the item in favorable terms, giving it a
narrative, since for me it may still hold the vestiges of a memory or
reference another life phase. Witness the pink plastic toys (that I did
not purchase) from Tess's third year, the cracked vase I fell in love
with at someone else's yard sale, a favorite sweater with a (minor)
rip, evidence of a mishap, another story.

151

I showed a gold blouse to a woman, who touched it and said, "I don't wear fabrics like that anymore."

Who was she to judge my standby ex-holiday outfit? Further, she was unaware that this shimmering shirt was dry cleaned fifteen years ago so there is pressure to wear it at least one more time. But she was right. I stopped wearing fabrics like this too. That's why it was out there. I thought it was the padded shoulders.

I was embarrassed for a woman who coveted a broken dish and was willing to pay $10 for it. I ended up giving it to her, feeling bad that she could want something I didn't or that had no intrinsic value and we both knew would be by the garbage bins at the end of the day with a FREE sign.

A tablecloth spread its wings with untouched objects for re-gifting. Many had price tags or never made it out of their wrapping. Many I'd had so long that they were no longer relevant. As gifts they missed the mark. I couldn't give them to someone else because I didn't like them enough to do even that: they weren't "me." The recipient would know I didn't choose them. I couldn't remember who gave what to me and feared I might re-gift something to the original giver. They were likely the only ones with whom I would have paired them.

An ex brought back a necklace from Ghana. Although without wrapping or a price tag, I knew it cost about $5 with a little bargaining. The string of maroon beads was one of those fake-looking stone necklaces you find all over the world, likely from China, hawked as though the stones came from the little village you are visiting. I remember buying necklaces like this as a student traveler when they still may have been locally strung. They were all I could afford, and I knew no better. This shiny red strand was brought back for me a few years ago, proffered to me sentimentally, by a man who considered himself sophisticated and well-to-do. I thought, *this is the best you could do?* as I *oooed and ahed* and thanked him up and down.

So along with humiliation, perhaps there's disappointment out here.

When I searched through the profiles of different women on Match.com years ago for an art project I was working on, I came across an older woman whose sole hobby was "yard sales." I think about that woman occasionally and whether she ever found someone to share her Saturday mornings, what she loaded into her back seat, and whether she might drop in.

At 2:00, a woman extracted herself from a Toyota. She fingered a few garish earrings and a blank journal. But before I could engage her, she was back in her car and said flatly, "Have a nice yard sale."

Bill, my retired trooper friend, stopped by in his very shiny, oversized, souped-up black Wrangler. Bill is a not big guy, but has a presence. I am eternally grateful to him because he patrols my property, making sure no cross-eyed, inebriated gun-toters trespass or hunt. He wants the deer and turkey to himself, and hunting season was coming up soon. I am fine with that. He kicked a bunch of ATV-drivers off the gas line border, and once encountered convicted felons on the lam. Without a gun, he got them to lay down theirs, and sent them packing to the police station.

Bill and I got to know each other over the past few years as I leaned on him during some run-ins with erratic caretakers—one who swam naked in my pool at high noon while I had guests over, another who threatened me with a buck knife. Bill watched out for me and somehow I was able to keep my credibility despite what could be construed as a pattern of self-inflicted drama. Earlier that summer, we sat in the Adirondack chairs and chatted over a glass of wine. He made out three bucks at the base of the field and counted their points from where we were sitting. He told me that his new RV was much better than his old camper, that he and his wife would drive out west to camp in August. They lived in a condo on the Hudson River with a community pool and good sunsets.

"Bill! How goes it? How's the yard sale in town?" I always broke into some Hochul-local accent when I spoke to him.

"Hey, Cynthia. Good. It's gridlock over there. How's it going here?"

"Quiet . . ." I rolled open the old target posters: a highly abstracted human torso with concentric lines and points assigned, highest near the heart. "Look at these . . ."

Bill nodded, "Yeah, those are old targets." Familiarity didn't allow him see them as striking visuals. A lot of police shootings, like in Ferguson, made these posters message-rich artist fodder. Questions had been raised about why a policeman didn't shoot a leg rather than the heart. There were no legs on the posters. Some part of me was testing Bill and the system when I showed him the targets.

I pointed out a box of nail polish that he could give to his granddaughters or costume jewelry for his wife. "I'll go get the wife. I'll be back."

Marc, my new tenant, had just wandered down the driveway to keep me company when a shining, bright red Audi pulled into the driveway. Bill got out of the car.

"Bill! Perfect timing. Meet Marc, my new tenant!"

"Marc? Nice to meet you." Marc extended his hand to Bill and smiled. Bill's wife got out of the car. "Cynthia, this is my wife Katy...."

"So nice to meet you, Katy. I've heard so much about you," I said.

"He's always talking about Cynthia McVay. You're not Cynthia. You are Cynthia *McVay*. It's nice to finally meet you," Katy said.

"Whoa! Look at this car, Bill!" I said.

"It's her car." Bill pointed to his wife with his head.

"He bought it for me," she smiled.

"How often do you wash it daily?" I asked. He knew I was playing with him and grinned.

Katy quipped, "Don't ask!"

I picked up an oversized watch with a brown leather band that I got at an Army & Navy store in St. Petersburg, when it was still Leningrad. I traded a single pair of black jeans for it and two decorated military uniforms and hats, which I was keeping for future Halloween costumes. (It is baffling to think that Russians couldn't get a pair of jeans in 1990.) A few years back, I dressed up in one of the outfits with a name tag that read *PUTIN-FREE*. Another time, years ago, a couple of Russian men watched me from a distance in a fancy restaurant (yes, I was wearing one of the uniforms out and about in SoHo). They approached me on their way out, and one asked, in a thick Russian accent, "Excuse me. Are you really a general in the Red Army?"

"But of course!" I answered, with a lot of throat. I was glad they didn't ask in Russian.

I didn't know why I didn't want this watch anymore, and when I described where it came from and modeled it for Katy, she told me I should wear it, that it looked good on my tanned arm. It came home on me.

Marc and Bill engaged as I showed Katy what was what. She ended up needing the stack of colored IKEA glass plates, much to Bill's dismay and silent protests, and I gave her a CD that I received as a party favor a decade earlier for her daughter's new store. I picked up a bag of Ashley Stewart dresses that had arrived at my home courtesy of a cyberthief.

"Look! These are brand new! Would you like them?"

"Don't you have any other chubby friends?"

"Please, I would love you to have them, if you like them."

A couple of women drove up. "Is this the yard sale?"

"Yes!"

"This is it?"

"Yes!"

"This is number 312?"

"Yes!"

"It's a madhouse in town. Unbelievable traffic with all those yard sales and almost nothing left."

Ah so. With a high concentration of yard sales seven minutes

155

away in a compact, gridded neighborhood, why would anyone make their way here? The women didn't get out of their car. They backed out.

The yard sale was over.

I found out the next day why the watch was in the pile: it didn't keep time. I gained an hour months before daylight savings time would tell me to set my watch back.

BAR SOAP

I was at the Sheep and Wool Festival in Rhinebeck, New York. It's an annual event, and for me an annual ritual. In years past, I bought reams of unspun wool, which I use as pillows; that day, I was focused on sheep and goat milk soap. I had already bought a half dozen bars, and I was sniffing my way through more, each wrapped in patterned paper and love. Peppermint. Licorice. Jasmine. Lavender. I couldn't narrow it down, so I bought all of them. I reasoned they make good gifts. I couldn't resist a paper bag full of slender tan soap squares perfect for the Airbnb cottage. Soap is one thing I buy without guilt, and I do so with impunity.

Soap reflects what we value and, I submit, is a metaphor for how we approach life, whether the bar is common or extraordinary, branded, fragrant, creamy, or clear, just as a restaurant's crusty bread and home-whipped butter gives us a hint of the kitchen. Local, homespun soap—which reveals a lot about me—is one of the first things I give a friend who doesn't think about it much, maybe prioritizes convenience and value and stocks his bathroom with a half-dozen Lever 2000s, seduced by a Sam's Club deal.

An embossed name or telltale original shape obscures over time, as the bar's employment, its journey, and imposed contours, overtake its provenance. A sink dweller cinches at the waist. A bar that lives in the shower is gentle and rounded. Perhaps it has one flattened corner—evidence of slipping from hands or the bathtub's curved edge, careening onto the hard tile floor. Whether it lives in the shower's direct spray in its own juices—a soap soup—or near an open window where it has a chance to dry between uses, reflects its owner's attentions, thoughtfulness, and commitment to its longevity. Deep cracks indicate that it's been a while since the outdoor shower or guest bathroom was used. I consign such a bar—along with mini, half-used soaps I've brought home from hotels or leftover from my Airbnb guests—to the kitchen sink. I try to get every wash from chips and fragments by gluing them onto larger bars with a gooey, soapy mortar. As a guest in someone else's home, I worry about soap dishes offering new, crisp soap. Where do the slightly used go?

A worn bar of soap is a small sculpture, crafted by its user, rolled and turned in wet hands. A byproduct of a grooming ritual, a bar of soap is a window into the psyche and etiquette of the lathered. Like an ancient stone staircase or wooden banister, a bar of soap is an artifact of time and process and touch, molded by a person or pod of people.

When soap is shared, its character is diluted by multiple, frequent wettings or varied cleansing strategies. The way a bar of soap is treated may become a source of friction for a couple or among roommates. A hair, of any kind, demeans and demotes a bar of soap, renders it untouchable. Living mostly alone, the bar in my soap dish is a direct product of my own handling.

An unsung hero in the invention lineup, soap is taken for granted and has been cast aside by a myriad of inferior substitutes. But the humble bar of soap, in breaking down dirt and oils lifted away under running water, is in part responsible for our survival as a species. Most of us spent more time washing our hands during the pandemic (contemplating doing so, reading about it, weighing the pros and cons of alternative sanitation methods) than over the course of the rest of our lives. We counted to twenty. We sang *Happy Birthday*. Or not. Truth be told, I washed my hands a little more than usual in 2020 but find twenty seconds to be a very long time. (Separately, in an informal survey, it turns out few of us wash behind our ears.)

Like how we eat our corn or what we do with our napkin at the end of the meal, the shape and condition of our bar soap says something about us, how we spend our intimate moments, in our own nakedness—when (generally) no one else is looking. Our soap has been up close with our private parts and crevices.

Bar soap is personal and revealing. There's a tinge of vulnerability in a naked bar sitting in a soap dish. Perhaps this explains why many choose liquid soap, with a buttoned up, built-in standoff-ish-ness.

I resist, easily. Aside from the benefits of its notable intimacy and tactility—the complete experience that bar soap offers—it wins hands down for environmental reasons. The key ingredient of liquid soap is water—scarce, heavy, and bulky, requiring energy to produce, package and transport. In addition, most body washes have synthetic, non-biodegradable ingredients. The bar soap I buy has fewer, cleaner, locally-sourced ingredients and biodegrade. Bar soap comes in infinite varieties to address allergies, sensitivities, chapped hands, and acne.

The plastic bottle of body wash or liquid soap will end up in a landfill on a good day, or the ocean (and in the belly of a whale) on a bad one. According to Reduce Plastic Waste, an estimated 250 million Americans buy some 1.4 billion bottles a year. A plastic bottle can take 450 years to deteriorate. The calculus may be different for public restrooms where liquid soap is bought in bulk and dispensed in permanent vessels, and there's a lot of people passing through. Buying liquid soap can make sense if bought in volume, from a local refillery, filling a refillable container.

Although soap was originally made from animal fats, most are now derived from botanical or nut-based oils—coconut, palm, almond, avocado, and essential oils such as lemon, lavender, and rose, and infused with floral or herbal aromas. No matter how efficient the process of packaged goods companies, carbon and toxic waste inherent in centralized large-scale production, packaging, and logistics—and cheap labor—is part of their equation. It might be a bargain for them, but not for this earth.

In a moment of weakness, I purchased liquid soap for guests at the start of the pandemic, believing for an instant non-science nonsense circulating that liquid soap was more sanitary. As the extra careful and paranoid avoided touching things—all things—they certainly stopped fondling soap in other people's dishes.

Soap—dry, solid, and unbreakable—makes for easy transport. A handmade bar may cost more than one made by a large corporation; a friend suggests that it may be out of reach for some. I submit it is a matter of priorities. The extra annual cost amounts to less than a couple beers, what many drink in bottled water or soda in a day, a single pedicure or small tattoo. And, for me, is an essential luxury.

I store a fragrant bar in my underwear drawer until I need a fresh one. And when I do, with tenderness, I unwrap the paper, and a memory or two.

BLACK RAT SNAKE

One evening, in the early 2000s, pre-barn, a friend and I were playing Scrabble in the cottage's living room. We heard a dull thud through the basement door.

"Paper towels musta fallen off the shelf," I said and smiled. I didn't get up to check.

The next day, we were out at the pool, and I went back to the house to get something from the basement. As I opened the basement door, having forgotten about the *thud* from the night before, something heavy and awkward fell on my head. I let out a blood curdling scream. It took me a moment to realize it was a snake, falling from the ceiling at the back of the chimney. Tess and my friend came running from the pool, thinking I had fallen or died. I was a pile of nerves and laughter when they arrived.

A convivial black rat snake (presumably the same one that dropped on the worker's head during construction years earlier) lived between the attic and basement behind the fireplace in the house. Not sure how to "take care" of the snake and recognizing we'd have many more mice in the drawers if we did, we learned to coexist by staying out of each other's way.

A couple times a year, when we lived in the cottage, I found a snake skin wedged in the chimney where my informal tenant scraped to shed its outer layer as it grew. One year, when I was extracting the parchment from the hole against the ceiling, ten-year-old Tess cried, "Wait!"

She ran from the room and returned with red gloves. She picked up the perfect specimen and laid it flat, from the tip with its gaping mouth and eye hole all the way to the tapering tail. She placed the yardstick beside—twice. Six feet.

After we moved to the barn, I wasn't sure whether the snake still inhabited the cottage. I hadn't heard about it from any renters, so I assumed it had moved on or a caretaker had taken care of it. But snake memory sticks with you. I never open the cottage's basement door quietly or quickly. I am careful to look around the gutters, and the garden, too, since I found skins there a couple times, and snake excrement which I came to recognize—looks a little like goose poop—on the worktable in the basement. I guess, on some level, I knew it was still there. I just hadn't seen it and didn't really want to.

A few years ago, I was checking on the cottage, after hearing the water filtration system beeping, alerting that the UV light needed to be changed. I opened the outside basement door, prepared to search the stone wall and ceiling for the snake. A papery skin draped right there, at the entrance. *Ach!* It hadn't been there a couple weeks earlier. I looked around before I extracted the skin from the insulation. It seemed longer than I remembered. A yard-stick happened to be angled up against the basement wall. I laid the skin beside it on the ground to measure it, almost three times. Eight feet.

Online research reveals that black rat snakes are usually less than six feet with a lifespan of fifteen years in the wild, but up to thirty years in captivity. Hm. Does living in my house qualify as captivity? It had been twenty years.

My pest control guy, with whom I've developed a relation-ship over the years as we tackled (with sensitivity) the Woodpecker Issue, Hedgehog Issue, Stinkbug/Fake Ladybug, Barn-Fly, and Wasp Issues, talked snakes. He likes them.

"Someone called me up to remove a snake, and I took it home with me to take care of the mice in my barn. If you get rid of the snakes, the rodent population goes through the roof." And everyone up here has snakes. They are everywhere. If someone says they don't, they just aren't aware. They are looking in the wrong places.

With Lyme disease an epidemic in the northeast, and rodents carrying ticks, snakes are on our side. Besides, because they're territorial, if you eliminate one, another one is liable to move into its place. Kind of a devil-you-know solution. I certainly didn't want a female to move in.

I consider myself fortunate to have a single snake that keeps to itself. I heard about someone who bought a Frank Lloyd Wright-like house whose central feature was a dramatic stone fireplace. When the new owners lit an inaugural fire to celebrate, thousands of (baby?) snakes slithered out of the chimney. I know someone else who razed his entire farmhouse to the foundation because dozens of snakes lived in the walls.

What is it about snakes and our visceral reaction to them? Ancestors claw at my gut, warn me to stay away. How many myths, Biblical and otherwise, have stoked our innate fears? I have worn heavy boas on my body at science fairs and had encounters in the Amazon with anaconda, and routinely almost step on them when I take hikes (yikes!), as they bask nonchalantly in a sunny spot on the trail. Not a single snake has ever done anything to me personally or to anyone I know. And yet. As a biologist and environmentalist, I am ashamed of my irrational anxiety, the flutter. How is it that a fear passed down to me through the millennia can feel so distinctly my own?

Years ago, I had a small cabin built near the pool for over-flow guests. Before the barn went up, sometimes Michael and I slept in the cabin to be closer to the night, and often the coyotes, or when I needed an extra guestroom. The simplicity and proximity to nature rendered it a solid tent of sorts. A couple years later, I built a smaller cabin to accommodate a solar one-holer, or composting toilet, used infrequently over the years by cabin-dwellers and swimmers. The larger cabin was eventually turned into a gardening shed; the composting toilet was used with ever less frequency.

In part, because a second black rat snake staked claim on the little compound, moving between the two cabins. When I open the shed, I bang around on the door first, crack the door slowly, look up at the rafters. The coiled black soaker hose stowed in the back of the shed "gets" me every time. Once, I opened the door of the toilet, which seemed heavier than usual, and the snake fell out at my feet.

163

I think about what would happen if I decided to use the composting toilet, only to discover the snake above my head just after I've committed, pants down, on the seat. Or, worse yet, once on the toilet, whose basin cover presses open with weight, find the snake below my bare butt! That has never happened because the thought keeps me from any attempts.

This fear lives subliminally inside me as I walk towards the sheds. I find myself doing a sort of sidestep, looking up into the roof overhang which they favor, glancing around, perusing the woodpile, another hideout.

I asked Matt, caretaker for a couple years, to please remove the snake from the shed. Matt didn't mind snakes, indeed bragged about catching them with his bare hands. And yet his snake-charming skills were absent when I needed them. For nine months, he claimed he never saw the snake, even though it consistently was part of my gardening experience.

One day—in an improbable Venn diagram—I saw the snake and Matt was home. I alerted Matt and stood by, keeping an eye on the puny head with its flickering tongue in the eaves of the toilet hut until Matt arrived. After assessing the situation, he hooked a curved metal rod around the snake's "shoulders," to pull the snake through the rafter. He yanked the muscular body, but it would not release its grip. I swore the snake would rip or break in the struggle, but eventually Matt pulled the snake down and wrestled it into a black plastic bag. Matt stood there with the squirming bag, as we spoke casually about next steps.

Matt and I were not on great terms at the time. I recently had confronted Matt on his drinking, which had manifest in some questionable and dangerous behavior. While I was away that February, I'd asked him to prune the struggling apple and pear trees. When I returned, I gag-bawled when I found he had chain sawed every healthy limb, leaving them at their bases. I asked what he'd done. He said he'd "stressed" the trees to produce more fruit, which is the last thing they needed. Many of the trees never recovered.

164

And one Sunday afternoon, when Charlotte and I were taking a walk through the field, I heard shots behind us. I turned to see him a hundred feet back shooting randomly. When I shouted to him, he couldn't hear us and apparently didn't see us. Things began to feel unsafe. Firearms and alcohol are a potent combination, and I knew I had to deal with him and his fiancé carefully. I let it be their choice. After a conversation, they agreed to move out.

Here we were face to face, with a wriggling plastic bag.

"What are you going to do with the snake?"

"I'll take it down to the river and let it go."

I was on my way out that afternoon, so I never saw Matt do it.

A few months after Matt and his fiancé moved out, I found a snake skin inside my barn-home, by the door closest to the shed. I found telltale snake poop behind a nearby chest. Maybe a snake had gotten in when I left the door open another day, but I always wondered whether Matt had a good, last laugh.

I stepped carefully for a few months but have seen no sign of that snake since.

WOODPECKERS

Early midwinter mornings, I awoke to the tormenting, persistent knocks of woodpeckers on the walls of my barn-home. Dozens of times every morning I jumped up, ran out, clapped and shouted, hoping to startle the little fiends. The pattern became predictable.

At first, my arrival was discouragement enough and the bird took flight as I opened the door. Over time, I had to clap or flap or shout. That stopped working too. I banged a garbage can to get its attention and jumped up and down. It flew away only to return minutes later.

From its perch twenty feet above me, the woodpecker looked down and chirped for every shout. *Chirp, chirp, chirp!* It was not until I clapped loudly and threateningly with antagonizing persistence that it took notice and flew away. Sometimes it flew twenty feet down the side of the barn and settled in again. I followed, clapped some more, beat the side of the barn, and it moved with zero commitment. We went all the way around the barn, stopping every twenty feet like that several times.

After a half-dozen exchanges, the bird looked at me, remained in its high perch, threw a chirp in my direction, and continued to bury its face in the siding and insulation. Torture was doled out not only through the reverberating drumming, but also in the knowledge of the very real damage the birds wreaked on my once tightly insulated home.

I learned that in spring the males are advertising, banging away, marking their territory. Some, however, are creating comfortable cave dwellings within the walls. If there are a series of holes in a vertical row in the siding, they are after bugs in the boards and walls—and you have a much bigger problem. No clues existed as to what these woodpeckers were up to for the onslaught I endured, but they seemed to prefer where the wall met the roof, the seam at the top of the barn side, between the boards, twenty-two feet from the ground.

Many were pileated woodpeckers, with their oversized powerful heads, amplified sound, swooping flight and white rumps. On occasion, a large pileated was accompanied by three smaller woodpeckers. I inferred they were a family, but later realized that the smaller ones were likely a different species, the red-bellied woodpecker.

When my then boyfriend saw me run out to chase the woodpeckers away, he too jumped up. He took on my battle. On my heels, he chased away the woodpeckers dozens of times that morning with me. The following week, he wrote me daily asking how the woodpeckers were.

"They're good. I'm not," I bemoaned.

"Let's make cages and hang woodpeckers on the Christmas tree! They would make great ornaments," he offered.

I laughed. That was one of the funniest things he had ever said, but I was soon sorry for having encouraged him. It unleashed a storm of woodpecker bigotry: "I hate woodpeckers!" "Fucking woodpeckers!" "Kill the little fuckers!"

Whether he really hated the redheaded hammering birds, or he was just siding with me out of allegiance, his reaction scared me. I'd seen his disdain for other things too, so I knew he wasn't all kind and gentle as he seemed, as he tried to be, that there was something more going on under the surface. Even though the woodpeckers frustrated me to no end, made dozens of holes in my barn—and cost me thousands of dollars in repairs—I didn't hate them. They couldn't help their innate desires. As the woodpeckers made holes in my walls, holes appeared in our relationship.

The woodpeckers outlasted us.

One morning I found a dead woodpecker in the drip line. I sent a photo of it to another friend and texted, "I swear I didn't do it." But how to explain this carnage, the punctured chest? When I turned over the still-soft, black-and-white bird for more clues, a small stone stuck in its face. Its head dangled on a limp neck.

At the same time, Tess texted me from college in St. Louis, that she had "counted seven dead birds on a two-hour walk." When she sent me a picture, I couldn't believe it: It was a red-bellied woodpecker. "At least three of them were like this one, with black and white dots," she texted. Why were woodpeckers dropping from the sky?

Despite the coincidence, my dead woodpecker did not fall from the sky. It was killed and left, bloodied. Who would do this? A hawk? A squirrel? Did I run out in the wee hours of the morning and kill it in my sleep?

A pang of guilt plagued me as I looked at the carcass. I didn't want the bird to be dead, but I felt as if I had willed its death. And now what? Should I leave it to warn the others, or toss it into the high grass? I let it lay there for a day but found that it did not act as a deterrent to its feathered brethren, and so threw it into the brush, out of sight and smell, but findable should I be interested in its skeleton in the spring.

We eventually solved the problem by sealing the crease at the top of the barn walls with old barnwood, leftover from another project, which happened to have thousands of nails sticking out, leaving the little guys a very uncomfortable place to land.

Silence. It's mostly been silence. So far.

CANINE COMPANIONS

Charlotte's time came in 2015. A wrenching decision.

Until then, it had puzzled me that many dog owners put down their dogs; rarely did dogs die a "natural" death. It seemed convenient for the owners. But when Charlotte was hanging on by a thread, for my sake, and so miserable, I understood.

I was running a non-profit office as an interim executive director in downtown Manhattan. I spent so much time in New York City, that I left sweet, accommodating, elderly Charlotte in Princeton, New Jersey, with my parents. When I was home without her, the barn felt empty. It was a long, snowy winter but circling through Princeton to pick her up on my way back upstate made little sense.

We recruited someone to run the organization and so I was released from my duties. When Charlotte came home in the spring, she didn't want to wake up in the morning anymore. She'd always risen early, like me. By then, sometimes she'd sleep until noon. She refused her breakfast, unusual for a Labrador, and her, notorious for eating with haste and abandon. After a little experimentation, I discovered that she hadn't lost her appetite; she just didn't want to eat dog food anymore. Who could blame her? So, I doubled up my dinners and fed her baked yam with quinoa, boiled chicken and brown rice, scrambled eggs in the morning with torn bread.

When the thyroid tumor on her throat got so bad that she gagged instead of breathed, and couldn't sleep because she couldn't breathe, it seemed unfair. Sleeping was the only thing she tolerated. I canceled the appointment with the vet twice, but the third time kept it.

Charlotte made it to her thirteenth birthday, which fell on *Cinco de Mayo*, 2015. I suppose I planned it that way. I scheduled the vet visit for a couple days later.

I had written Tess who was in Australia to tell her I had

made a decision. She called almost immediately despite the time difference. I saw her twisted, crying face in my cell phone and realized I had texted her so she would try to convince me not to do it.

I explained why it was necessary. I was being The Mom. Even though Charlotte's discomfort didn't meet all the criteria for imminent demise according to online pundits (incontinence, not eating, inability to move), it would be selfish to keep her alive.

On a beautiful spring Friday, early evening, Charlotte and I watched the sun go down over the field, although, to be fair, she had her back to it. I heard the rumble of an approaching car. The thin, vegan vet, who had visited the previous month, got out of the car with a guy who worked for the Humane Society. They were wearing matching red polo shirts.

I felt guilty that I was going through with it out of convenience—I had to go to the city the following week—but the vet assured me *it was time*. The vet called Charlotte *Lady*. She stroked her bony body, felt under her chin, peered into her cloudy eyes, and said that next week *she will be that much worse*, that even a month before Charlotte had more meat on her.

With one shot, then another, Charlotte lay still in the grass. When Humane guy went to get a brand-new blue body bag and unzipped it, I went inside. Through the window, I saw him take the much heavier, full bag to the car. He didn't make the bag look seventy pounds. A few long minutes went by, and the vet brought me the bill in her meticulous handwriting.

A week later, Charlotte's ashes came back in a red leather box with a frame on the lid where I was supposed to put a photo but never did.

A friend, who knew how much I loved Charlotte, asked whether I would taxidermy Charlotte. Seemed like an odd idea, especially if she were stuffed standing, or barking, or just her head were mounted like a bear or lion. But maybe Charlotte sleeping on her cushion by the window would have brought a modicum of solace. I'd walk by her as I have many times over many years.

Charlotte left a hole. A hole in my mornings, my routines.

Without constraints, I traveled some. But there came a time—I waited 18 months—when I didn't want to go through another winter with little to no affection, a cuddle, someone to spoon. So along with OkCupid.com, I started trawling Petfinder.com. I thought I wanted another Labrador, although I was wary. No dog could live up to beautiful, smart, funny Charlotte. In my search, I filtered for large breed, female, puppy, within a 25-mile radius. Then a 50-mile radius. Then a 50-mile radius of places I was going—Berkshires, Adirondacks, New York City, Princeton.

I reminded myself: If you don't want a puppy, do not look at a litter of puppies. I started searching too early, before I could handle another dependent. I was obsessed with puppy porn for much of the summer as a sleep inducer. I submitted applications to local shelters, only to find that the pups were still in North Carolina or Georgia. I wouldn't be able to meet them before I put money down, which didn't seem right to me, especially on a dog with ambiguous provenance. And just like online dating, I learned they rarely looked like their photos in person.

One morning, I drove two hours to claim one of two irresistible chocolate Lab/Australian sheepdog mix with mushed, splattered faces. I arrived at 10:00 AM, the shelter's opening time, on the day they would be up for adoption. Twenty-six people were ahead of me; some had been there since 7:00 AM. I saw the puppies I came for go home in the arms of the first two people in line. They deserved them. I stood in line for another hour while my application was processed in case there were other puppies of interest. I really had no business getting a puppy in August when I would be traveling to Italy for two weeks in September. Even though I had just blown my morning, I was relieved not to be taking them home with me.

When I returned from Sicily, I began in earnest to search for a puppy. I walked up to (handsome) strangers with handsome (predominantly) Labradors to inquire where they came from. I

171

coveted a Weimaraner Labrador mix I saw in the street—a taupe, slender Labrador with blue eyes.

A friend recommended a breeder in Vermont. I looked at the link he sent and called.

"Hello?" a man answered.

"Hi. I'm calling about Labrador puppies?"

"You'll need to speak to Anne. I'm down in the barn right now milking the cows. She's the one who can tell you everything. I'll hang up, and you call back and leave a message on the answering machine with all your information."

"I can send you an email with—"

"We don't do email. Just call back and leave the information. We'll get back to you within 24 hours."

Anne called a few hours later. "We don't have any Lab puppies right now, but we have some English Setter pups that'll be ready in a few weeks."

By the time I hung up, Anne had convinced me that English Setters were perfect companions: smart, affectionate, athletic but calm. Not over bred, like Irish Setters, which were larger, high strung, and had hip issues. She also told me I wanted a male—they were more beautiful and slightly larger. There were three males to choose from, and a small female; all the others had been spoken for. She would send me an email with photos. It might take a few days; their internet didn't work very well.

"I don't know why English Setters aren't more popular in the United States. People just don't know about them," she said.

I found out why a few months later.

I received the promised email with the mug shots and knew the third male in the line-up was the one. I practically kissed my phone, he was so adorable. I asked Anne to save him for me and wrote a check for the $200 deposit. The envelope sat on my dashboard for a week. Reality was setting in. Could I handle a dog on my own? I had no caretaker, no backup. My parents, who were becoming elderly, could still handle a dog if I went on a trip, but were two and a half hours away. Who would cover for me when I ran into New York City for the day or night?

I sent Tess the picture of the puppy.

"Awww!! We need to name him!" she texted.

We bantered about a whole bunch of names. When she suggested Dexter, that was it. No other name came close. He was without question a Dexter.

A few days later, my friend Dan came for dinner. He'd had a Lab before, like me, and missed having a dog. When I mentioned Dexter, my dilemma, and showed him the picture, without my even asking, he said, "I'll babysit."

"Really?"

"Sure. I'd love to." Dan has a way of saying things definitively, which makes him an excellent businessman. He processes information quickly, intuitively, and makes decisions fast. No waffling. "I want a dog but can't have one myself right now. But we could share him," he offered. "You could bring him to my office when you need to go into NYC, or I could stay at your house with him."

Deal. I sent off the deposit, without a stamp—oops! It was returned, I sent it again. Forces kept offering me a chance to back out, but I didn't heed the warnings. Dan and I scheduled a time to pick up the puppy in Vermont a couple weeks later, on Election Day 2016. We thought there would be lots of goodness to go around that fateful day.

I was the third person at the voting booth in my tiny hamlet's fire station. From there, I met Dan at a park-and-ride, and we headed to Vermont. We talked about his business and his succession issues, our children, politics. We always had a lot of ground to cover; our conversations were not clouded with complications like romantic interest. We arrived too early (the breeders would still be milking), so enjoyed an excellent lunch in a nearby town, sitting in the window of a farm-to-table diner.

We inched up to the suburban house off a dirt road,

surrounded by fenced fields and barns. Anne was tall and gaunt, with a Laura Dern demeanor. She led us into their ranch-house kitchen. I impatiently listened to a half hour of instructions and excellent advice, with a modicum of attention, before she went downstairs to retrieve our puppy.

When she brought up a tiny, eight-week ball of fur, we held Dexter and all his sweetness. She continued to talk about his care as she took him to the sink to wash him. He was a compliant little handful for what seemed a lengthy process. She blow dried his fur. (To this day, on the rare occasion that I blow dry my hair, Dexter appears in the bathroom, sits attentively, waiting for his turn.) The shorn lawn seemed high when we took him outside. He followed every step we took and hung onto our heels. He sat when I stopped walking. He was already trained! I was in love.

On the way home, Dexter sat on Dan's lap while I drove. Dan's booming voice suddenly seemed too loud for our new passenger, resting against Dan's chest. An ugly crate I was told to purchase was far too large for this little guy, and we couldn't imagine throwing him in there when he just wanted to snuggle. For some of the time while I drove, little Dexter sat on my lap, curled on my legs and in the crook of my arms.

We turned on the radio to listen to what was going on in the elections. It was late afternoon; many of the states were trailing on voters. Things were not going the way they were supposed to.

When we got home, Dexter and I hung out on my bed, which seemed immense, with the election streaming on my laptop. I sent pictures of Dexter to Tess, who was glued to the election results. She had worked for six months for Hillary, managing Ottawa County, in Port *Clinton*—of all places—Ohio, a county which had predicted election outcomes for years, and had already elected Trump. Tess learned so much about voting dynamics and what it would take for Hillary to win. She saw the tallies coming in and knew. NPR and *The New York Times* still held a strange, smug confidence and were waiting for the democrats to swing the vote when they eventually went to the booths after work. The media was not hearing or seeing or believing what was going on in our country.

But that day, Election Day, the world changed. Trump was elected, of course, and I had a new puppy, which is almost like having a newborn. I haven't sleep well since.

Dexter came with me on my daily walks. At first, the five-mile trail was too much for little him. But I couldn't imagine leaving him home while I exercised, so I carried him part of the way when he was tuckering. He was off lead much of the time; his legs were so short I could easily catch him when he strayed. Mostly, he walked right next to me and sat every time I stopped. Or ran ahead and waited for me. "Thank you for waiting!" I said as I reached him and gave him a pat. He'd run ahead again, and wait at the next turn.

He grew, his legs stretched. The following summer, we went for walks in the high field, and he raced the trails and picked me up on his next go-round. I brush hogged extra trails through the five-foot grass, to keep him from running into the woods. He was a blur as he came around the bend and raced by; only his intoxicating smile and jubilance were visible.

I leashed him when we walked down the road to the preserve and let him off when were on the trail. When we got back to the property later, he turned to look at me every couple of steps, asking for freedom. Off the leash, he tore into the woods, and I heard bark-shrieks in the distance as he chased deer. Ten, fifteen minutes later, he ended up at the barn's door.

After a long walk, on a hot day, Dexter's tongue hung to the ground. We watered up at the outdoor spigot, and I encouraged him to get into the pool to cool down. I wanted him to get used it. But instead, he ran off to the stream by the road, and then to the road.

He wasn't running away; he was just doing what he was meant to do. He was a sport dog, a hunter, even if he'd never heard a rifle. I loved watching him run, his glee and competence, his incredible athleticism, but I worried. And it was time- and emotionally consuming. Before long, I spent hours every day getting Dexter home. I found him on the road, peeling roadkill from the asphalt. He was next door visiting a dog who'd been left in a small fenced-in area. I heard him yelping deep in the woods.

I bought hundreds of dollars' worth of shock collars and long metal leads. I won't go into the details here, but nothing worked. I could not shock him after I tried it once. He was running away with the usual enthusiasm, and I squeezed the button. He cried with such agony it brought me to my knees and tears. They don't show that part on the videos. I did more research and spoke to everyone who knew anything about English Setters. I called Anne. We went to training class where he was a fast learner. He was the perfect student inside, in a controlled environment. But when we were out in the field, and there was a squirrel or a deer, he was gone. He was hardwired, and so different from Charlotte. He didn't just bark at deer or squirrels; he ran after them until he got them.

Dexter spent more time on the leash, both of us frustrated. He pulled hard, yanking me from one side to the other as he darted through the grass, tail wagging high. He was all joy, but I was miserable. It was not merely annoying; I feared he would dislocate my shoulder.

A friend, who had had three English Setters in her life, said that the only way to control them was *containment*. After much consultation and consideration, I had a fence installed around the barn, enclosing all but the front door. It took months. In the interim, I leashed Dexter as we went from the barn to the fenced-in pool area, the only place I now felt it was safe for him to "run," which was nowhere at all.

Just after the fence was up, I took a week-long, snorkel-ing-kayaking trip in Baja California and left one-year-old Dexter with my parents in Princeton, where they had an acre in the woods enclosed by deer fence. While I was away, and out of touch, unbe-knownst to me, Dexter escaped through the front gate, not once, but three times. And, true to form, he ran straight down the driveway to a busy road. The first time he was lost for a day and someone delivered him to a shelter. The second time, my mother was able to cajole him back in. The third time, he raced down the driveway and within moments was hit by a car—hard.

When I was able to check emails at the end of my trip, emerging from a week of underwater activity, Dexter was in intensive care. His broken pelvis required surgery, but blood needed to clear from his lungs before they could operate. After returning on a red-eye flight from California and a few days' wait, a five-inch plate was installed in his fractured pelvis with five long screws. A lengthy, stapled incision ran down his backside which he could reach with his lizard neck despite the Elizabethan collar. He refused each of the daily sixteen antibiotic and painkilling pills, no matter how I presented them. I wrapped them in cheese and liverwurst, crushed them in his food, and tried to drop them at the back of his tongue and close his mouth. He was relegated to a crate, immobile, for eight weeks to make sure his pelvic screws didn't come loose, which would instigate another unbearable round of surgery. Those were two very tough, very long winter months for both of us. I wasn't sure we would make it.

In early spring when the snow began to melt, I was able to finally let Dexter out into his huge enclosure. He ran at such a speed and with such joy it was infectious. I fell in the snow laughing. It was all worth it.

OPEN WINDOW

I sleep with the window open. Wide. It's not just the window but the wall that opens. The five-by-five-foot pane sweeps over Dexter's pillow, brushes the foot of the bed, and is secured by a two-foot stump against my bureau full of winter sweaters and pajamas I rarely wear. The Great Outdoors lies just beyond a sheer nylon screen. The pulsing, screaming, shrieking, clicking, crashing, fluttering, threatening, unabashed nocturn washes into the room. And so, I am a voyeur of the night.

I adored living in a tent in the Peruvian Amazon decades ago, but I don't go camping. There's no need. I have the benefits of camping all the time. My bed's proximity to nature is akin to sleeping in a tent, but with a good deal more comfort, among Belgian linens and a down-stuffed duvet, propped on a half dozen pillows.

For reasons not entirely understood, Dexter—as well as deer, coyote, birds, and, for the most part, mosquitoes—accepts and respects the screen as a barrier, much the way safari animals don't give humans trouble on the back of a Land Rover. I am amazed and thankful that Dexter, alert and bursting with excitement having heard a howl, will not even paw the screen.

As a puppy, Dexter sat outside in the grass by the open window at dusk, and into the night, while I sat inside on my bed, with laptop or book. Now he sits on a comfortable chair, which we sometimes occupy together, scouring the field for movement. Occasionally he jumps and runs to the edge of the lawn, to the fence, to investigate or intimidate an intruder. Dawn and dusk are his favorite times at his perch, on watch. When he's had enough, he comes to the window and stares me down almost patiently until my eyes meet his, then I him at the door.

At night, the reading lamp reflects on the screen to create a visual obstruction, a large dark square, punctuated by whatever presses up against it—moth triangles, or tonight, the underbelly of a praying mantis, angling in a billowy 18th-century hippy hoop skirt. I pray she will amble out of Dexter's reach, who is on her side, outside, before he comes to check in with me and spots her.

When I turn off the lamp, my eyes adjust to the moon's light in the room and outdoor world beyond. Without the distractions of sight, the litany of sounds and activity floods the room, seems louder. The air is moist. I sense possibility and my own vulnerability. Thirty feet outside the window, a stand of poplars, also known as dollar trees, because their leaves shimmer silver on their stems, amplifies the slightest breeze.

Before I erected Dexter's four-foot-high fence, at night, coyotes padded and yelped right outside the window. They would have taken playful, innocent Dexter like they did the orchard's sheepdogs next door. I found coyote feces atop the four-foot round bales in the field—and recently saw one lounging on top of a bale all afternoon. Surely, they could clear the dog fence, but for whatever reason don't. Perhaps, even with their menacing and fascinating howls, they are shy. When I hear them, I use my stern voice—*Come. Now. Inside.*—to call Dexter. He races back to the door, sensing urgency. It occurs to me that, when I hear them, it may be too late, that is, too late for Dexter. The coyotes likely lurk nearby, quietly, long before they become vocal and make their presence known.

When Dexter's inside and safe, the biologist in me tries to follow individual voices, without success, to count how many are in the pack. On a clear night, if I sneak to catch a glimpse, to assess whether their yips are contact calls or coincide with a kill, for example, the slightest movement in the dark—even behind a closed window—used to silence them. Not any more.

At an informal talk at our town's environmental board meeting, a biologist mentioned that a house built in the woods on five acres impacts thirty acres of ecology around it. I am aware I leave wounds and imprints, but it is hard to believe nature hasn't moved back in when I hear all that goes on. It seems I am forgiven my trespassing, released of my human presence, as the nocturnal creatures

let it all hang out. Shrieking owls, cooing and hooting ones. Screaming rabbits and jarring squeals.

On spring mornings, I roll over in bed to see robins spaced
out every six feet, pull and snap elastic worms from the short-
cropped lawn. I keep a meadow beyond the lawn to encourage
wildlife that has nowhere else to go in a mostly populated, tilled,
and otherwise wooded region. We've lost three billion birds over
the past fifty years in the U.S. and Canada, in part because their
midwestern habitat has become commercial agriculture. Many of
those birds have found their home in the more hospitable northeast,
and perhaps some in the field outside my window. At least I hope
so.

In the wee hours, when the deer wake and move from the
deep grass where they've bedded down for the night across the field
to the apple trees, Dexter senses movement, stands at the window,
points with his whole body, alert, tracking. He emits a supra-sonic
whine, or stands looking at me by the bed, until I let him out to
chase the deer. Sometimes he stalks slowly, over minutes, almost
imperceptibly, and then bursts into a barking frenzy to surprise
them. It's the best he can do, since he's contained and comparatively
small. Mostly they don't pay him mind, aware of his limits. Sometimes I join him, go to the window or door, and do a deer-bark, their
warning call, a heaving cough that comes from the chest, half seal.
"Huh! Huh!" I clap my hands or run toward them. Dexter throws a
glance my way, pleased by our collaboration.

Despite the lure of the nocturn, I am a morning person. I
often lay awake in the final hours of the night in anticipation, not
wanting to miss dawn's magic: the orange-pink smear of sun behind
the poplars or angling on the field catching the morning dew, the
fog rising from the meadow on a cool, moist morning.

Before the fence, a half dozen turkeys paraded, strutted, and
gobbled at arm's length outside the window mornings. I lay witness
to courtship and competition. Turkeys can fly, of course, but their
preferred mode of transportation is waddling. I have not seen them

inside the fence.

Visitors—and I include Tess and my parents in that group—rarely leave open the window when they sleep. I so want friends and family to experience nature the way I do, but, inevitably, the window is closed to "tilt" or shut completely. My daughter dons an eye mask and ear buds and draws her curtain, the only curtain in our barn-home. I have never had curtains in my bedroom, not in my entire life. In most places I've lived, no neighbors are within sight, even when I lived in the city, so there's been no need. A curtain would shut out the natural light. Why would I do that?

And so, visitors miss the night. They miss the morning, too.

Can it really be too cold? Do the lights in their room attract mosquitoes? I'm not sure, and I don't press. But I suspect it is the unvoiced, unarticulated sense of vulnerability that precludes guests from experiencing what I so adore, indeed seek and need.

Or perhaps, simply, they desire uninterrupted sleep. Admittedly, it's been a long time since I've slept through the night. Far too much is going on to do that. I have always been a light sleeper, a requirement as a single mother, so am easily roused by distant coyote calls, even Dexter's body tensing before his barks pierce the night.

From late spring until mid fall, the window remains open for weeks at a time until a thunderstorm threatens to throw art off the walls—as it did a couple months ago, knocking a porcelain lamp to pieces—or heaves rain at angles soaking Dexter's pillow. When a storm is in the forecast, or the sky turns slate, I watch the windows on all sides to see which way things are going and blowing, then edit the openings.

Mostly, the evenings hover around sixty degrees. Hudson Valley summer nights cool my home, unlike in New York City where the asphalt radiates heat it's collected all day. One week in August often has unbearably hot, still, humid nights, but those are rare. Those nights, I toss in bed to find a spot that hasn't yet been warmed and moistened by my own body, shifting from pillow to pillow, flipping them to find the cool side. Dexter lies on the concrete floor.

The open window at night is an extension of my day outdoors on the laptop or tractor, in the garden, pool or field. I can't help myself: my life and spirit, my being, are oriented to exist in nature. I've created a life and home to indulge this obsession. Most days, from May until October, I begin at dawn working by the pool, surrounded by dense clusters of irises, a stampede of Echinacea, a village of black-eyed Susan, cyclones of trumpet vine and wisteria, ambitious but fragile climbing roses, fleeting red and flirty orange poppies, tall, persistent no-nonsense stems of sunchoke and lush ornamental native wild cranberry bushes. The garden is nature lightly curated.

Most summer mornings, as I make my way to the pool with my phone, towel, and latte, Dexter is ahead of me at the gate. He knows where we're going. In this light, on those mornings, at that hour, the pool is still and meditative. The pool pump has not yet kicked on. We head to the outdoor sofa in the shallow end, and on the way, I glance at what's fallen in—a bright-orange spotted newt, leggy spiders, fleeced bumble bees. If I see a ripple, something is likely still fighting for its life. I lay the towel on the water-beaded cushion and set down my coffee. I grab the pole-less net and return to fish out this morning's catch: Mostly leaves, a couple daddy long-legs doubled up on themselves, a small black beetle, an enormous one. I contemplate whether to save an invasive, no-good Japanese beetle. I feel a pang of sadness when I retrieve a limp dragonfly.

Events, seasons, and cycles are reflected in the pool too: trumpet vine leaves, maple seed pods. Hundreds of whiteflies dot the water's surface in August, the pool an unwitting pest management device for these destructive leaf eaters. Once a month there's excitement: a star-nosed mole, a blind mole, a drenched mouse, a pickerel frog with a camouflaged spider hitching a ride, a splayed praying mantis, a large brown spider laden with hundreds of babies on its abdomen. She took some care: I wanted to extract her without leaving her progeny behind.

One morning, a mockingbird with a crooked neck floated, alive. How did a bird end up in the drink? I noticed that the snail that had been camping near the stairs was cracked. Did the mockingbird dive for it the way a pelican goes after a fish, only to discover the unforgiving stone the snail was on?

Once, Dexter chased a squirrel into the pool. I had to shoo riveted Dexter outside the enclosure and think fast about how to scoop—with a short net—a very confused, frenetic rodent in a way that would avoid it running up my arm and biting my nose. The squirrel was saved, there may have been a shriek. It was not a moment of exceptional grace.

I wipe the dew off the pool sofa's cushion with a towel and lay out the dry part to sit. Dexter shoulders up against me and my laptop. He likes routine too. I've created different spaces to work, justifying and allowing time with sky and fresh air. Fortunately for me, most Airbnb guests who stay in the cottage prefer the pool in the afternoon heat, rarely experience the pool at dawn, its gentle serenity, so I have it to myself. Before the pump kicks on, the still water doubles the flowers and any cloud formations. The early light catches a distant apple tree and golden meadow.

If inside on a beautiful or even "mediocre" day—whatever that means, even rainy days have their seductions—I become irritable, in something tantamount to claustrophobia. Thanksgiving on the 14th floor of my sister's stunning New York City apartment makes me physically uncomfortable. I feel caged. In the car, both driver and passenger windows go down as soon as I turn on the engine. Once, a potential mate asked me to close the window as we barreled along on a country road on a beautiful spring day. In that moment, I knew we were incompatible.

I've always been this way. Clues were there all along: I'm the one in third grade who asked to hold class outdoors. As a young teen, I spent time in the woods alone, which turns out to be a common experience for nature writers, a penchant which defines us. While living in New York City, I found ways to spend a couple hours every day in Central Park. For health and fitness, I trail run or hike. I garden extensively, prune and wrangle vines from trees. I took up rowing on the Hudson River in 2016. I can't imagine spending time on an ergometer or other machine indoors for exercise.

In early October, when it becomes too chilly, when the pool is closed for the season, my day begins in the Adirondack chairs overlooking the field, where the sun hits the meadow at rakish angles and warms the earth.

One day, I saw a friend at midday, and she asked why I was wearing a sweater. When I told her I was cold from sitting outside in fifty degrees for hours, she remarked, "You are not taking care of yourself."

Au contraire. This is me taking care of myself. I need this, these moments, nature in my day. I miss them when I wake in the city, or elsewhere, or in winter, when the experience is muted by glass and hibernation.

People nod. They, too, like to sleep in a cool bedroom. They tell me how they set their AC to sixty, missing the point entirely. If this is not yet clear: I am not a climate-control person. I mostly take whatever nature serves up. It's not just about saving money or the planet, although that's reason enough. I will resist shutting out the outdoors, under humming AC or a bubbling furnace. Perhaps if I lived beside industry or unbearable traffic, I'd succumb. But I have the luxury of—and am ever grateful for— a natural context. I am lucky, yes, privileged, but I submit that most people have choices and options. I purchased this property for what many spend on a home in a trailer park, or a studio in Queens, or a condo, after seeing dozens of properties, weighing all their pros and cons. I chose this piece of land with all its demands and generosity, as a single, working mother of a young child. I consider myself privileged in recognizing its bewildering treasures.

October mornings, the temperature in the room will drop below 50. When I climb under the covers to warm my nose, the night sounds are muffled, inaudible, compromised. The window needs to close soon. But I know this is not a casual decision. This is not just closing the window for the evening, but admitting the seasons are moving on, winter is nigh. I already mourn the summer smells and raucous activity. I remind myself as I swing the window closed, that this, too, is part of nature's cycle, that things are quieting down out there. The crickets and peepers are tucked away. Through the glass, I will just have to try a little harder to hear the owls and coyotes.

*   *   *

A few winters ago, at 2:00 AM, Dexter sat up. He sensed something.

Barking filled the bedroom with urgency and horror. The night was broken; my sleep, my precious sleep, interrupted again. I sat up. Outside the window was a presence: The dark silhouette of a large deer, a smaller one beyond. Dexter raced to the door so I could let him out to take care of things. I opened the (unscreened) window, the window at the foot of the bed, the one I rarely open, and did the deer alarm call as loudly as I could. The huge animal scattered, ran to the fence, kicked over, and in a moment was gone. Dexter was confused, barking at the door. He returned to the bedroom just as I closed the window.

The next night, a repeat.

And the following.

This went on for weeks. We no longer woke at 2:00. Dexter and I laid awake in anticipation of our visitors. Weeks of interrupted sleep. A friend said, "Put up curtains!" as if it was just the sight of the deer that was upsetting. It was upsetting to have them there eating the hisbiscus and lilac, but more: there was something disarming, unnerving, about a 200-pound animal right outside the ceiling-to-floor window. I'm not sure a curtain—that is, not seeing it—would have solved anything. I would likely lay awake and wonder whether it was behind the curtain, then get up several times a night to check.

When I had just finished constructing the barn but wasn't living here full time, I worried that a deer would jump through the large windows, and thrash around inside in the middle of winter, that the furnace would not be able to keep up, and everything would freeze and crack. I would be miles and weeks away and not know.

And then there was the image of a friend's mother, who was in a cast up to her hip watching television when a deer crashed through a sliding glass door and couldn't find its way out, blood and glass all over the place.

I called Bill, the ex-state trooper who hunts deer in September. He told me he couldn't shoot without a permit.

Sleepless, I called the Department of Environmental Conservation, on the verge of tears.

"I need a non-season permit to kill a deer."

"We don't give out permits for—"

"This deer is right outside my window every night."

"Did you put up a fence?"

"Yes, but admittedly it's not a deer fence," and I explained. "We have too many deer! They have no natural predators. Not only do they eat everything in the area, we hit them with our cars and they have ticks that carry Lyme disease!"

"Have you tried everything?"

"Yes."

"Sprays? Critter-Gitter?"

"Critter-Gitter?"

Critter-Gitter is a sensor-activated light and sound system to frighten deer away. Our conversation was over until I agreed to try Critter-Gitter.

The day I went online to purchase Critter-Gitter, the deer stopped coming. I guess it worked.

When it arrived a couple days later, I hung the little black box anyway. After Dexter came in for the night, I went outside to turn it on. I had 30 seconds to get out of range before it sounded.

I snuck out at dawn to turn it off before I let Dexter out, which puzzled him to no end. It would inevitably chirp, activated by movement, before I was able to wrestle it to sleep.

A week went by. The deer never came to the window. The alarm never went off.

I decided to move it to another part of the yard, where the deer snacked on the conifers. The night I hung it there, the deer appeared outside my bedroom window.

And when I moved it back to my bedroom window, they stopped coming again. It never went off.

I called up the manufacturer. "Is there a supra-sonic signal emitting when the alarm is off?"

"No, ma'am."

"There's no way a deer hears it before the alarm goes off?"

"No, ma'am."

I have been thinking about telepathy lately. I am not a New Age kind of person, but there's lots of evidence that deer (and Dexter) are tuned in. If you consider how much information is conveyed between our smartphones, couldn't our brains—even more complex and operating with their own physics and frequencies—pick up more nuanced things? Maybe the deer could tell I had a weapon of mass destruction. I've been losing sleep over all this.

Maybe I need a curtain.

LIFE AT THE MARGINS
Crepuscular and Other Adaptations

One early April day, before Charlotte passed, I was raking and cleaning the garden, excited for spring. In her antiquated state, Charlotte was up to something in the irises nearby. When I went over to investigate, I found she had unearthed a nest of tiny, pulsing bunny bodies—on Easter! I gently shooed Charlotte away and re-covered the nest with the dry grass blanket provided, but not before I took a little video, which I posted on Instagram—*Happy Easter!* The exposed nakedness made a lasting impression. I returned daily to check that the little ribs still heaved. Concerned I never saw the mother, I wondered if we had contaminated the clutch and whether I should take it into my care.

No, is the short answer. According to an internet search, wild bunnies do not fare well in domestic settings, and more: Mother rabbits spend only five minutes at dawn nursing their progeny, explaining why we hadn't seen this one.

A few days later, their eyes opened, they grew, they squirmed. I went to the city and when I returned a day later, I immediately went to check on them. I was disappointed to find the little bodies stiff and cold.

I also learned that rabbits are *crepuscular*—active at dawn and dusk. Many predators, such as felines and coyotes, are out at night, and other predators, at high noon. Rabbits, rats, mice, ferrets, among others, adapt to avoid predation, operating at the margins.

A biologist by training, I studied animal behavior and ecosystems. Even so, I'm not sure I knew the term "crepuscular" until The Bunny Incident, but love the concept and, on introspection, identify as crepuscular myself.

I wake before dawn, possibly because I can sense Dexter tense, attuned to the activity outside the window in the form of—

yes, more, many—rabbits emerging from the high grass and deer moving across the meadow. I'm part of a little ecosystem of behavior, an indirect byproduct of *crepuscular adaptation*.

To be fair, I have always been a morning even crack-of-dawn person, in an irritating way to those who are not, like my night-owl daughter. I spring out of bed and use an alarm only if I need to get to an airport at an ungodly hour. Although I immediately turn on the espresso machine, I don't need coffee to get going; sipping a perfect, foamy latte is just one of the many reasons I love morning.

In summer, I often wake at 5:00 AM in anticipation of dawn. Once awake, I find it difficult to roll back into slumber, even though I am chronically sleep-deprived. I relish the sun breaking through the morning clouds, the stillness which gives way to ornithological jubilance, and the gentle, tender roll of light and movement unfurling across the field.

Many activities compete for the early hours: I prefer rowing with less wind, low sun, and few other boats on the creek. I do my best writing at that time, sitting by the meditative pool in the shade. The morning news, and, lately, Wordle demand my attention. Dexter prefers a cool morning walk.

When I drive down the driveway to my morning row, a half-dozen rabbits shoot out, in, away, every ten feet. On the road, I take it slow, navigating all the crepuscular land mines: chipmunks, deer, turkey. I note another adaptation: Squirrels pull up their tails as I approach, reducing their chances of getting caught under the braking tires.

I find dusk equally mesmerizing. Who doesn't love a sunset? The changeover is imbued with romance, drama, conclusion—yet promise—light, and mood changes, color play in the clouds, a chorus of peepers in spring. Even the word "twilight" sparkles like the fireflies in summer.

In my first decade here, I never left the field before sunset, but now I recognize there are other places, too, to witness the resplendent show. I rarely head into a theater or indoors at dusk. I make sure, if I can, to be in a good spot, with a front row seat for the sun's descent, dedicated, to fully appreciate the moment wherever I am. When I am home, Dexter and I watch together. He is back on duty. After sleeping most of the day, he takes his perch on the outdoor lounge chair, beside me, to watch over the field.

Like Dexter, I get sleepy in the middle of the day. This has been a trend over the past decade, and my doctor—with no apparent empathy or interest—says *it's just age, you're getting old*. Maybe it's because I don't get enough sleep, what with jumping out of bed with only six hours of shut-eye. It concerns me, but not enough to miss dawn, or go to bed at nine, or stop rowing.

All this time, I thought I was a morning person, but I've come to realize, like rabbits, I am crepuscular. Not matutinal (active only at dawn), nor vespertine (at dusk), but bipolar.

I wish there were more *crepuscum*—that the day were entirely dawn and dusk.

*   *   *

Tess was visiting. Having just returned from Europe, her jet-lagged body almost aligned with mine. She voiced a desire to rise earlier; perhaps she's getting a taste of how lovely the hour is. Her inclination—and she has been like this from the get-go—is to push into the night and sleep until late morning, which saddens me. I feel she misses so much. Others remark, *that's teenagers*. But she has not outgrown her nocturnal nature even in her twenties, and I know that for as long as I can remember, I've woken early. I've slept past 9:00 AM a handful of times in my entire life. We're just wired differently.

I took a riveting course on circadian rhythms in college. Circadian rhythms, of course, are our biological clocks. Since then, new research has shown that our brain plus tens of thousands of genes regulate not only sleep but appetite, digestion, hormones, susceptibility to alcohol, urination, medication absorption. Our internal clocks approximate a day; the sun keeps us on schedule. Morning people have shorter clocks; night owls' run longer. If left to our own devices without the benefit of sunlight, my body wants to shorten the day; my daughter's wants to lengthen it.

Our entire ecosystem works off this circadian notion. Those of us who live close to nature have intuitive expectations for what we see at dawn, during the day, at dusk, and at night—that is, what's natural, and what is cause for concern. We know that our headlights will catch different animals on the road at night: raccoon, possum, cats, skunks. A possum is ugly-cute in the broad daylight; a raccoon could be rabid. In part, this notion of what's natural makes a matinee (or even a nap) a tad scandalous; it goes against the grain to succumb to darkness during the day.

In the Hudson Valley, coyotes are nocturnal. According to friends who live in Montana and Colorado, coyotes are diurnal. Westerners don't have the luxury I have, the tacit agreement, in which the coyotes have adapted to humans, and so have "gone under" into the night, possibly because of the large spaces and lower density of human settlement.

I used to hear them howling once a month, then weekly. Now I hear them almost every night, sometimes twice. Are they increasing in number, or I am more vigilant?

Last November, already pitch black by 4:30 pm, I heard a commotion. I ran outside. Dexter was up against the fence, barking, holding his own, defending our homestead against an excited pack of yipping coyotes just on the other side. Trembling, yelling, I dragged reluctant Dexter back into the house. I'd been living with the notion that everything was okay so long we operated at different times of day. But it seems the coyotes adapt too—to their prey and the lengthening night.

On occasion, I see a lone, lean coyote during the day, lazily zigzagging across the field in the distance. I assume they are beta males who've been cast from the pack. But I am seeing loners more frequently. And I've read that when a coyote is out during the day, it serves as a warning, that they are emboldened.

One morning, after a strenuous early morning row, I took Dexter for a walk, wearing high rubber boots in the tall grass. As we came up the hill, a bark sounded in the woods. A large, confident, well-formed (read: wolf-like) coyote stood thirty feet away. My heart stopped, but my feet began to run.

We were a thousand feet from the house, and safety.

Dexter pulled back on his leash every few steps to bark.

"Dexter! Come!"

When I turned, I saw the coyote trailing, fifty feet behind. In those boots, I had just enough energy and adrenaline and speed to make it back to the door.

Phew.

It turns out, I should never have bolted, rather shouted, thrown things, and looked big. But I was concerned the coyote might recruit its brethren. Surrounded by a pack, the ending could have been quite different.

I could bring an air horn and a stick next time. Or, maybe, just not go for walks too far afield for a while. I'll avoid the ticks and the occasional coyote in a temporal, spatial adaptation.

PETER RABBIT

I was weeding in the pool area when puppy Dexter moved around the fence corner, just out of sight. Judging from his erect, pointing tail, posture, and barely visible movement, I sensed Dexter was onto something. I stood up and ambled around the corner feigning disinterest in case I needed to swipe something from playful Dexter who turns everything (a glove, a sock) into a game. He poked at something gently. I was not prepared for what I saw.

A full-grown rabbit hung from the fence, its haunches caught in the wire, its nose a few inches from the ground. Peter? Peter Rabbit? The visible eye was half open. Neither limp nor stiff, the rodent, while close, was not yet occupied by the stillness of death.

Dexter! I cried inside, assuming he was responsible. Twice, when he was tiny, he pushed half his body into holes, tail wagging, and brought up the heads of full-grown rabbits. The first time I didn't believe it, despite the fresh bloody tangle hanging from the base of the neck. But then I saw him do it on a walk. I chased him, his jaw clenched tightly over a three-lined snout clamped inside his own, two soft velvety ears sticking out the side. Dexter was obstinate. Even when I caught him, I could not unlock his jaw to wrestle free the rabbit head. I couldn't leave it in his mouth, either. The thought of Dexter playing with or dismantling the head, imagining his teeth coming down on the eyeballs, the fur being stripped from the hard skull, was too much for me.

How long had Peter Rabbit been hanging—minutes, hours?

I wasn't sure what to do, but I knew it wouldn't be with Dexter around. I grabbed him by the collar, and he dragged me inside; he too knew I would do this alone. I had no choice but to put the rabbit out of its misery, and the only way I could imagine doing that was by drowning it.

I grabbed a brown shopping bag, an old rag, and a tall composting bin. I filled the bin with water from the wheelbarrow at the edge of the roof line, an informal water catchment system. My heart was pounding. I knew I wouldn't be able to stomach holding Peter's body down in the water, even with a rag. I didn't want to feel him squirm and spasm for breath in his struggle for life. Moral pundits explain that it is easier to kill when there's distance, tools, an apparatus, which is why military drones are so troubling; they're distant from the targets, could just be a video game.

I found a stick, long and sturdy enough to push and hold Peter down in the water. It would also keep me from being bitten, although it didn't occur to me that Peter would be a threat, that he might twist and try to do so. I needed the stick mostly to protect my fingers and conscience from the deed.

Dexter barked from inside the house as I sighed and stepped forward. I held out the bucket, my head away, back. Almost without looking, definitely without seeing, I wrestled the bin under Peter's body. The vessel was the right shape and configuration, long and tall, but I had to tilt it while lifting Peter's body with the stick—and I lost some water over the lip as I did. I wondered whether the water was still deep enough. My doubt was fleeting. As I lifted the container to submerge Peter's head, he came to life, struggled, and bent away, more flexible and livelier than I ever imagined. Where did this surge of energy and strength, come from? Should I stop? Should I save him rather than kill him? It was too late to think about whether I was doing the right thing. I pushed harder and steadier as the mercy killing became a battle. I wanted to pull back, for it to be over, but he didn't. Did I get it all wrong?

While Peter wrestled for his life, in cold blood I studied his haunches up close. I tried to figure out how Peter got himself into this situation. It seemed he jumped through one of the wire rectangles in the fence and his muscular haunches were caught behind, mid-jump, saturated with action. His left hind leg was rubbed completely fur- and skinless, down to the raw crimson muscle. Maybe Dexter instigated a chase from the other side, from the cloak of the juniper bushes, and Peter tried to fly through the fence. But

Dexter was not really the culprit here.

As I pushed the flailing body harder, trying to steady both hand and mind, I wondered whether this bunny was really Peter. Could it be Lily, or Josephine? Was this the rabbit whose nest Charlotte found among the Siberian irises on Easter Day, with eight tiny blind and hairless kits?

I held the athletic body for as long as I could.

"Ah!" I cried out loud. I let go and stepped back.

Now what? I had made things worse, creating more stress for this rabbit, if I were to retreat and try to save it. Tears of guilt, remorse, and frustration welled in my eyes. The situation needed immediate attention, but I was done. Done! I could think of only one person: Bill, my hunting neighbor. He was okay with death and dead animals. I called him.

"Bill. Do you have a minute?"

"What's up?"

"There's a rabbit stuck in the fence. I can't kill him. I can't get him out. I was trying to drown him, but it's not working."

"I was on my way to New Jersey."

"Oh, okay. I just thought—"

"I'll stop by on my way down 9W. Lucky you caught me."

Right after I hung up with Bill, the rabbit seemed more still—dead still—but all I could see was its haunches. The rest was submerged in the compost bin. I really didn't want to confirm and was not sure how.

I texted Bill. *I think it did drown. Sorry to bother you. No need to come by. Thanks though.*

Moments later, Bill pulled up. Lucky, too, because I realized I would have a hard time wrestling the dead body out of the fence without retching. Bill grabbed Peter with the rag, pulled him out of his awkward acrobatic state, stuffed him into the brown shopping bag, and folded it over.

"I'll leave it for the coyotes by the road. It'll be gone in no time."

"Dexter will find it." The fence had not yet been built. "Could you take it somewhere farther way?"

"There's a dumpster just before the thruway. I'll throw it there." That's the kind of thing an ex-trooper knows—where dead bodies go.

"Thanks, Bill. You're so sweet to come by. I just couldn't do it."

"No problem, Cynthia."

CHAINSAW MASSACRE

During the pandemic, people discovered or confirmed the restorative power of nature as they took their lives outdoors. The likes of Henry David Thoreau and John Burroughs as well as many other writers and scientists have long suggested how to observe, honor, and allow in nature. A recent spate of contemplative, informed, eye-opening books hit the market cataloging trees' magic and mystery. (*The Hidden Life of Trees: What They feel, How They Communicate*, by Peter Wohlieben; *The Overstory*, by Richard Powers; *Finding the Mother Tree: Discovering the Wisdom of the Forest*, by Suzanne Simard; *Sprout Lands, Tending the Endless Gift of Trees*, by William Bryant Logan, to name a few.)

The family across from me on our designated "scenic road" in rural Hudson Valley removed dozens of mature maples, oaks, hickory, and tulip trees on their five-acre plot, leaving a scant few. The owner showed me the pile, proud of his conquest, as if it were the head of a lion. His neighboring father and brother did the same, completely flattening and denuding their own five-acre parcels. While plenty of people I know have figured out how to live with and in nature, there are holdouts. For them, the lawn is king.

Some go on to "beautify" their barren yards with ornamental bushes and non-native trees, red-dyed mulch, but mostly a grass monoculture that will thirst for the very water a leafy canopy would have helped retain. Pesticides are employed to ward off dandelions and clover. These men—almost always they are men—wrangle and tame, spray Roundup, weed whack, blow every last leaf off their grass. They spend Saturday mornings sitting on their mowers burning fuel and time, leaving stripes like a vacuum on wall-to-wall carpet. Meanwhile, invasive vines encroach on the newly minted forest edge.

A few months after seeding his lawn, my across-the-street neighbor came to retrieve free foot-tall saplings in a giveaway I participated in as a member of our town's environmental board. The irony stung.

This has been going on for some time on this (once) scenic road. A while back, the new owners of a vacant perch overlooking the Hudson River lopped off every tree on the steep slope, and then spent years and thousands of dollars erecting fake stone concrete retaining walls so their double-wide wouldn't topple onto the road below. The razed slope is now covered in brush, vines and weed trees that block the view more than if they'd pruned the lower branches of the existing trees.

Another neighbor took down a healthy fifty-foot oak, whose trunk was three-foot in diameter. It fell into a stand of woods onto my property, creating a tangle of branches and toppled trees. I can not begin to understand why he would rather look at that confused mess, when he instead could have enjoyed the significant cooling shade of a majestic oak which posed no threat to his modest home. But this is the same man who has dumped oil and fish tanks and concrete slabs into my woods over the years. He mumbled that the tree was dead—never mind that its core was solid, and the crown full of leaves. A few weeks later, he hacked off every branch hanging along our shared border, leaving a jagged, angry edge.

If I cut down the woods between us, I wonder if my neighbors would be less inclined to denude their own. I suspect they enjoy having the woods separating us, framing their lawns. But they are not willing to live with something half-feral that might have its own mind and agenda, something that might drop acorns.

I understand that some trees need to come down: those diseased, hollow, dead, dangerous, and tilting toward a dwelling. Maybe, also, to open a view. Or for proactive, planned wildfire management. But the massacres I describe go well beyond curating a healthy stand—and the views they create are of asphalt and passing cars. I also appreciate the desire for a lawn for children to play, although I have not seen any on the lawns across the street.

I suspect some version of the white-picket fence syndrome

is at work here, a staking of claim. These men have pioneering, dominating spirits that won't give up. Perhaps they fear nature in all its glorious complexity and seek comfort from being in the driver's seat. Yet imposing an unnatural "order" requires an enormous amount of work and produces its own kind of pressurized chaos. They take a forested lot and render it suburbia. I am baffled that someone would choose to purchase five acres of woods and decimate it, rather than start with a lot that is already cleared— or simply choose to live in town. Why live in the woods and then remove them?

We owe trees respect for all they do and are. They buffer climate change through carbon sequestration, reduce flooding and erosion, retain moisture, support wildlife, filter our air and produce the oxygen we breathe. Trees offer visual privacy as well as sound barriers from screaming or barking neighbors and droning highways. In city streets, trees have been shown to save money and lives by reducing asthma, crime, and heat—services that also flow from urban parks. As grand as they can be, trees are humanizing and intimate. The very presence of trees *creates* a neighborhood, a place to rest, pause, hang a hammock, anchor a picnic, lean to read a book.

Many seem to appreciate the magic. But how to explain the open, visible hostility with which some Americans confront trees, nature, and wildlife? Even if they care little about climate change, or aren't drawn to the bookstore's nature shelf, how can they not appreciate the sheer majesty of a generous, gnarly sugar maple or the gentle breath of a hemlock? What is it about these men that makes them want to eliminate every tree on their property, bulldoze it flat, and put in a lawn, stripping the land of any vestige of authentic topography, habitat and ecosystem?

We will never understand nor accept one another's approaches. At least, I admit that no amount of listening will help me accept their perspective. But here, nevertheless, is a modest proposal: that the fate of trees be a responsibility we shoulder, at least to some degree, together. Because whether it's a stand of cedars lining a scenic byway or a row of London planetrees on a city block, trees are, in addition to so many other things, a common good.

My town, like most, requires a building permit to put up a fence, but not to clear-cut 150 trees. Some towns have successfully implemented tree ordinances, requiring landowners to submit a proposal to the town board to take down a certain number, kind, or size of tree. But this is tough for some to stomach. Few want to mandate or even suggest their neighbors make thoughtful, community-based decisions about our shared natural assets, even though we all rely on them directly or indirectly. American municipalities are more inclined to mandate their residents mow their lawns (even those who are unable either financially or physically) than to keep a healthy tree standing. Landownership agency remains a strong concept in this country of individuals. Those who own their land will do what they want to it. But as part of our futures together on this fragile planet, we need to start thinking about trees and other natural spaces as all of ours, not just the property owner's who can undo a century worth of growth with a $200 chainsaw. I consider myself a mere custodian of my land and weigh every move I make to honor and promote its wildlife inhabitants.

In 1986, as Latin American Program Officer for World Wildlife Fund, I helped establish the Monarch Butterfly Reserve in Central Mexico, where, at that time, 140 million Monarchs overwintered. Their hibernation requires a specific, delicate microclimate that could be altered by the removal of a single Oyamel Fir. Doing so could let in the sun and make it too warm, bringing the Monarchs out of hibernation (and threaten their ability to return north) or expose them to wind and cold and so freeze them. As part of the *ejidatario* system, the local residents, of limited means, leased their land to lumber companies; they had to "use" the land to keep it. Understanding their needs, we helped to develop alternative uses and income streams, including from the plenitude of tourism that ensued, to take the pressure off logging. Every tree mattered.

Every tree matters.

I mention this because the people who lived among Mexico's Monarchs, had even more reasons to fell (and sell) trees than my neighbors here in the Hudson Valley. A change of attitude and perspective seems eminently possible.

And yet, as denizens we accept the brazen approach to maintaining power lines all over this country. As I drive on Route 9W, a stand of once noble Norway spruce catches my eye, every time. Dozens were planted over a hundred years ago, demarcating the generous grounds of a former religious retreat. Surely, these trees were there before telephone, cable and electric poles were installed, but no matter, over decades the line crews have excavated the heart of the trees to dramatically reshape them in unnatural, disturbing ways, testimony to the violent, silent whims of utility. They cut healthy trees, lop off whole sides or tops of maples and oaks, disembowel them, often not limiting their cuts to the thirty percent rule that ensures survival. If they were thoughtful, tree-loving arborists, they would remove the invasive vines which have been granted photosynthetic access by the road's path and their cuttings, which further destabilize the wounded trees. In many cases, it is the vines and instability after the "pruning" which topple the trees onto the power lines during storms, which lead to extensive outages, damage, and death. We are accustomed to seeing tree branches and leaves vie for the sun to fill their canopies symmetrically and completely. It takes a toll on all who view the magnificent, now-disfigured stands. We live with their pain every day, unconsciously.

Many of the wildfires in the west were sparked by electrical lines—more than 1,600 California wildfires over six years were caused by Pacific Gas & Electric—presenting not just inconvenient outages, but danger and destruction on an enormous scale. "Solutions" to date stipulate more regulation and additional tree cutting. To be clear, I am not challenging the need to manage forests to ensure underbrush doesn't contribute to the spread of raging fires, but we should consider alternatives—like burying the lines.

But why? Why are we so beholden to the utility companies, allowing them to butcher trees on land that rarely belongs to them, when they have failed us time and time again? The obvious solution is to bury the lines, like gas and water, as they do in Europe, some cities, and new developments. The utilities' stance is that it's too expensive to bury the lines. Many have bought into their narrative. Not I.

Laying conduit for wires under the road cannot be more expensive if we calculate the true, fully-loaded costs of above-ground lines, erecting even taller, heavier, and more dangerous poles, tree teams, wildfire damage, preventative and storm-induced outages, need for late-night repair crews, millions of people without service and homes, deaths, and all the lawyers employed who fight to maintain the status quo that is: centralized industrial utilities. It would require thoughtful planning and some spontaneity, reorganizing processes and departments, coordination with the highway department, working in an incremental and opportunistic way, such as when roads are due for repaving, or they are excavating water or gas pipes. I warrant political, organizational, and communication failures, the way funds are bucketed and allocated, and lack of innovative problem-solving keep the lines from being buried, not the cost.

Human's disregard for trees and this planet goes far beyond these close-to-home examples. I mention these because, with a change of attitude and perspective, they seem manageable, doable, and because the chainsaw I hear in the distance is a constant reminder.

On the upside, visionary Mayor Yvonne Aki-Sawyerr of Freetown, Sierra Leone, committed to planting one million trees of fifteen different species over two years to increase biodiversity and reduce landslides.

Someone once told me, the best time to plant a tree is twenty years ago. Better yet: why not just leave the ones that are standing?

AMERICA ON THE CREEK

On a serene fall morning in the Hudson Valley in 2020, my eyes savored the billowing, exuberant orange, yellow, red, and still-green treetops, as a friend and I set off in two single sculls on the water-glass of Rondout Creek. I took up rowing in 2016 but became obsessed in 2020, as we moved to singles and doubles. Larger boats were off limits during Covid. Rowing saved me those pandemic summers from isolation's grip, giving me a routine and ability to see friends, even distant. But whatever solace it brought came tinted with the fractured world beyond.

We headed east towards the Hudson River. Low tide revealed what was underwater all along: sunken trees and moss-covered docks laden with invasive purple loosestrife's long fingers. A blue heron stalked the shallow water. Cormorants clung to buoys. When I glanced over my shoulder to see what lay ahead, I couldn't tell whether the rippling water signaled a floating log or a duck, until it flew away. Ospreys nest every year atop the rusty 30-foot arm of an arthritic crane, which reaches towards the heavens in a state of perpetual supplication. I carry a low-grade unease that a town planner will "clean up" this waterfront, mistaking its complex, adaptive ecosystem for unredeemed industrial wreckage.

We rowed toward where the creek spills into the Hudson River. We gauged the river's hospitality by the Rondout Lighthouse's American flag: If it shivers horizontally—which it did often, lately—it's too windy and we turned around. Even a slight breeze is difficult in a single scull, and so we rowed less frequently on the regal but intimidating river. The Hudson is a draw for its long vistas, the luxury of taking a dozen strokes without having to turn to see what's ahead—as we travel backwards—and the excitement-cum-terror when an immense ship approaches. But what beckons most is its sheer grandeur.

"To Eddyville?" I asked.

"Yep."

We headed back up the creek—which, to be clear, is no com-promise; it has historic, aesthetic, and natural treasures all its own, delivered on a personal scale. Four bridges offer delectable shade and segment the three miles to a waterfall.

We pulled by the low-slung, blue-and-white houseboat that a long-haired, bare-chested Cuban outfitted as a B&B the previous year, and a vomit-hued hospital ship ripe for creative re-purposing. We passed the sheriff's dock, got a whiff of bacon from Ole Savan-nah's southern brunch, heard woodworkers tapping in the barn at the Hudson River Maritime Museum. Each of several marinas we pass has its own character. The Hamlet of Connelly leans toward sailboats—some verging on yachts—and sports a vast rusty hanger. At the far end, some part of it has been UNDER NEW MANAGE-MENT for as long as I can remember.

On a warm afternoon, but not that day, small children with bubbled arms jump and shriek in the water I hope they don't swal-low. There's a little Mexican restaurant, a cluster of fuel pumps, waterfront acreage for sale. A few trailers create a courtyard around an inviting, smoking barbecue.

We headed toward the Wilbur train bridge. If we hear a rum-ble and a hoot, we decide whether we can make it or to wait out the locomotive. They seem to go on forever, slowly: oil tanks, Maersk containers, multicolored trailers, flatbeds, and container skeletons, cars increasingly labeled Amazon, heading in equal measures north and south. Sometimes we yield to impatience and take our chances, pulling quickly, hoping the train won't kick a rock or worse as we pass 150 feet beneath. So far so good. When I see them, I wave at an older couple who while away the day on a large sailboat below the trestle. I wonder how they trust the century-old structure.

I turned to take a good look before navigating the next part through Feeney Shipyard, where barges and tugboats dou-ble- and triple-park and sometimes release debris we dodge in our tippy, fragile sculls. For over a hundred years, Feeney's has been fixing and building marine vessels— a microcosm of America at work. It was busy, almost jubilant, during the pandemic, under Trump. What did that say about global shipping and America's economy? Were the ships out of commission while we got things straight with China? Or was there so much commerce that demand for more capacity reached all the way back here? *STATUE CRUISES, Statue of Liberty and Ellis Island* rested here, too, that pandemic summer, her windows masked with strand board, a metaphor for our fractious and fraying republic. New York tourism was suspended along with the hopes and dreams of immigrant children.

We rowed alongside the vast vessels, their sides smeared in orange and green like Richter paintings, scraped by the lock walls of the Panama Canal, or the port of Newark. We watched PILOT NO. 1 metamorphose from oil spill response vessel to pilot-boat mothership. Cranes at rakish angles hoist American flags hundreds of feet into the sky. Workers in hardhats and protective visors scrape and paint. Even on weekends, sparks fly. In the scrapyard at the far end of Feeney's, a four-taloned claw wrangles a pile of old cars and lawnmowers. I applaud the efforts to recycle, but I worry the tall stack might topple into the creek. Despite my environmentalist bent, I appreciate the shipyard's authentic, productive industry.

Just beyond the shipyard strait, a 20-foot motorboat revved into high gear—heedless of the NO WAKE zone—creating a large, threatening wave, which can easily unsteady my vintage, 26-foot-long, scull. After passing me, it bore down directly at my friend as if playing a game of chicken. She pulled over toward the creek's banks and shook for ten minutes.

All summer, we dealt with an unarticulated political rift on the Rondout Creek. Rowers, sailors, and kayakers seemed to share a connection: physical exertion, poetry of motion, proximity to nature. Motorboats and fishermen tended to gun their way down the creek, blasting music and heaving blue exhaust mixed with cigarette smoke, American flags on the bow and Trump pennants on the stern. Many boat names contain whimsy, but some are imbued with aggression or hard partying, like *I CAN'T REMEMBER*.

For much of the row to Eddyville, a motorboat crept along behind us, its disconcerting presence hard to read. The boat was not only following us, but the rules—going slowly so as to not create a wake. The boat stopped near a wetland inlet just short of where we turn around. As we passed the boat on our way back, I made out three men and a couple of children. The morning sun caught a translucent line as a reel was cast. I debated if I should thank them for going slowly. My instinct is to acknowledge good behavior, but I've learned it can backfire if it rubs up against the wrong sort of masculinity, the kind that rejected masks and common courtesy as a threat to individual liberty. I decided to take my chances.

"Thank you for going slowly."

"Sure," he said.

I smiled in relief.

Just then, I sensed a flutter, a shadow. I looked up. Flashes of white popped against the blue sky overhead.

"Look! A bald eagle," I exclaimed. It landed in a nearby, leafless tree.

"Hey, kids. A bald eagle!" The boat dipped as they all moved to one side to see.

We watched together.

When they were named the national bird in 1782, bald eagles soared in the hundreds of thousands. By the mid-1960s, habitat destruction, hunting, and pesticides reduced their numbers to 450 nesting pairs in the continental United States. Thanks to environmental protections, bald eagles came off the endangered species list in 1995. When we see one on our rows, we still pause in awe.

I nodded to the family and carried on. I exhaled as I drove—pushed with my feet, my hands hanging off the oars, feeling the resistance of the water—and inhaled on recovery, as I rolled up the slide. That's what that year was: constant recovery.

I wanted to believe the eagle was an omen of good news. We were battling for our country and everybody in it, for the American flag and all it represented, for the planet's future. Elections were around the corner.

Fall was in the air, the days shortening. Soon the boats—sailboats, motorboats, our sculls—would be put away. Docks would be removed. I would miss being out on the water and the profound solace the creek offered as winter locked up the waterways, but I would have something to look forward to in the spring.

SUNDAY TIMES

Like many in the tristate area, Michael and I ritualistically spent Sunday morning plowing through *The New York Times*, discussing global events and getting nowhere on the crossword puzzle. No matter how many postcards I received encouraging me to subscribe, and I called to do so, the NYT would not deliver to rural Field Farm where few of my neighbors shared our zeal to stay connected to the outside world. So, Michael drove into town to buy the newspaper, while I made the morning brew.

Michael and I "competed" in our support of two different stores.

Michael traveled north into the small hamlet of Port Ewen to Smith's, aka Smitty's, an old-school deli with a big white plastic sign advertising 7UP. On Sunday mornings—and possibly others —the owner, Fred, and a posse of men leaned around the bagel bin area shooting the breeze. I think Michael liked that scene; I wasn't against it, but it wasn't one I fit into easily. I had no idea what they talked about, since they generally went silent when I walked in. Michael returned from his jaunt with a tidbit of local news along with the paper.

When I was alone, I headed south on 9W to the Country Store, with a gazillion signs and promises in the window, and adjacent to a Sacred Heart church. I often arrived as mass got out. I liked to support Dave, the young, hardworking and serious owner behind the register, who delivered an earnest "Good morning, Father" to a collared customer, with change and a brown bag. If the place wasn't too busy, I ordered an everything bagel, toasted with cream cheese. If it was, I made eye contact, dropped a five-dollar bill on the counter and mouthed *thanks*. Other than the Sunday crowd, this was a deli—like Smitty's— that seemed to cater to early morning laborers with drip coffee, egg sandwiches, glazed pastries and powdered donuts or poked with jam. For lunch, roast beef sandwiches, a pickle, chips and cold sodas. Italian bread, not baguettes.

About ten years ago, the Country Store was reconfigured. Dave cut back on his inventory and got rid of a couple of large refrigerators. He told me that his electric bill was a crippling two grand a month. A few years later he put the place up for sale, but, as he says, no one wants to work seven days a week, so he still operates it.

Another time, Dave had a bunch of vintage items—an old cash register and tools on the lower shelf near the papers.

"Where'd these come from?" I asked as I stooped to look them over.

"My father," Dave said.

I assumed his father had died and he was clearing things out. Did I say, "I'm sorry" out loud? Did he correct me? It turned out his father was fine, and that his father was Fred, owner of Smitty's up the road. Ha! Michael and my divided loyalties were feeding the same family.

Since I took up rowing, I drop in at Smitty's on Sundays for the paper on the way to the Rondout Creek. I have become a Sunday regular at Smitty's.

At 85, Fred has lost most his eyesight; Dave drives him to the store each morning. When I go in to grab a paper, I am usually in a rush to get to the water. Once, early on, I parked on the wrong side of the street right in front, to make my jaunt into the store faster, and told Fred so. He thought that was funny and reminds me periodically that's how we "met." Now I leave a few minutes to spare, park on the correct side of the street. I generally find Fred around the corner, chatting it up with the guys. I don't wait long for an opening.

"Fred, someone's here for you," one of them will say.

"Good morning, Fred."

"Is that Cynthia? How's it going? Have you been out on the water?"

"Not yet. On my way." He moves around to the back of the counter. As I hand him a couple bills I tell him, "That's a five and a single for the paper."

Dave grows tomatoes out back of the Country Store and they both sell them. Sometimes he has heirloom tomatoes. When I *ooed* and *aahed* about them a few years ago, Fred laughed, puzzled. "You like those funny looking ones?" Since, if he has them, he saves them for me. I often pick up a couple meaty ones while I'm there. Problem is, he won't charge me for the tomatoes.

"They don't cost anything!" Fred says. Or, "I just steal them from my neighbors at night."

I try to sneak a twenty on the counter when he's not around, but his employees tell me he'll fire them if they allow me to pay. I know the newspaper is a lost leader, in that there is no profit margin in it for the store. They sell the paper hoping that people come in and buy a coffee and a bagel. In my case, he *gives* me tomatoes. I have to live with that.

Dave was in the store behind the counter at Smitty's the other day, helping his father. When I complimented him on his tomatoes, and how I find it impossible to grow them myself, he says he works hard to keep all the critters out of the tomato patch.

Fred piped in and laughed, "He plants poison ivy around the edges, so people don't steal them!"

Dave stopped selling lottery tickets and they both stopped selling cigarettes. They didn't use the word *unethical*, but Fred said, "It's a waste of money. I've been here fifty years and seen people die. They used to come in and buy one, two, three packs a day. You can smell it on them when they come in. Then they stop coming."

"Don't you make money on the lottery tickets?" I asked.

Dave said, "Six cents on the dollar. Not worth it, watching people throw their money away. . . . Hey, Dad, I'm working on getting the newspapers bundled."

I turned to Fred. "You have to bundle up the returns?"

"Yeah. They pick them up on Sunday nights and they make pizza boxes out of them!" Fred says, laughing. Good to know.

I asked him, under my breath, "What do you guys talk about

around the corner?"

"Mostly their wives," Fred grinned. "The wives wouldn't like what they say. We poke fun at people to keep their skin from getting thin. Sometimes they don't come back for a few days. But eventually they do."

Last October, I told him I wouldn't be in for a few weeks because of spinal surgery, but that my daughter would be visiting and would come to get the paper.

When Tess returned with the paper, she also brought home an envelope. Inside, was a handmade card with a collage of a woman who looked remarkably like me in a row boat filled with tomatoes. Someone had carefully written above the printed Get Well Soon, "I hope these hold you until next season." Fred wrote with a ballpoint pen, "Hope you are doing great, Fred."

I was so touched. When I thanked him a couple weeks later in person, he said, ever humble, "I didn't make it. I had someone make it for me!" It was the nicest gift I received during my recovery.

Fred asked how I was doing for weeks. This is the kind of exchange and humanity we all missed during Covid. The casual pleasantries, witty banter, and anchors in our days and weeks.

I'm rowing again, so back to my old routines. I'm picking up *The New York Times*, and a couple tomatoes, checking in on Fred, every summer Sunday.

Last Sunday, when I walked in, Fred said, "I've been thinking about you all night."

"Uh-oh." I said. "That doesn't sound right."

"Yeah. I been stalking you," he laughed, and went behind the counter. He came back with an enormous, ripe cantelope and handed it to me. "Look what fell off the coconut tree."

IN THE LAND

"*The very least you can do in your life is figure out what you hope for. And the most you can do is live inside that hope. Not admire it from a distance but live right in it, under its roof.*"

— Barbara Kingsolver, *Animal Dreams*

SUN-KISSED FRUIT

In the summer of 2010, on our trip to Turkey, Michael and I spent several days in the mosques and markets and streets of Istanbul— and then jumped in a car. We drove east into the interior town of Göreme, a World Heritage Site in Cappadocia, one of the most extraordinary places I've ever been. One civilization after another has passed through this plateau— Christian, Byzantine, Roman, Turkish, Armenian—settling among and within toothy formations of soft volcanic rock people hollowed out to create surreal dwellings and sites of worship. It is a realm where civilizations as well as anthropology and geology collide. How does an archaeologist or preservationist contemplating the dome of a fairy drip castle decide whether to restore the 16th-century frescoes, the 13th-century gilded ceilings a few inches beyond, or the 3rd-century Roman drawings? What a dilemma!

We stayed in an unadorned castle-cave and rose in the morning to trek along the rim of the Ilhara Valley. No one else was there. You'd think it would be jumping with tourists, but we were alone, discovering and savoring one breathtaking, intimate room after another. Inside some, gold leaf or paint glittered from dusty walls. Lines of dozens of rounded, small openings puncturing the walls brought in light and from the distance created a visual rhythm in the landscape. These nooks, we learned, were of more recent vintage—carved in the last century by pigeon keepers who occupied the spaces.

When we'd had our cultural fill, we descended into a vast expanse of trees, happy to find shade for our walk across the valley. When we looked up, we saw that the back-lit, bright green trees were gilded, too—with bright orange balls. We were in an apricot orchard, each branch jam-packed with perfectly-ripe Turkish apricots. I freed a soft, blushing one and rolled it in my palm. The warm, velvety, juicy morsel found my mouth. The flavor was nothing like the apricots we eat in the States—that is, they had flavor, bursting with intensity that recalled the dried variety. Low on water, we inhaled dozens of succulent apricots as we made our way through the valley to the other side, in search of more archaeological sites.

Still there was not a soul in sight. There were no signs posted, no one to ask permission for our walking harvest or to offer recompense. At the time, we didn't feel like trespassers, but appreci-ators.

This unexpected apricot bounty reminded me of half a dozen stocky, white peach trees I had discovered on my own defunct orchard in the Hudson Valley. Perhaps the previous owner Jim had mentioned them, as he did his grandmother's heirloom rose bush, three pear trees, and the watercress in the stream—which I didn't find for years. But I think I discovered those quiet, bent white peach trees on my own, dotting the slope behind the lean-to. In survival mode, gnarly and weather-worn, the trees were on their last legs. But when the fruit arrived in August, I parked myself in the shade of the largest tree, reached up and pulled down an orb. As my teeth punctured the taut skin and bit into its rose-infused flesh, the juice exploded. It was, to this day, the best peach bite I have ever eaten.

But I wasn't the only one ravaging the peaches. Beetle borers had settled into the trunks, and the fruit was covered with black holes and sticky spots where the juice bubbled and gelled. I ate as many peaches as I found, savoring one or two bites per fruit avoid-ing those scary spots. Is that why they tasted so good, even more precious?

A few years later I took down the infested by then unpro-ductive trees before they became poison ivy magnets so the tractor could get through. I mourned their loss for years.

The amazing thing about fruit trees is how much fruit a single tree can generate. Many of the couple dozen apple trees that came with the property I excavated from poison ivy, pruned, and nursed back to life have toppled over the decades. But the one clos-est to the house, and largest, produces so many apples I eat three or

216

four a day in the fall to keep up. The tree has overwhelmed me for years, yet it still astonishes me anew each season.

Meanwhile, two Bartlett trees, drop dozens of pears daily littering the ground below. If I leave them, they attract bees or are smushed by the lawnmower. The pressure to keep up is immense. But what a problem to have: too many perfectly ripe pears! Unlike the apples, which are *very* organic (read: spotted and warped), the pears are mostly unblemished and there are so many at once that every cheese plate is adorned with sliced and lemon-spritzed pears at my Labor Day Party. I enjoy fresh pear nectar as well—ripe pears blended with ice and water and lemon, to be drunk immediately. I poach peeled pears in sugar water, with whole cloves and a ribbon of lemon rind. Guests dutifully eat them with farmer's cheese or drizzled chocolate liqueur from the Amalfi coast. I dry, freeze, and puree them. I give them away to everyone I bump into. Bags and bags and bags.

When Charlotte was still with us, she used to check under the pear trees first thing when we arrived from New York City for the weekend. Dexter doesn't eat the pears but dives for the apples on our walks through the field.

Eating from the land provides immense satisfaction. I anchor the seasons in my daily walks, with what I stumble across. Foraging in spots I know about and picking from old fruit trees carries an element of comfort along with renewed discovery every year. In the spring, asparagus pushes up through the thick grass in the meadow: warm, fresh, exquisite. I resist. I bring it home to assemble a critical mass for a meal. Fiddlehead ferns and most mushrooms, are, of course, toxic when eaten raw, so nibbling from the forest floor carries the risk of a bad stomachache, or more. I look forward to sauteing them with garlic and chili flakes.

In July, taking a walk through the field, I hover on the edge, among the blackberry and raspberry thickets. My hands rummage for flawless ripened raspberries releasing from their torus, sometimes too quickly to apprehend. I press the amalgamation of 100 drupelets onto my tongue. *Mmmm.* I remind myself that blackberries are better cooked, as jam.

I am fortunate to be able to casually graze my land, but the demise of those white peach trees left a void. I must have mentioned them frequently, because not long ago, Tess gave me three one-foot peach saplings.

"You loved your peach trees, right, Mom?"

I planted the small sticks in my garden, near the house, so I could keep an eye on them, and think of Tess when I see them, which is daily. They have grown a yard a year, and already one has more fruit than I can keep up with.

Last year, small, rock hard, greenish fruit dropped from the tree, perhaps prematurely. I gathered them from the garden floor and brushed them off. Sadly, in their raw state they were almost inedible. I was considering fertilizing and pruning them to see if there's a way to sweeten them next year. But maybe I won't. After drying, poaching, and stewing them in sugared water, they remind me of those Turkish apricots. Of Cappadocia.

And on the off chance that a certain Turkish tree farmer should stumble upon my tiny orchard on a holiday of his own, it would behoove me to have some ready at hand.

IN THE WOODS

Out of nowhere, a strong cool cloud-breath flustered the still-innocent spring foliage. It made me look up, reminded me there was more. Though I knew the delicate leaves were the palest of greens, the canopy was dark against the gray sky. The mockingbird overhead was shrill and nervous. The turkeys in the meadow called for love-love-love-love-love-love. I wondered how much more time I had before it rained again. I had been scanning the saturated earth, training my eyes on the rotting leaf detritus, the bases of maples and ash and elm, trying not to get distracted, as I often am, by nature's casual arrangements of beauty on the forest floor. But how could my eyes not follow the alluring muscular curves of a naked trunk, defiantly vertical in its deathness, whose nude blond skin would catch the sun on another day? I was thankful for the many healthy trees in this stand, but it was these that drew my attention: the bare trunks and the character-laden, gnarly insect and fungal warehouses with peeling bark, blunted branches, and rhythmic cavities made by persistent woodpeckers. Each held a story.

The early, warm, seductive spring retreated with the coming of the endless rain. May showers. I was between men and among trees. I was more whole alone.

Where were they? Could my eyes just not see them? Were we looking in the wrong places? Morels respond to a mix of rain and sun, so maybe they were waiting for the sky to clear. At the lecture the previous night, the mycologist said it was morel season right now. I rushed home worried I might have missed them, filled with dread and urgency. After an hour of searching and no luck, I wondered whether they did get away. The lecturer's pictures from the 1980s depicted large, phallic morels leaning up against a classic collecting basket. He reminded us that mushrooms are more closely related to animals than plants, something that is hard to understand, since they are less relatable. Almost a third of humans don't like to eat mushrooms and many young humans find them slimy and weird, maybe because of their association with dark moist places and fairytales. Learning to appreciate mushrooms (and cooked carrots) is a culinary rite of passage, a threshold to adulthood.

The reproductive spore-bearing vessels of mushrooms spring from underground networks, connected more like nerves than root systems, one reason you can find mushrooms in the same spot year after year, periscopes emerging from their underworld. Like the large fish of the sea, mushrooms accumulate high concentrations of compounds, in their case, from whatever is in the soil. Depending on what tree they reside near, they are delicious (elm) or inedible (sumac). Mushrooms by the side of the road can sponge up petrol, and morels, which favor the drip line of old apple trees, often contain lead arsenate, a pesticide used heavily in orchards before DDT. A little lead arsenate did not deter this forager, when I did find, finally, a single blond morel under the one still-flowering apple tree. The government biologist many times warned of the over-enthusiastic and uninformed forager's mistakes, but even so paused and—I think— salivated when describing how to cook morels in butter, shallots, and a dash of Pernod.

Whoa! Resting right there in asphalt blackness was a pile of fresh poop—I mean, scat. Clean and glistening, nary a leaf had shifted to cover a soft coil; that is, no time had brought pollen dust or insects or touch to alter the weighty mass. The air wasn't cold enough for the pile to steam, but the freshness gave a feeling that the mound had just been put there. Put there by a what? A bear? A raccoon? I would have been disappointed if these feces came from the coyotes I hear outside my open screen summer nights but admit that to face off with one at that moment would nonetheless provide an adrenaline rush. It didn't look like the coyotes' stool I regularly see in the meadow's paths with felted hair, calcified white with bone, or full of apples. I wanted this excrement to belong to something new, bigger, more dangerous. I so wanted it to be a bobcat, but presumably wild cats, like domestic ones, bury their feces. No apparent seeds or fur or porcupine quills provided clues. I took a photograph so I could ID the mass later. And when I did query "fecal pile in woods," the first page of search results was about pest control. Sad that's what came up, not answers for the curious, the ones who crave a little thrill from The Great Outdoors, but remedies for the fearful who view animals as pests and who want to quell them. One of the first things the pest control entry said was DO NOT TOUCH IT. Funny. Would these same folks who were looking to eradicate pests touch the excrement? It was like a bad joke.

When I was picking fiddlehead ferns last week, a similar heap of scat gave me a jolt. I was crouching atop the antique garbage dump in the woods, harvesting the treasured spirals amidst old bottles, a dented coffee percolator and a rusty radiator. A house burned down a century ago leaving a stone foundation and a cave-hole that likely served as a basement or root cellar. On the corner of the stone wall, a yard from that dark opening, an accumulation of waste lay quietly, variegated by time, as if the site had served as a creature's commode over days or weeks. I had never known an animal to do that before. I knew animals marked their territories with urine, but this was different. The cave, just beyond the pile and so close to hunkering me, suddenly seemed darker.

This fecal matter was fresh. I felt as though I was being watched. In over two decades, I had seen a bear only twice. Once, from the other end of the field, from the house, I saw a black velvet creature galumph into these woods, where I was at that moment. The other time, I saw a bear running towards that stone foundation, towards the den and fecal pile. It could just be a coincidence, not a pattern, but I was feeling bear.

I looked up. Isn't that where bears go? I saw a white pine with its dead lower branches radiating skyward. No bear there. I had been scouring the small stuff, seeking morels on the ground and enokis under the elm bark, but realized maybe I should be also looking up, beyond, out. In case. My eyes had been focused at four, maybe five feet, not on the horizon line, not around the forest in front of me.

Heading towards the clearing, I followed the narrow, slightly ambling trail, ground-grooved by the deer. I often stick to the deer's intention lines through the woods, as they do the mown path through the meadow. It wasn't as if the brush was thick, but the path was convenient, easy. Choices had been made. Within seconds, my scalp started to itch. I felt ticks all over. Was that a wisp of hair brushing my forehead, or . . .? My clean hand lifted to scratch off a small scab.

A bottle rested at the base of the big oak. Was this the same bottle I found years ago, or was this a new one? Did I leave it behind because I didn't want to carry it out? The white and red label was pristine, fresh, with a line drawing of a friendly fox face. FOX SCENT. I wondered why a hunter would want to smell like a fox for the deer. Amazon sells a one-ounce bottle of RED FOX URINE for $6.99.

> This intense, full-bodied, all-natural urine product
> is a true Deer Hunter's Grade™ Masking Scent/
> Fear Reducer - the best available. Use in areas where
> animal activity is noted, to help bring in otherwise
> skittish game.

Full-bodied fox urine, like a Barolo. *Mmmm.*

I often find empty bottles of spirits where hunters lay in wait. Always comforts me to know that they are drinking while they're shooting! Damn hunters. I never have met someone who owns a gun who doesn't drink. Maybe because they feel so klutzy in nature's grace. Does wearing fox urine as cologne drive them to drink? Or do they numb themselves before they blow the life out of animals who look them in the eye, whose intelligence we are only beginning to comprehend? How else could they live with themselves? Does shell shock play here too? Some part of the brain must absorb the ricochet of the barrel. Maybe the same pain that drives a shooter to drink, drives him to kill.

A few winters ago, I saw a fox for the first time on this land, a delicate, playful canine perambulating atop the snow, appearing here, then way over there, a few moments later. I watched for and followed him through the window for weeks, picking out his rusty blur amid the white. Once, when I was sleeping in my daughter's room while my parents were visiting, a couple of my unfinished paintings were leaning up against the ceiling-to-floor window. When I woke, the canvases blocked my view of the field at dawn, which I didn't want to miss. I got up to move the paintings and just as I did, the red fox jumped five feet straight into the air and pounced on his prey, unaware of his audience behind the glass. I marvel at what stirred me to get up at that exact moment.

Nature doesn't care. That's what Ashley Mayne said at her book reading. Nature doesn't care or judge. In a way, we are invisible out here in the woods. But we're not, of course. As a child, I visualized the compressed worms and beetles in the dirt. We alter where our foot presses down, even when we tread lightly. Animals flee. Parenting birds go crazy trying to distract us when we stumble near their nests. We probably wouldn't have noticed the nest, but the commotion has the opposite effect, alerts us. *Where is the nest?* Nature doesn't care, except that we humans have ravaged this planet on such a large scale, nature does care. The natural world recoils. Nature submits or retreats or fights back, devastatingly so. I understand Ashley to mean just the nature around us, this immediate patch, this here, this land, these woods don't care. Nature says, we see you! We see you and we don't care you're wearing your old jeans!

Every spring the earth rebounds fully, diminishes and laughs at me, the landowner. Ha. What does that even mean—owner—to this bear or oak who just go about their business? Yet, humbled, and as invisible as I might try to be, right then I felt like I was being watched.

I left the bottle of *FOX SCENT* at the foot of the oak to find it ten years from now. I was at the clearing.

FORAGING ASPARAGUS

I can't wait for April, as dreary as it can be, teasing and testing my patience with rain and mud. I look forward to the cheerful daffodils and aromatic hyacinths pushing up near the barn, but, really, I long for the soft pussy willow, the dogwood blossoms embracing the field, the orchard's pink riot on the hill, the maple's red leaf buds against the crisp blue sky, the delicate bright green leaves of the poplars, the haze of Hudson Valley light at dawn breaking over the field.

It is also prime time for foraging the fleeting fiddlehead fern—which has only a week's window before it unfurls and becomes toxic—and wild asparagus. I look at my photographs and Instagram posts from the previous year, and time walks to accommodate all those delicate gifts of hope and bounty and culinary delight that comprise Mother Earth's annual reawakening.

Foraging provides a valid excuse to go for a walk, to be outside, reacquaint with the property, check on things. To take Dexter on a jaunt. There is something immensely satisfying about eating off the land, off my own land, and I am lucky to have several extraordinary meadows and ample woods, which are particularly generous in early spring when the garden still sleeps. Friends plant and tend to productive gardens, reap trunks full of tomatoes in July. My clay soil nor the deer are worth fighting—I have tried—and so I let nature decide what she will give me. And there is something about finding food rather than shopping for or even growing it, that makes a plate of tender wild greens particularly precious.

I admit that foraging is a bit of a misnomer for what I do at this point. I know, for the most part, where to find the delectables. I discovered an extensive stand of ostrich fern years ago, and so I make a beeline to that spot after hitting the stream for watercress. My secret, inadvertent crops become destinations on my walks. I scour the field and forest floor on my way and sometimes I stumble across unexpected dividends which become part of future rounds.

I have a half dozen places I seek asparagus, although because they are spread over acres, it is hard to remember exact coordinates. Every year I tell myself that I will map them, but don't. The Christmas tree each asparagus spear becomes when it grows out (complete with red bulbs) would serve as a marker if they weren't taken down by the brushhog with the grass. So, in a way, I still must re-find the asparagus each year.

Before we head out the door, I harness and leash Dexter since he can't be off-lead, what with all the distractions—turkeys and squirrels in the distance. I put on my tall black Hunter boots to reduce the possibility of being fodder for ticks and poison ivy, but both still pose significant risk. In mid-April, the meadow is low, the spears are visible. I push away the grass and poison ivy with my toe and break the stem close to the ground. Just a month later, the two-foot-high grass obscures the asparagus. By that time, if I find asparagus above grass height, it is gargantuan and—save for the last foot—inedible. By end of May, the grass is three-foot—Dexter can barely get through—and most of the unharvested asparagus has likely gone to seed.

Once, I waved a handful of asparagus in front of Dexter's nose and said, *asparagus!*, hoping to train him to sniff it out. And he does, especially when we are close, in an area I know has yields. Problem is, he seems to like asparagus, or at least he likes seeing me riled up. If he gets there before I do, he nips off the top, treasured inch. *Noooo, Dexter!* I hold him close and am cautious in our approach.

To be fair, half of my asparagus harvest comes from the garden. I transplanted some from the field a decade ago, and it has spread among my perennials. But even in the garden, it's not straightforward. The delicate, helmeted head doesn't come up exactly where it was before. From the same underground root system, or perhaps the result of a previous year's blowing red seed, it pushes up behind, through, under other plantings a foot away. While I visit the field daily, I check the garden twice on a sunny May day; it can grow six inches in a single afternoon with sun and rain. I keep an eye on coy Dexter to make sure he stays away from that part of the garden. And I rarely plan weekend getaways during this time. A long weekend can mean the asparagus will grow out. The season over, curtailed.

I place whatever I've harvested in a glass with an inch of water until I am ready to cook them, generally when there's a critical mass. The asparagus continue to grow, sometimes another foot if I wait a day or two. It's comical and a tad creepy. These are not twenty stems of equal length and girth in a purple rubber band. Each spear has a character all its own, bulbous or slender, curled, crooked, or bowed.

I grill, roast, sauté or boil them. I have had to become inventive in their preparation, as for weeks they are a diet staple. I throw them into a risotto with ramps and fiddleheads or savor them alone. My latest, favorite dish is asparagus roasted in olive oil and sea salt, cut into bite size pieces, tossed in their cooked oil, French feta, and juice of half a lemon. Magic.

When people set out to forage, they are usually after the big five, like on a safari: fiddleheads, morels, truffles, chantarelles, ramps. There are many other abundant or invasive edibles with high nutritional value that interest people less, such as stinging nettles, watercress, garlic mustard, lamb's quarters, sorrel, elderberry, (young) milkweed shoots, walnuts. And people love to eat flowers in salads or waters or teas. I have a hard time sacrificing peonies, pansies, lilac, and roses, and, truth be told, they don't taste as good as they look. Nasturtiums might be the exception.

Asparagus is not generally on the list, it seems. Perhaps because it is uncommon, or not really wild, but feral, having escaped domestication. Sometimes I wonder if someone a century ago grew asparagus here in the upper field. I heard that there used to be an asparagus farm nearby that was chopped into a housing development. Asparagus pushes up in their lawns between above-ground pools and trampolines. I ponder how many of those homeowners recognize—or are oblivious to—their good fortune.

Foraging has become a bit of a rage, almost a competitive sport, in part driven by the foodie movement and reconnection to nature. I wonder sometimes where people are foraging. Public parks? Private property? A neighbor-friend-chef texted, asking if she could come forage my property. She was after morels, which have been rare in the past few years. I didn't want to sound or be stingy, but if I find a cherished morel, I'm keeping it for personal consumption. She had been out foraging with someone else who found forty pounds of morels on someone else's property. *Forty pounds*, sounds almost wrong, an assault.

I found only three funny-looking morels this year and held them with tenderness. I soaked them overnight in salt water to extract the bugs, drenched them in flour and sauteed them in leftover Hudson Valley bacon grease, black pepper, and garlic. I served them with a clean palette of boiled asparagus and savored every morsel.

ON THE ROAD

Rounding the familiar curves of 9W, I spotted something up ahead on the road that didn't fit the normal patterns of movement. A blur, two red smudges hung in the air, together, then separated. Again. The activity was illegible, didn't make sense, and was barely perceptible in the mottled sun and shade. The unfamiliar commotion possessed a persistence, a gentle jaggedness. What had I just seen? I pulled over just after I passed.

As Frans de Waal, with whom I share schooling, laments, biologists and anthropologists were shamed for anthropomorphizing animals, that is, imbuing other organisms with human emotions or motives. I wonder if this shaming can be chalked up to not the need for scientific rigor, but our desire as a species to guard our superiority, distance, and difference—intellectually and emotionally—from other organisms. I understand that it is not wise to make assumptions about behaviors—animal or human—but sometimes it seems so obvious what is going on, that to describe something clinically is more dishonest than leaping to projected conclusions.

Once I deciphered the movement, I was not contemplating my responsibilities as a scientist but rather found myself stirred by a flash of tenderness: a male cardinal was trying to pick up and shuttle a female, of muted hue and life, from the road. He succeeded in lifting the female three or four feet off the ground and, just as I approached, lost his grip. I could only imagine that the male cardinal did not want his mate to be hit again, irretrievably lost to an unswerving vehicle. What an effort, laden with risk, he had undertaken!

According to Audubon, like the golden eagle, whooping crane, and Laysan albatross, cardinals are monogamous and mate for life. They are together year-round and share in household duties. The male brings the female materials to make the nest. A biologist might conjure that the male is guarding his potential offspring in helping his mate, but I submit this handsome male could find another lover elsewhere. There was something more to his doggedness. This was important stuff.

I got out of my car and approached slowly. The heroic, caring cardinal hopped into a bush on the side of the road out of view. Although motionless on the asphalt, the female was not visibly damaged. I stooped to cradle the always-lighter-than-you-expect two ounces of feather and bone. The tiny heart knocked fast and faint in my cupped hands.

I gently laid her down out of harm's way in the direction of her lover in the bushes. It was all I could do, the least. I hoped that my scent did not render the wild untouchable, that she recovered and the two reunited. That one did not die of internal bleeding and the other of a broken heart.

THE FIELD

In the early years, I paid the previous owner, Jim, to brush hog the fields for a couple thousand dollars. He seemed to enjoy being back on his property, rolling a couple of long days on his old, big-wheeled tractor. While Jim said the meadow should be mowed two to three times a year to keep the grass healthy and more pure, I could only justify, and afford, doing it once. And I enjoy watching the field grow tall and letting the wildflowers bloom, and often seed, which leads to a vicious cycle of impurity, and beauty.

When Jim moved on, I hired others, who charged $50-$65 per hour.

Bob, a school bus driver, carried a Santa Claus belly. He was a jolly sort and we seemed to get along. Meanwhile, I had interested some local farmers to graze their cattle on my property and had been waiting for them to put up a fence in early July. When they didn't show, I asked why, and they told me that Bob had told them my meadow was of poor quality. I didn't like Bob talking behind my back, and didn't call Bob the following summer.

I hired a group of shorter, heavy-set locals who hung out under the apple trees drinking beer, and occasionally climbed on their tractors to mow, even though I told them I didn't approve of drinking and driving. I found out they were collecting workers compensation from the highway because they allegedly had hurt their backs mowing medians and edges, but here they were on tractors in my field. That didn't sit well with me.

I found a website called hay.net. Listings by landowners went on for pages, describing the kind of grass available, cost per bushel, location, conditions, and contact information. Most offered "grass and clover" or "alfalfa," and then there was the euphemistic "grass mix" which seemed to apply to Field Farm. I undercut every-one's price per bushel and indicated that the interested party was responsible for baling. I would have been happy if they came and took it for free, but I thought I knew how marketing worked. I got one hit for my listing, a couple asking: "Is your grass as good as it sounds?" I was astounded how it felt like a sexual inquiry. I hadn't, after all, made my grass sound that good, or good at all. I didn't respond.

I called local farms listed in the phone book. They turned out to be orchards, raspberry farms, schools; none had animals or the desire to bale hay. I called the last one listed.

"Hello?" a man answered. After a short pause, not long enough for me to respond, he continued. "If you're trying to find my fiancé, Susanna, she is not here right now. She's in the field fucking Pete. She said she was working long hours but when I came down to visit with her, that's what I found that slut doing. She's in the corn field with Pete, drunk as a pig." The recording clicked off, beeped, and waited for a message.

When I called back a week later, a woman answered the phone. "Hello, this is Susanna."

I waited a second to make sure it wasn't a recording. I resisted asking for her side of the story, how Pete was, but found out that, no, they didn't need hay either.

Then one day a tall, auburn man in his thirties jumped out of his pickup in the driveway.

"I'm Robby. Ralph said you might be interested in having someone bale your hay."

"Ralph did? Next door?"

"I used to work for him at the orchard, when I was a kid," Robby said. He pulled a piece of grass out of its stem and stuck it in the side of his mouth.

We walked the fields together as he assessed the grass and topography, commenting on how Ralph can be tough, but was a good guy, and that he'd mellowed after he married. I agreed.

Robby is one of the hardest working guys I've ever met. Along with rebuilding county bridges and roads, Rob had a cattle and pig operation in a neighboring town. That July, after it had been dry for a spell, Robby arrived with his dad, his brother, and a flatbed loaded with a tractor, a twelve-foot-wide mower, a Yorkshire rake for turning the cut hay, and a baler. Robby's dad was in his eighties, but he was an active participant. I remember him operating the then-new Bobcat, with a tusk like a Narwhal whale to prod the bales, move them together in the field for eventual flatbed loading.

Ever since, in mid-June, Robby pays a visit to see how the grass is faring. If I'm home, I make a point of going over to him to catch up on things. He's a hardworking Republican, and up until recently he thought I was too, although we usually steer clear of politics. He's educated me on animal husbandry, how he has to schedule the butcher a year in advance, how his cows are all spoken for three years out. Each of his cows are individually inspected, but those in large-scale industrial producers are only inspected one per thousand. "I look my cows and customers in the eye. I know every one of them." Doesn't seem fair.

I like to watch Robby scroll across the field in his big red tractor, looking back over his shoulder, at the sickle mower. He can cover the whole field in one long day. It's tough to watch the tall supple grass, golden rod and purple loosestrife, Queen Anne's Lace, and multitude of flowers removed from my vista, but the short-cropped field has its own beauty. Bobby returns a few days later to turn the cut grass to dry the other side. Once dry, the cuttings are vacuumed up and rolled into bales, spit out of the baler, strung with blue nylon. The whole process relies on there being no rain for close to a week.

He makes hundreds of large wheels out of the field in short order and has done so for more than a decade. Although the grass would improve if it were cut twice or more a year, the grass isn't worth baling twice. Sometimes Robby leaves the bales into the winter, if the fall is wet and the field is soft, or he's extra busy. I love having the large rounds out in the shorn meadow throwing shadows, creating visual interest, particularly in the snow, so I discourage Robby from taking them away, which he ignores; he just does what he needs to do. The bales legitimize Field Farm somehow, even if all it produces is mediocre hay.

One spring, Robby arrived smiling. He had just had a baby boy. A few years later, Robby lost his dad and, more recently, his brother dropped out of the business. Robby shook his head about his brother, so I didn't ask, although I saw his name on signs running for local office. So now it's just Robby and his freckly, redheaded son working my fields. His son operates the Bobcat, relocating the large round bales. He did that even when his feet didn't reach the pedals. He almost flipped the machine as a kid, as my heart did its own flip in my chest. Robby just laughed, as his son's face turned pinker.

Another time Robby showed up, the timing seemed off, so I asked him what he was doing here early in the year.

"I got these guys breaking Ramadan."

"What do you mean?"

"Back at my place. They need to slaughter the cow themselves. So, I left. Funny, the guy who's doing it is the head surgeon at Vassar Medical or something." So, despite his Republican-ness and whatever one might assume goes with it, Robby was hosting a small crowd of Muslims at his farm.

Folks at the Cornell Cooperative Extension ask me whether Robby pays me or puts nutrients back into the soil, since he's carrying them all away in the bales. No, is the answer. I am just thankful to have him take down the field at all, competently and regularly. He cuts and takes the best grass, which is not very high quality to begin with, some forty acres, and leaves the rest behind. That's the part that I contend with—the scraps and edges, the smaller fields with lower grass-to-other ratio.

ROCKS, GOATS, AND DRAGONFLIES

Do I spend too much time driving this tractor, alone?

One friend asked me if I do it so I can tell people I do it. I don't think so, although the thought has crossed my mind.

It never occurred to me to not clear the fields. This is the way I found Field Farm and I have never questioned the open sky, open space. For the same reason that people are drawn to water's edge, fields soothe and restore. Evidence suggests that the horizon line is a natural antidepressant, despite man's penchant to build vertically. Besides, if I didn't mow, the field would not turn into a lovely woodland. Once, I "let it go" on the hill near the driveway, hoping woods would spring up to block my neighbor's flooding lights, but that patch turned into a bigger mess of multiflora bramble, not a maple or oak forest. Maybe in the field around the corner, where there are hundreds of baby trees mixed in, a red maple stand would develop, but that meadow offers a wetland, and a specific ecosystem.

When a Department of Environmental Conservation wildlife biologist and I walked through that field one spring, at my request for help with invasive species, our voices flushed four woodcocks into their upward 300-foot bolt. He said wild dogwood bushes taken down every other year make perfect nesting grounds for woodcocks in the spring. (He didn't help me with the invasives—said my property was perfect the way it was, I should keep doing whatever I was doing. Damn woodcocks.) So, in part, I brush hog to maintain the meadow, cultivating a grassland, hosting critters not found in the surrounding stand of woods.

Michael was in my life for a good swath of time at Field Farm, and he engaged and embraced the land fully. Handy as a carpenter, and practical, we built things and spent a lot of time out in the land together, battling invasives, putting up boxes for kestrels, bats, and bluebirds, and discovering new trails in the area.

Michael brought an old red Ford tractor with big wheels and housed it in my lean-to. The tractor looked great and moved naturally through the field. We cut paths through the high grass to vary our walks and vantage points throughout the summer. In the winter, we cleared fallen apple trees where the poison ivy and grapevines formed thick, impenetrable mounds. But when Michael and I parted after years of yo-yoing, when it became clear that he could not, would not control his drinking, he took his tractor with him. Manless, tractorless, I was on my own.

When I pulled into a John Deere dealership in 2013, it might have seemed like a spontaneous visit, but I had been researching tractors for months, even years. As much as I had wanted a classic older tractor with big wheels, I am not mechanical nor could I make sense of the listings of secondhand tractors. I needed a new tractor with a service warranty and a dealership, where someone could help me when something went awry. Even though most swore by Kubota over John Deere, this novice felt the draw to a John Deere. One of Deere's smaller tractors also had a mower deck, with an allegedly easy switcheroo mechanism so it could be a lawnmower one minute and a brush hog the next. I figured I could save thousands of dollars on lawn mowing too. Buying the tractor was a big decision, a big purchase. I didn't want the machine to be another tool that sat and collected mouse nests. I bit the bullet and bought a green 1025R with a front-loader, sometimes with a brush hog behind and sometimes a lawn mowing deck beneath. The tractor has over ten years on it now, and hundreds of hours. It no longer looks or sounds new. It's scuffed and dirty in all the right places, like a pair of old tennis shoes.

I am at peace on the land, in my field, but I am not sure how much I actually love being on this tractor. A part of me does— having a good excuse to be outdoors, productive in a way. I get close to the gnarly apple trees to see how the apples are doing, and to gauge whether to come back another day to fill a large basket of these market-less fruit. I bump along carefully watching the row of uncut pasture on my left to remember what I will be cutting on the way back. I relish the discovery—of eleven types of grasses, a foxhole, pressed spots where deer have nestled for the night. But I do not enjoy obliterating those places with the whacking blade.

Despite the relentless drone, I would rather be on this tractor than have others do it for me. I find it hard to listen when others brush hog—others, like the "caretaker" from hell or the boyfriend in my life at that moment. From the house, or an apple tree, I hear them hit rocks, rocks I generally know about and would have avoided. My heart goes out to the little John Deere as it bangs and grinds and fails. The engine turns off, and in the minutes of silence an assessment is made, things are moved out of the way. I bite my tongue when they return to the house. I don't ask what happened and whether the tractor is okay.

"We should move the rocks, or mark them, ja?" My then-boyfriend Christopher suggested. Although he was slight and had bad posture, Christopher had a dose of competitive pride and perseverance. His smudged glasses slipped.

"Yes. That would be good," I said.

Another thing to do that we would never get to. There was a very strong chance that he would not last a year, but he didn't know that yet. I take close mental notes of where the rocks are from year to year to mark them, poorly, in my memory. It is said one remembers things that carry emotion. When I hit a rock, I remember it almost as well as I remember the men. Besides, I don't know what kind of marker I could tolerate. It would have to stand seven feet to clear the grass, so it doesn't also become something that is hit, but cannot intrude on the views I hold so dear.

Christopher, whose family owned an informal blueberry farm, went sailing in Greece but ran the tractor before he left. He seemed to know what he was doing but acted victorious when—after I heard the telltale screech and grind—he brought back half a rock freshly cut by the brush hog, as if he'd caught it. The rock remained in the front bucket while we worked on the tractor, weighing the tractor down, as the thought of his battle with the rock did me. Christopher took a long time to take down that piece of the meadow, and I later realized why: He had gone over it a couple times to get it close to the ground, something we had discussed, and I had said was not worth doing. There is so much to brush hog that to mow an area twice is a waste—in consultant jargon, not "critical path." If we were going to mow twice, then one of those cuts should have been two months ago, not in a single day. I was hoping he'd deal with some of the more difficult spots if he folded back into my life on the trajectory we established before he left for Greece. Would that make him feel like he was taking care of me, as I suppose he needed to, and as I would have liked him to?

Men rarely say *I'm sorry*. Rather, they give me advice about how to do this or that with the stones in the field, tractor, pear and apple trees, meadow, house, pool, my extensive garden, my squash game. I wonder how it is that these advice dispensers know so much about these things—apparently more than me—but rarely possess a tractor, or a field, or an apple tree of their own. I have friends who consider themselves superior gardeners because they have a 10' X 10' deck of potted trees and plants in Brooklyn with irrigation on a timer. I have owned this property for over twenty years. I have assembled and managed all this, with some of their help and generally welcome suggestions and collaboration. When they offer unsolicited advice, when they start their sentences with *you should*, however, a defensiveness inside me kicks in to explain why I haven't gotten to it. It is on the list of *A Million Things To Do*. But after reciting the reasons so often, I try now to just nod and listen, allowing them to be right. That is what it is about. It is about them being The Man, and to permit them a very, very indirect apology for having hit a rock with my little tractor.

Before they head out, I give them bits of knowledge in an apologetic tone about where the rocks might be or suggest an area that is less problematic, but I find their eyes rarely follow where my arm points. Generally, I tell them some of the pitfalls of previous farm help, conveying how I feel about certain issues, how to handle others. They assure me that they know all about tractors. They saddle up as if the tractor were a stallion and throw it into high throttle.

I contemplate whether I secretly enjoy when they hit a rock, even though it hurts.

Often, they don't know why the tractor overheats or how to read the temperature gauge. Once, I hired one of those prideful, outdoorsy guys, covered with tattoos, to chainsaw, but he wanted to spend the afternoon on my tractor instead. He drove it until the engine turned off on its own, overheated, dozens of times. He sat back for a smoke until it cooled down, but did not clean the filter nor screen, and then started her up until it shut down again, within minutes, of course. He smoked a pack of cigarettes that afternoon. I would have fired him on the spot if I had known, but he was in the meadow around the corner, so I could not hear the rhythms of his incompetence. He wasn't even familiar enough with tractors to know not to admit this indiscretion to the tractor's owner.

Young Jack, who helped one weekend while I was away, claimed to know all about tractors—he'd grown up on a farm further upstate—kept pouring oil into the engine, seeing a yellow light, not realizing that the light meant the Power Take-Off, the mechanism that gives the brush hog motion, was working. He poured and poured into the wrong hole, until there was oil all over the engine and the thing smoked and almost took to flame. The mess cost me hundreds of dollars to clean and repair. I guess I should be happy the tractor didn't blow up.

Even I, who claim to know nothing about tractors, know to clean the screen when the temperature gauge starts getting close to the red area. I pull in under an apple tree and open the hood, remove and dust the screen, and brush the front of the tractor of wisps and seed fur. I give it a moment to rest as I pick some flowers or dried-up weeds with dramatic profiles, such as the great mullein, that I will take back with me to the house. I carry a water bottle, steal a warm sip before I relegate it to temporary vase, and take out my clippers to cut wildflowers still in bloom to save from the brush hog's undiscriminating blade. I imagine I am one of the few tractor riders who find golden rod, one day shy of full bloom, a perfect flower, with its draping, heavy, knitted, bottle-blond, Rastafarian head.

*   *   *

So today I am riding this tractor again.

Hitting a rock or a big branch gives me a jolt, an apoplectic *oh my god*. Instincts, which are not mine, take over as I instantly pull up the whipping blade from the mass, turn off the PTO and move gently forward or back to adjust and relieve the pain. But the sound plagues me for another few rows and makes me extra careful, the way I slow down after getting a speeding ticket, to mind things a bit more closely, respect the law. In this case, it is the law of nature, the land, the hidden rocks, to which I succumb and do not pretend to control.

I am in awe and fear of how high the blackberry bushes have grown this year, unabated, and wonder whether I'll ever get through them without their flogging back at me and taking out an eye despite my sunglasses. I hold my hand on the other side of the lever to protect it from the onslaught, and sometimes I back into a large bramble rather than take it head on. The spines are relentless, the bushes dense. Did I forget to cut this last year, or has the cutting made them this much stronger and persistent?

When Tess was young, we coveted the blackberries that bore fruit on the outcropping near the orchard. We watched the bushes carefully in early summer until the berries were large and ripe, and then picked gallons. Puppy Charlotte jumped for berries. Young Tess ate mostly everything she picked, coming home empty-bucketed. I tried to impress upon her that blackberries were better as jam than fresh, but her mouth and face dyed purple were childhood incarnate. I didn't mind. Her little hands and short reach were not

239

part of my harvesting plan. While we picked, I told Tess about how my sister and I used to pick blackberries when we were kids, up the road from where we lived in New Jersey, across from what later became the Johnson Estate. Soon after, the blackberry grove turned into a McMansion. Fifty years later, I still experience a dull pang when I drive by that spot on my way to my parents.

Tess and I marked midsummer with blackberry tart, but it has been years since we picked blackberries. I miss them, but not the white hieroglyphic scratches that remained on my tanned arm for the rest of the summer. We forewent harvest for legitimate reasons for a couple years and lost our tradition. I must remember the blackberries next July. I have added new things to my foraging list every year and have inadvertently removed the old mainstays in my excitement for novelty, as with men, perhaps. I wonder whether these imposing blackberries will be part of next summer's harvest, or whether these bushes are angry and fruitless.

I come across several tall, feathery asparagus plants. Before they bend under the front of the tractor, I lean over to snip one more than three feet tall, and perfectly symmetrical, to bring home and place in a vase on the coffee table. I take note of the others, hoping to find them again next spring, when they are simple, edible spears pushing up through the soil, barely visible in the meadow grass. I briefly contemplate transplanting them now, but I have goals for the tractor today, plus moving them to the garden would steal the excitement of uncovering them next year. Remember, I must remember, where they are.

Something springs from the brush ahead, spins in the air, and lands ten feet away: a praying mantis. I don't remember seeing so many, but I am a month earlier this year. I will see this mantis a few more times before I am done with this corner of meadow. Robby says I have more mantises than anywhere he mows.

Something else hops in front of me: a woodland jumping mouse, bouncing three feet at a time, all tucked together with its long tail hanging limply behind. I saw a bunny today, too, darting

ROCKS, GOATS, AND DRAGONFLIES

into the blackberries. I don't know if I hit its home or just a rest spot. A small garter snake esses its way off to the already cut meadow, so I won't have to think about it next row. It reminds me of the black rat snake that Robby ran over that looked like a bleeding tire.

I cringe to think what I don't see and meets the blade. I worry about all the hideouts I am flattening and upsetting. At least now is better than earlier in the year when the Coopers hawks hunt and turtles nest. The migratory woodcocks and other fledglings are now long gone for the season, so I set the brush hog on low where the poison ivy crawls along under the grass and golden rod and dogwood bushes. The insidious vine is everywhere, but less so on the paths that are mowed regularly.

I see a raptor overhead. With the motor running I cannot hear if it is a red-tailed hawk with its long, rasping recognizable call: *kree-eee-ar, kree-eee-ar.* Three big birds circle overhead now. Ah, they are just turkey vultures teetering then swooping in to find what I have left for them—mangled, unearthed, homeless.

There was a moment, when I first bought the property, that I was close—very close—to putting a pond in the middle of the field. I'd met an excavator during the house renovation who showed me a pond he had carved into a bucolic property a few miles away. He got me thinking I wanted a body of water in the low wet spot, where springs throughout the lawn and field feed a natural swale in the landscape. I called off the project the day before he was supposed to come with his backhoe, wary of how it would end up green, festering mosquito larvae, or a barren dry scab at summer's peak. And it wasn't an insignificant financial decision. I felt bad leaving him in the lurch, but I am thankful I left the field the way it was, with its infinite visages through the seasons.

That's where I planted a six-foot weeping willow a decade later which grew to be fifty feet tall and wide. It looks as if it's always been there. In the willow's sweeping skirts, in August, the native ironweed and supplicating, reach-for-the-sky loosestrife form a purple patch.

On this tractor, this gentlewoman's tractor, every small incline is a steep hill. Even a large clump of grass, a messy blackberry bush, or a small depression imbalances the tractor. I hear myself gasp and exclaim, over the engine, surprising myself with what I emit in unedited moments: "Shit!" or just "Ah!" "Ay-yay-yay" is an expression I picked up in Mexico as an exchange student at age fifteen; it amazes me how it comes out naturally today. When I hit an incline of more than twenty degrees, or a mound slopes in two directions at once, sometimes I turn into the hill to avoid rolling but am no longer on my planned course. Other times I back up and try a different route. What seems like a straightforward rectangular field warranting non-negotiable back-and-forths becomes a random maze of crossed paths through the tall grass. I will look at the unmown chunks of field with a critical eye and go back to eliminate them, if I can, from a different angle. The efficient McKinsey consultant in me, who optimizes most of my life (even relaxed moments), is disturbed by the inefficiencies created by the knolls and holes. I am especially embarrassed when Robby drops by and might note the irregularities.

My heart sinks as the tractor braves another uncomfortable angle. My mother is on my shoulder, pleading: *Be careful, Cindy!* My parents, who to my knowledge have never ridden, let alone owned, a tractor, warned me about tractors.

"You shouldn't do it alone. I worry about you out there doing all these things by yourself," my mother said.

"Thousands of farmers die every year when they roll," my father quantified. Let's double check. According to the Bureau of Labor Statistics' most recent data:

> A total of 146 workers suffered fatal injuries in incidents involving tractors in 2018. This was the lowest number of work deaths involving tractors on record between 2011 and 2018. Among fatal incidents involving tractors, 103 of the 146 deaths in 2018

occurred to workers age 55 or older, and 67 deaths were to workers age 65 or older.

Their concern was warranted, but it annoyed me that they didn't trust my instincts or judgment or figure that I knew perhaps a hundred times more than they did. There is some truth to their worries, but I already know that. Christopher's brother, who is in the landscaping business, confirmed that if you feel insecure on a tractor, you are. Maybe my annoyance is my fear. I am scared, but what's the alternative? I am alone. I try, when I can, to brush hog when Robby is here baling hay, when I see workers in the orchard next door, or when I have a tenant in the house. I wonder whether my sense of duty to the land—and my fear—take on a different hue because I am a woman.

"I always carry my phone, just in case," I reassured my parents.

My annoyance is also rooted in my aloneness. To be fair, I wasn't as alone as this account portrays, but intense experiences (particularly in nature) often occur with the heightened awareness of solitude. But my mother was pointing out, again, that I am alone. Why, after all these years, am I single, with dozens of men entering and exiting? I know she doesn't mean to hurt me, but she is forever reminding me that I am by myself, and how she feels bad about it. I feel bad about it too, but she puts me in the position of having to defend myself. It hits a nerve. I have not figured out one of life's most basic joys, one that she has celebrated for close to seven decades.

Christopher asserted that one chooses to fall in love, which is contrary to what I had always heard—"love finds you" or "you can't choose who you love." I have tried to choose love, commit to some- one who has most of the essential qualities, believing that arranged marriages are as successful as marriages for love. I have told myself, *I am going to give this guy a real try.* I go along with it assuming it will and must work. But it hasn't. It certainly didn't with Christopher.

When I have a man in my life, if he's handy and willing, generally I am on the tractor, and he is running the chainsaw. We work in the same field, me navigating the bumps and clumps, while he eliminates the dead branches from the apple trees. One thing I don't do is chainsaw—with or without company. But there are many more hours to put in on the tractor and I will inevitably be brush hogging when I am alone. I am not being macho (macha?) or prideful. I am doing it because it needs to be done, and to hire someone to do it seems grandiose and a tad indulgent.

I just looked up "macha," thinking I'd find the feminine version of the overused Spanish word for an aggressively masculine man. According to Thalia Took:

> Macha is an Irish war Goddess, strongly linked to the land . . . associated with both horses and cows. . . generally thought of as one aspect of the triple death Goddess the Morrigan . . . both sex and battle Goddess, and Her personality is usually described as both warlike and alluring. She is known to be a prophetess: the Washer at the Ford is said to be one aspect of Her, Who appears to those about to die. She is an omen of death. . . . Goddess of the land. . . Like many supernatural lovers, She warns [her husband Crunniuc] to tell no one of Her existence; but he boasts to the king of Ulster that his wife can outrun the fastest chariot.

This is crazy. Strongly linked to the land, warlike and alluring, and ironically, ran a race in Ulster, which happens to be the name of the town and county where I live: Ulster Park in Ulster County, New York. I am also a quarter Irish. When I was young, I was a fast runner, outracing the boys in the neighborhood, as well as my very athletic cousin Dan, until I hit puberty. But it is this sentence that really makes me pause: "Washer at the Ford is said to be one aspect of Her, Who appears to those about to die." Is this a reference to the animals that meet the thwacking blades?

I digress, perhaps. Each row is tricky and takes careful time.
All these hours on the tractor, just to take down a scrappy field,
not even to till a crop. Orchards are common in the Hudson Valley
because in many places like mine the soil is clay and rock. The fine
clay rots the roots of plants that require drainage; many crops don't
fare well. A friend in the farm business looked at satellite maps and
said my soil is good for agriculture, which baffles me, as I struggle
to grow lavender and hydrangea and blueberry in my garden en-
riched with topsoil and mulch.

A century ago, a squatter had a vineyard and orchard here.
Craggy apple and pear trees dot the landscape, and undulating
ground among the stand of birches can be found where the vineyard
stood. Every year a couple more apple trees go even though I ripped
out all the poison ivy that smothered them when I first arrived and
pruned them in February when the snow was not too deep. As I
brush hog I try to remember where those downed fruit trees were,
in mourning, as well as to avoid artifactual and rotted out stumps.

I am pleased to report this year I will have a bumper apple
crop. A handful of remaining trees will drop bushels of apples
in mid-October after the first frost. I don't pretend to know what
varietals I have, but there are several types of reds—McIntosh for
sure, maybe Macoun and Red Delicious—and some yellow ones—
Ginger Gold? Every tree has its own personality and profile, and
possibly apple. Perhaps there are heirlooms that I should nurture or
graft, but it's probably too late for that. I will fill a half dozen brown
bags with apples this fall, many unblemished, many more destined
to be baked. There are more to be gathered, but I'm not sure what
to do with them all. I dried cookie-sheets full a couple years ago,
but that required so much work, coring, and slicing, and they were
far too easy to eat. The ratio of skin to meat was high but did not
interfere with their consumption. This year, the apples are much
bigger, and I might get more from the drying, but I'm not sure my
wrists are enthusiastic.

Every day I eat several apples, generally for breakfast—

grated up and mixed in my muesli with yogurt and coconut milk. Apple milk, just apples and milk blended (which I first drank in Argentina when I was 12), is also easy and delicious. I make baked apples for dessert and serve chunky cooked apples with a pork loin. If I had an apple press, I could make juice, cider, hard cider, or beer, or maybe even try distilling them into vodka. Until I figure out how best to employ them, the bags of apples will occupy the cottage's basement in a pseudo-refrigerated state. The prettiest apples sit on my dining room table as an adornment, shrinking in number as fall wears on. Apples are an integral part of my life for several months.

The pears are doing well this year, too. They are the largest, best pears ever. Pear trees stand in the field, or on the edge, outside the stonewall. Most of the Bartletts on the two trees near the pool came down in August, well before the apples. Birds and bees love the perfectly ripe pears as much as I, so I try to collect the fruit before they are irretrievably punctured by beaks and mandibles. Of those I can reach, many are on the ground and already shared. The Bosc pears come later, pregnant golden weights pulling down, impatient to be harvested. I can see them now from the tractor.

Christopher and I picked Boscs with a fruit picker that Michael left after he moved out of my life. He had written and attached a pink Day-Glo label in his male block print, NO NEED TO SETTLE FOR LOW HANGING FRUIT, which I had not removed, possibly to warn future pear-picking companions. Christopher lost that label in the field, by accident, I think, but we brought home a basket full of difficult-to-reach and still-hard Boscs. Christopher wanted to see which pears fared better—unripe or ripe ones from the tree. He rejected all those on the ground, which I usually gather. Mostly he wanted to prove he was right, even though I didn't have an opinion, other than wanting to collect those on the ground which seemed most urgent. He will be gone before he gets his answer. Like many men I've dated, Christopher was attracted to my independence, then moved in quickly to control me, arriving at odd hours early in the morning from his distant home unannounced. He put his coffee in my espresso machine before he'd even tried mine. But, really, in the end I lost respect for him, when, after all his mansplaining, he had accomplished little in his own life. It's hard to take advice from someone who hasn't actually done anything.

The pears, like the men, are fleeting, almost all spent, eaten, or secured in syrup long before the apples arrive in abundance.

I think about the history of this farm as I roll close to the edges of the field, near the woods, where the stonewalls are now buried fifteen feet in. The *Rosa multiflora*, the invasive rose bush found all over the northeast, native to eastern Asia, was planted here, like in many places, to fence in the cattle with its dense, aggressive thorniness. The rose bush borders the entire field. Many years later, it has become the literal thorn in landowners' sides, and mine, as it has taken over fields and forests, sometimes reaching 25 feet in length into the trees. Its barbs, vigorous growth, and lack of predators have made it a nuisance and hard to remove. I have pulled it out of maple trees, poplars, and dogwoods and wrestled it to the ground. In the spring, the flat, white flower gives off a lovely rose aroma, as if to sweeten its blow, which I find hard to enjoy knowing that each flower has its own malicious intent.

Today, I ride through clumps of multiflora cutting it in a losing battle, aware that I am pruning it, which may encourage it to come back stronger next year. To dig up the bushes and re-move them, as is recommended by some conservancy groups, is not practical—there are hundreds of large thorny bundles. Michael and I lassoed them and tried to pull them out with his tractor, but the rope broke multiple times. Spraying with Round Up is not an option I will consider. Goats, however, might eradicate them. From a time-management, environmental, and aesthetic perspective, goats are the most palatable of options. Imagine goats in the landscape!

On LinkedIn, for years, my title read "Future Goat Herder," right above "Director of the Office of Innovation, Peace Corps," "Strategy and Management Consultant, McKinsey." Some people understood the irony. Others asked me how the goats were, and I

replied by bleating first, and then noted that I was a *Future* Goat
Herder, perhaps always in the future. I have been researching
goats, their habits, types, weighing meat vs. dairy and wool goats
(surprised to find that Mohair comes from the Angora goat, and
rabbits), thinking about what it would take to keep them through
the winter rather than as seasonal help. I heard that the region was
8,000 goats short, what with a significant Caribbean population in
New York, and Muslims breaking Ramadan. In the ungulate tent at
the county fair, goats occupy one side and sheep the other. When
I ask the attendant owners about their relative benefits, the goat
people say, "Sheep are dumb!" The sheep people bleat, "Them goats
is wiley!"

A few clever goat owners have developed goat rental pro-
grams to clear medians on highways or stands of invasive phragmites. I heard about a family who rented goats for a couple days
to eat the poison ivy in their woods. When they came home in the
evening, the goats were inside on the sofa.

On the job, fifteen goats will eat about a quarter acre in three
to five days. So little! That translates to 240 days/acre/goat—about
two-thirds of the year. I would need at least 20 goats to get through
the bramble on 20 acres. Maybe if they eat the brush when it is
emergent there is less for the goats to eat so fewer would get the job
done. They could eat all the riffraff, and acres of wild oregano and
grapevines mixed in. The milkweed, however, is poisonous to most
animals other than Monarch butterflies, whose caterpillars hang on
the underside of the leaves. I have lots of milkweed and briefly contemplated selling milkweed credits to support the Monarch's needs.
It is not clear whether goats would avoid the milkweed, or eat it and
fall ill.

Dexter, who has the coloring and stature of a goat,
seems goat enough for me. I can't handle six of him, let alone
20. Acknowledging I cannot raise goats on my own, I have been
looking for someone who can "do" goats for years. They need to
own the goats, or they might just abscond one day, and leave all

those fence-jumping, tree-climbing ruminants with me. I had an evergreen listing on Cornell's Cooperative Exchange, and I posted on a bulletin board at the Vet School at Cornell, and NOFA. The job requires someone with experience, stamina, and resourcefulness and is at a juncture in their life. Over the years, this algorithm has produced zero prospects. I suspect that someone who is dutiful and skilled already has their own place and doesn't need mine, although with the reenergized back-to-the-land movement, additional resources and connecting networks, maybe I should try again. Perhaps I looked too early.

And recently I've become more interested in pigs. They eat everything, root up and fertilize, and respect a single solar-electrified, low wire. I wonder if I can find someone who wants to run pigs. Would that make me a swineherd? I'll have to practice my snort.

Back to now, on this tractor. I look at the edges of the field, where bittersweet finds its victims, shooting out to strangle trees at warp speed. There are two varieties of bittersweet—one native and scarce, the other an invasive, abundant immigrant. It is the latter that is aggressively attacking our marginal forests. Host trees are laden with heavy, healthy vines and leaves that vie with their own, until the trees pull down. Bittersweet twists around branches and trunks and itself so tightly that I cut it every other turn to unravel and wait for the vine to die before I yank it free. Even then, the tenacious vine might decide to grip indefinitely.

The day I broke up with Michael for the final time—while I could still hear the gravel under the tires of his Volvo pulling out of the driveway—I grabbed a handsaw and large shears and stomped off to the bottom of the field. I would fight the bittersweet where the vines had become thick as thieves in a huge confusing knot. I sawed and cut through my sadness and anger, crying and groaning. I could barely see what I was doing in my frenzy. I was trying to prove to myself that I could manage all this without him, I think. I was freeing the trees, just as I had liberated myself from the controlling clutch of a man who might have loved me, but seemed to love his vodka more. I didn't need him! I couldn't count on him, but hadn't realized how much I came to depend on him, how he showed up at every turn around every tree. How he really was part of my life here on Field Farm. What I didn't know then was that he always would be. A day hasn't gone by when I don't think of Michael. I see him every time a hawk floats overhead. As much as I don't want to, I compare subsequent men to him. He unwittingly became the benchmark. I want him minus the drinking.

The following spring, for every cut there seemed to be fifty new vines, already snaking their way up the few remaining, smothered trees.

You might ask: What is the "sweet" part of the bittersweet? One forgives the vine in the fall. For a moment in late October, the female vines bear deep-orange pods that pop through a yellow skin, on the sun-exposed branches at the forest's edge. The birds love the berries, as do I. I have taken my shears along on a walk to snip yards that become a wreathe or a snarl of color in the corner of the dining room in time for Halloween and Thanksgiving. Hundreds of seeds drop off as I drag the dry, withered vine out the door in late December. Undoubtedly, some of those seeds find a new home, another victim.

An old hoe, tiller, wagon, Yorkshire rake, and flatbed on the edge of the woods become visible in the winter, although their stories remain buried. I wonder how they arrived there, abandoned in those spots, and how the farmer finished his task. Every tree that topples—and there is at least one a year—becomes a magnet, a haven, for vines, creating an impenetrable tangle. The mound grows every year making it more and more difficult to pass, and becomes another project to pull apart and dissect.

It takes a lot of concentration, and a modicum of skill, to be on this tractor with its small wheels and big personality. But is this really a good use of my two master's degrees and worldly business experience? Therein lies my conflict: All the time and love I put into this field could be spent doing something bigger, more important, something with impact beyond my own turf. Should I dedicate myself to eliminating ocean plastic or saving the Bornean elephant? Happiness comes from purpose, they say. What is my purpose? Can I have one without being in an office, avoiding the fluorescent lights, the cubicles, the politics, incessant meetings, pettiness, airports? I just want to get things done, have my hands in the dirt. I try to contribute by serving on the boards of impactful, global and local organizations.

I subscribe to Richard Louv's theory of Nature Deficit Disorder. I am happiest out here on the land or in my garden, although I wonder if I will tire of it eventually. I watch the end of the meadow up against the tree line—my horizon—or the tops of the trees, and it gives me immense pleasure, a calm. I know many of the canopies by heart, the stand of poplars, the smaller stand of birches beside, the dogwoods that line the edges, the dark hole where a tree came down last year, the bare trunk of a dead tree left standing. Three seasons out of four, I don't need meditation or yoga for my sanity. I don't really get lonely out here by myself, although people keep asking me, as if I should. I do feel the need to be social, for companionship, touch. I envy those on Facebook celebrating their 30th wedding anniversary, but I get to my fair share of exotic places, often with a lover. When I go to parties or drive into New York City to catch up with friends or get my cultural fix, expectations run high, since I've given up a sunset on the farm, generally, to be there.

My eyes follow another fleeing insect into the air. I gaze at the sky and see several bulbous dragonflies hovering and darting skittishly. As I refocus, I see that there are hundreds, every few cubic feet, hanging over the field. I declare it Dragon Fly Day! Like the fireflies earlier in the summer, they are spaced out, demarcating blocks of sky, making air three-dimensional. Where did they come from? What are they up do?

They remind me of the early days of September 2001, before the horrifying Trade Towers destruction, we looked up into the

Field Farm sky and saw a family of bald eagles overhead—a mother and three juveniles. There is a regular nest on the nearby Kingston-Rhinecliff Bridge, so they are occasional visitors and a noteworthy presence. The following weekend, after 9/11, Tess and I escaped from Manhattan like many others. When we looked up that time, the sky was heavy and loud with military helicopters. A different American symbol.

Back to dragonflies. These small helicopters are considered totems of change and transformation and adaptability, if you spot them. Am I to believe that because I see dragonflies, something is occurring within me, or is nature just doing its thing and I am a mere witness? Imbued symbolism of this kind seems awfully self-centered—to believe that all these dragonflies are swarming on the chance that I will see them. Dragonfly swarms occur at the beginning of fall, when many people are going back to school, or work, after an August vacation. If you see a dragonfly swarm, you are likely outdoors and observant and connecting with the natural world, and maybe yourself, anyway.

But maybe change is in the air here on Field Farm.

I search the Internet for the biological explanation for the dragonflies. I had posited that perhaps they form leks, groups of solicitous males, like red-winged blackbirds and mosquitoes, and sometimes humans. Instead, I read about swarms, static and migratory. People posted sightings of dragonflies in large numbers over the past few days, in neighboring towns and across the country. Someone else just mowed his grass and witnessed the dragonfly swarm. It may be time for change, but he and I are both stirring up things in the grass, and dragonflies emerge to clean up the etymological debris. Migratory birds are often on the heels of the dragonflies, taking advantage of the abundant protein-laden prey.

I agree that I am seeking and perhaps laying the groundwork for a personal transformation, although I am loath to go about it in a New Age sort of way. I confess that I have been reading my horoscope frequently for clues. It keeps telling me that the answer is *right there,* in me. Being mostly relationship-less through the Trump years and the pandemic made for a few challenging years. And there's so much to deal with on my own. I was an anomaly in the landscape twenty-plus years ago—a single mother scoring this expanse. I may still be.

*   *   *

I look over all the acres to go. There is no relief, little shade. Today's a scorcher. I remind myself that I chose this life, this field, this tractor, so I can't complain. I've driven away hired men and romantic interests who might have helped me take this field down. I haven't yet found a goat herder to run goats. I will be on this tractor every fall for weeks until I do. I will learn this field, bump by bump, and earn its respect. Am I Macha, the Goddess of the Land, the fast runner who has finally slowed down? The alluring warrior battling the bramble on my own?

Fall lands in the field first. Some grasses keep at it: pushing six inches of fresh green growth, taking advantage of a late summer rain. Other tall grasses have called it over; salmon and sienna run through their blades. Burgundy poison ivy crawls through the grass and around the milkweed's pale yellow, erect stalks. On the wood's edge, surrounding the meadow, dusty, crimson dogwoods, lean and blunted dead trunks naked of their own leaves, host bittersweet and bright red Virginia creeper that reach for the heavens. While the stand of maples beyond holds onto summer, the meadow dials in the fall.

When I return to the Adirondack chairs at sundown, I watch a flock of starlings fly low over the cut field and turn in unison like a stingray, their white underbellies reflecting the last light. A crow passes in front of them, in the opposite direction, cawing, cleverer than it sounds. The meadow is quiet in the distance. I know more about its crevices, the small mounds, the rocks, its many micro-ecosystems, but only a few of its secrets.

EPILOGUE

A tornado whipped through this spring. The leaning lean-to which
has been here since the beginning of time collapsed on top of the
tractor, and all the rest of it. For months, I've had to reckon with the
wreckage, the accumulation of old wood, tools, toys, boats, fencing.
A part of me is glad to be forced to deal with it. I am reliving
projects as I dig and unpack and assess each board and post. I
remember many individually; I had dreams for some. Now I'm
chucking much of it into the firewood pile and creating new projects
for the usable to avoid feeding a distant landfill.

I hired Calvin, a skilled carpenter, to make a bedframe for
the cottage and he's replacing burlap in the barn with handsome
tongue-and-groove left by a tenant. Calvin will redeploy the lean-
to's lumber and corrugated metal roofing to build a chicken coop
on his own property. He's also expressed interest in my tractor since
it no longer has a place to roost. I will deliberate that one, but may
concede. Robby has taken on more of the fields than at the start,
so there's less for me to do. Although, last year, thick, persistent
Canadian wildfire smoke and crazy weather precluded his coming
at all. The ground was so wet, he couldn't even retrieve bales from
the previous year, which continue to soften, sprout and submerge
in this year's growth. He dropped by a couple weeks ago, and said
he hopes to be by soon. He mentioned that he started raising goats,
given the sizable market for them. I offered my place if he wanted to
expand his herd. He shook his head. He doesn't need more land, he
needs more time in the day—and goats are complicated. I already
knew that.

The flat graveled spot left by the lean-to's footprint offers
opportunity, shaded by a maple, a hickory, and a wild cherry tree
that grew up alongside, and a couple weedy mulberries that I've
been whacking back for years. Now they all have room to spread.
Perhaps it is a setting for a sculpture, a tiny home or a bench. If I

wait long enough, it may decide for itself.

I am learning to let go, allowing nature to rectify and reinstitute balance. I am no longer obsessed with staying on top of invasives, unsure whether it helps or matters. Every year, a different epidemic or insect dominates—mites, carpenter bees, ground hornets, mint rust, lily leaf beetle, rabbits—with unclear prescriptions. Just as I get motivated to tackle the issue, it goes away. In the past, I dutifully plucked thousands of Japanese beetles off the bush cinquefoil in summer; this year I didn't, and the blooms seemed as abundant. Rather than cutting everything back, I am leaving the garden standing this fall for the birds to pick through and to give the beneficial insects and other critters places to cosy up, tuck in. Some leaf litter will decompose in place releasing nutrients into the soil, and it'll be easier to rake through in the spring when the leaves and stems are limp and loose.

I've been here long enough, that it's not only the hours and months and seasons and migratory birds cycling through—and the same stubborn potholes reappearing in the driveway—but the next generation of escapades and renovations and thrills.

Tess turned thirty and will marry kindred Sam here next spring. I planted dozens of peonies and hundreds of tulips for the occasion. The pool got a new liner, long overdue, and the split-rail fence pushed and compromised by the ever-expanding junipers needs addressing. In the spring, the barn siding will be cleaned and stained—maybe a transparent barn red— to extend its life. Local, handmade turmeric-colored Adirondack chairs replaced the outdoor furniture blemished by acid rain and lichen. Their hemisphere arrangement gives homage to the golden rod burning bright this fall. Even when I can't make it, the chairs watch the sun go down, along with one old soft chair for Dexter.

Calvin has been reflashing the barn's windows, getting it right this time. The house has been painted twice, has a new kitchen and appliances, and its third hammock. I have welcomed and enjoyed the company of hundreds of Airbnbers, and washed and folded infinite loads of sheets and towels, which helps pay the bills. Some guests are regulars, some are friends, many are windows into the world beyond, all are a study in human behavior. Several have moved to the area after spending time here and remind me, in part, why I wrote this.

As I looked at old photos, I see images from ten years ago that defy imagination—at least mine. Wisps of saplings are now thirty-foot trees. Dexter's fence delineates an outdoor space hugging a hill that was previously boundless. The six-foot weeping willow I planted fifteen years ago has grown to sixty feet and anchors the field. Most of the apple trees are gone, but a couple hollow ones are making a comeback. The landmark blue spruce succumbed to disease. After living in denial for years, I finally had it removed. Last summer a microburst toppled a stand of poplars outside my bedroom window onto the fence. This month, I witnessed a dramatic display of northern lights through the remaining, contorted trunks. There is always something to deal with or discover. Expectations remain fluid. Time passes in many ways.

Men too mark time here. They have come and gone and left their imprints and memories. I thought this meadow would provide a backdrop for romance, a setting to build a life together. Although I was hopeful, in the end, none stood a chance. I have come to realize that Field Farm is the lead relationship, my surrogate partner, dominant and complex, keeping me tightly tethered and true. I thought it was Charlotte and Dexter who limited my movement, and they have, but I confess I find it hard to wake anywhere but in my field. And so, as much joy as it affords, Field Farm has hindered my ability to find a life partner, even made this notion discretionary, less urgent.

I've always maintained that if someone I adored came with a better situation, I'd be willing to let go, move on. But not in all my time scouring the (other) field—the field of potential mates—have I encountered a suitor who met Field Farm's high bar, who could offer me more than this loyal, fierce, calming and sympathetic landscape. Many men my age have scaled down, pared back, live in the past not the future, see little, walk slowly, have moved into condos, are tethered by their own circumstances, or don't understand the need for sky and an open window.

I look down at my big, square, doer hands, which are older than I am. There's the gnawing fear I cannot continue to manage all this alone, do this land justice, even as I hire others to do what I used to. As I enter the next life chapter, I am contemplating how and where to grow old. I have one eye on apartments in New York City, where everything is walkable, accessible, and less maintenance. Maybe without Field Farm in the mix, I'd fall for a cerebral foodie. But given the just-in 2024 election results, I think Dexter and I will need this meadow—its solace and distractions—for at least four more years.

ACKNOWLEDGMENTS

APPRECIATION

So much appreciation is in order, to the many friends and family members who patiently listened to my stories by the cauldron, and who encouraged me to share my experiences and love of Field Farm. To my parents who inculcated the love of the natural world, written word, and innovative design, and who listened with unbridled enthusiasm to new installments. My co-conspirator and daughter Tess accompanied me in much of this adventure and indulged my crazy ideas and my writing; she in turn cares deeply for the planet, and is working to save it, for which I am most grateful.

I have shared gardening tips, long farm-to-table meals and essays with many friends, too many to mention. I appreciate members of the St. Croix Writer's Circle for their humor and encouragement in our seasonal weekly gatherings. The two rounds of Bread Loaf Orion and Bread Loaf Sicily participants and leaders kicked off this writing a decade ago. I owe enormous gratitude to Dana Davison who provided unflagging support in helping navigate the technical aspects of book design. I appreciate my collaboration with Trey Popp, at *The Pennsylvania Gazette,* who polished several essays with a delicate editorial hand.

Long before I arrived, Field Farm, in the Town of Esopus, belonged to the Esopus people, a tribe of the Lenape Native Americans, who made their lives in the Catskills and what is now Ulster and Sullivan Counties. They lived in small groups and hunted, foraged, and cultivated a diverse set of crops. They lived to be only 35 or 40 years old—about the age I arrived. The Esopus were forced west by colonists, and they eventually ended up in Oklahoma, Shawano County, Wisconsin, and among the Munsee-Delaware Nation of Ontario, Canada. If any of the Esopus tribe read this, please contact me. I would be honored to walk the land with you.

PREVIOUSLY PUBLISHED

- A version of "Smitten" appeared online in *Ragazine,* in 2017, https://www.ragazine.cc/cynthia-mcvay-creative-nonfiction/
- A brief excerpt in "Origins" appeared in "Homestretch," *The Blue Mountain Review,* December 2023
- "Bar Soap" appeared in in *The Pennsylvania Gazette* as "Bar Soap. An Ode," July/August 2025
- A version of "Open Window" appeared in *The Pennsylvania Gazette* as "Through a Window, Darkly," November 7, 2022, https://thepenngazette.com/through-a-window-darkly/
- An excerpt of "Canine Companions" appeared in *2019 Orison Anthology,* as an excerpt of "Morning Kenyan," winner of 2018 Orison Anthology Award in Nonfiction and finalist in the Bridging the Gap Awards at the 2017 Slice Writer's Conference
- An excerpt of "Chainsaw Massacre" appeared in *The Pennsylvania Gazette,* March/April 2022, https://thepenngazette.com/chainsaw-massacre/
- "On the Road" appeared in *DaCunha's Anthology 2,* and won Editors' Choice, daCunha's 2017 Flash Nonfiction Competition and was performed in the UK October 2017
- A version of "America on the Creek" appeared in *The Pennsylvania Gazette* as "Up the Creek and Back," February 2021, https://thepenngazette.com/up-the-creek-and-back/
- A version of "Sun-Kissed Fruit" appeared in *The Pennsylvania Gazette* as "Orchard Bounty," July/August 2022, https://thepenngazette.com/orchard-bounty/
- "In the Woods" appeared in *The Ravens Perch,* July 7, 2017, http://www.theravensperch.com/in-the-woods-by-cynthia-mcvay/
- "Foraging Asparagus" appeared in *Goats Milk,* August 2021, https://goatsmilkmagazine.ca/2021/08/01/foraging-asparagus/
- An excerpt of "Rocks, Goats and Dragonflies" appeared as "All About Tractors" in *Orion Magazine,* Spring 2020

AUTHOR'S BIO

CYNTHIA McVAY was a strategy and management consultant for McKinsey and independently for two decades, advising household names, non-profits and startups. She served as Latin American Program Officer for the World Wildlife Fund and inaugural Director of Innovation for the Peace Corps. She holds a BA from Harvard in biology and studio arts, and an MA in international studies from the University of Pennsylvania and MBA from Wharton, as a Fellow of The Lauder Institute. Cynthia serves on numerous boards including the Rauch Foundation, Center for Large Landscape Conservation, and John Burroughs Association. She splits her time between the Hudson Valley and St. Croix, USVI.

Written, photographed and designed by Cynthia McVay
Copyright @ 2025 Cynthia McVay

www.cynthiamcvay.com
IG/cynthiamcvay

Some names have been changed.

All rights reserved.
Published by Living in a Place Press.
No part of this book may be reproduced, stored in a retrieval
system, or transmitted in any form or by any means, including
electronic, mechanical, photocopying or microfilming, recording,
or otherwise without written permission from the publisher and
author.

There is no permission granted in any circumstance without the
written consent of the publisher and author to use any material in
the book for AI purposes including training.

Second Edition

ISBN: 979-8-9918639-1-9

www.ingramcontent.com/pod-product-compliance
Lightning Source LLC
Chambersburg PA
CBHW071412090426
42737CB00011B/1441